The New Naturalist Library

A survey of British Natural History

Heathlands

Editors
Kenneth Mellanby, C.B.E., Sc.D.
S. M. Walters, M.A., Ph.D.
Professor Richard West, F.R.S., F.G.S.

Photographic Editor
Eric Hosking, O.B.E., F.R.P.S.

The aim of this series is to interest the general reader in the wildlife of Britain by recapturing the enquiring spirit of the old naturalists. The Editors believe that the natural pride of the British public in the native fauna and flora, to which must be added concern for their conservation, is best fostered by maintaining a high standard of accuracy combined with clarity of exposition in presenting the results of modern scientific research.

The New Naturalist

HEATHLANDS

Nigel Webb,
B.Sc., Ph.D.

With 20 colour photographs,
and over 100 photographs and
diagrams in black and white

COLLINS
Grafton Street, London

William Collins Sons & Co. Ltd
London · Glasgow · Sydney · Auckland
Toronto · Johannesburg

First published 1986
© N. R. Webb 1986

ISBN 0 00 219419 8 (limpback edition)
ISBN 0 00 219020 6 (hardback edition)

Filmset by Ace Filmsetting Ltd., Frome, Somerset
Colour and black-and-white reproduction by Alpha Reprographics, Harefield
Printed and bound by Mackays of Chatham, Chatham, Kent

Contents

	page
Editors' Preface	7
Author's Preface	9

1. **'A Waste and Barren Land'**   11
   The 'image' of heathland.
   Definitions, and the scope of the book.

2. **The Basic Requirements**   17
   Heathland zones and distribution.
   The influence of climate, soils, geology.

3. **A Primeval Landscape?**   25
   Early views on the origins of heathland.
   Pollen analysis – and the findings;
   Heathland pollen profiles.

4. **The Influence of Man**   36
   Farming, settlement, land-use and the effects.
   The documentary evidence. Grazing, fuel-gathering, etc.

5. **British Lowland Heaths**   53
   Flora, fauna, and distinctive characteristics of individual
   heathland areas throughout Britain.

6. **Heathland Plant Communities**   78
   The pattern of vegetation. The categories of heathland
   plant communities.

7. **The Dynamics of Heathland Vegetation**   86
   The patterns of change, and succession. Production and
   decomposition. Nutrients. The effects of fire, and
   post-fire succession.

8. **The Heathers**   107
   Distribution, characteristics, germination, life history.

9. **Other Heathland Plants**   121
   Plants of dry heath, wet and humid heath.
   Gorses, whins and brooms, Insectivorous plants.

10. **Heathland Invertebrates**   132
    Species and ecology. Ants, spiders, grasshoppers, dragonflies,
    beetles and bugs, Heather Beetle, butterflies and moths.

11. **Heathland Vertebrates** 161
    Species and ecology. Amphibians and reptiles, birds, mammals.

12. **What the Future Holds** 181
    The science of ecology. Conservation management, restoration. Criteria for selecting reserves. Burning. Bracken and scrub control. Protection of individual species. Recreation and amenity.

    References for Further Reading 202

    Heathland Nature Reserves 211

    Index 215

Editors' Preface

The success of Professor W. H. Pearsall's classic book *Mountains and Moorlands*, published in the *New Naturalist* series in 1950, made the absence of a complementary study on the lowland heaths of Britain an obvious gap in the series. Britain is unique in Europe in having such a wide range of heath and moorland communities, and in the eyes of many continental biologists the wide open spaces, often beautified by heather (*Calluna*) or gorse (*Ulex*) are the most remarkable feature of our countryside. As Pearsall explained, however, in his preface to *Mountains and Moorlands*, 'there are really two Britains – two different countries, their boundary a line that strikes diagonally across England from Yorkshire to Devon'. The moorlands belong to the 'region of mountains and old rocks', and the heathlands 'the newer, fertile land of the plains'. It is with the lowland heaths of Britain that Dr Nigel Webb's book is concerned.

When Professor Pearsall wrote his book, the science of 'historical ecology' had not been formally recognized – though Pearsall himself was a pioneer in this field, as in so many other branches of ecology.

Nigel Webb, therefore, builds on an important tradition. But his book, understandably, shows a significant difference in emphasis in three interlocking themes. The first is the explicit recognition of the artificial nature of the lowland heath and the importance of human activity: the early chapters amass the detailed evidence and produce a convincing picture. This picture is derived from recent research conducted both in Britain and Continental Europe, and the 'new look' at British heathlands as part of a wider NW European vegetation type constitutes the second change in emphasis. For this international view Dr Webb's career makes him especially qualified, for he studied for two years in Denmark before joining the staff of the Furzebrook Research Station of the Institute of Terrestrial Ecology in Dorset where he is now Principal Scientific Officer.

Tragically, what man 'creates' he can also destroy. The third new emphasis in Dr Webb's masterly study is the sombre recognition that our lowland heaths, no longer having a clear role in any rural economy, are disappearing at an alarming rate. The final chapter of the book is devoted to the challenge of conservation of this unique habitat with the rare plants and animals that it supports. Here again, Dr Webb combines special knowledge derived both from his professional career and from his work 'on the ground' as Chairman of the Conservation Committee of the Dorset Trust for Nature Conservation.

A final change in emphasis is worthy of comment. Until recently, the nature conservation movement has tended to be concerned, very understandably, with the fate of two main kinds of organisms: on the one hand, the flowering plants, since after all they compose and shape the habitats, and on the other the birds, since ornithology is by far the most popular and organized branch of natural history. Now there are signs that the lower animals are receiving their share of concern. Dr Webb is, by training, a specialist in the heathland invertebrate fauna, and the review of heathland plants and animals in the later chapters of his book show the value of adding this developing expertise to the conservation movement as a whole.

Author's Preface

At the outset, let me say that those who open this book expecting a definitive review of heathland ecology will be disappointed. I have approached its writing as if I were telling you about heathlands; about their formation, their vegetation, the plants and animals which live on them and the problems faced by conservationists who wish to protect and maintain them in perpetuity. I have attempted to do this from a more personal standpoint rather than that of the scientific reviewer. Although I have endeavoured to cover as wide a range of the relevant material as possible, some topics are dealt with in more detail and there are some digressions – for no better reason than they interested me and I wanted to share this interest with my readers. I daresay that you will have no difficulty in identifying them!

My own interest in heathlands stems from my earliest research on the communities of soil mites living in a Danish heathland soil. So fascinating have heathlands been that I have studied them ever since. A similar attraction must have been felt by many people, especially naturalists, for over the years, there have been numerous publications on many aspects of heathland natural history and ecology. For many heathland ecologists, the great landmarks have been Beijerinck's classic monograph on the Scotch Heather (published 1940) and the book, *Heathland Ecology*, by Professor Charles Gimingham of Aberdeen (published 1972). This latter work was a critical synthesis of heathland ecology at that date, and it provided a stimulus to further study of both the heathland community as a whole and of its constituent species populations. In the intervening years, there has been much research and interest in heathland, particularly into aspects which are relevant to their conservation: the time has now come when yet another critical synthesis is required. I do not feel that this book should be regarded as such a synthesis; it is aimed at a different readership. I do hope, however, that I have provided a text in which as much as possible of this recent work has been described, together with adequate references which will enable the more interested reader to follow the subject in greater depth.

Since the scope of the *New Naturalist* Series provides for a more personal approach, I have confined my text to the heathlands of southern Britain. That is to say dwarf shrub communities dominated by Ling (*Calluna vulgaris*) growing in sandy mineral soils. Upland moorland over 250 m (800 ft) communities have been ignored. I realise that botanically, both upland and lowland dwarf shrub vegetation are best regarded as one continuous type. However, this is a difficult distinction for a zoologist to accept, since animals show much clearer differences in their distribution patterns, both between the north and south of Britain and between upland and lowland.

Many naturalists would agree, if only from an intuitive feeling, that the heathlands of southern England are a formation which can be treated satisfactorily on their own. However, it is not possible to maintain a rigid distinction between moorland and heathland, particularly when discussing the ecology of Ling – for the simple reason that much of the research into this plant's ecology was carried out on upland communities, and much of it in Scotland. I have borrowed from this research in interpreting the processes of lowland heath vegetation, although the extent to which this is possible varies, especially when considering post-fire succession.

In the final chapter, I have tried to show how an understanding of the patterns and processes in heathland plant and animal communities is relevant – indeed essential – to solving the problems of wildlife conservation. The decision as to what should be conserved is not really a scientific one, since it is a subjective judgement in which ecological science has little part. But the actions we must take for effective conservation depend on our understanding of the structure and functioning of the assemblages of plants and animals. Finally, we must not forget that the influence of man has figured strongly in the history of heathlands; man was responsible largely for their origin throughout Europe and, until this century, heathlands were part of the agricultural system. Where heathland remains today in southern Britain, the problems of how to maintain it are considerable.

In the preparation of this work I wish to thank numerous friends and colleagues who have, both actively and passively, assisted me by influencing my thinking, with whom I have discussed various ideas or who have contributed directly to this text.

I am grateful to Dr L. E. Haskins for permission to quote from her thesis on the vegetational history of south-east Dorset and for allowing me to make use of her pollen diagram from Morden Bog. I am likewise grateful to Dr J. J. Hopkins for permission to quote from his thesis on the Lizard heaths.

Dr J. Rodwell of Lancaster University very kindly provided me with a summary of the classification of lowland heath vegetation in advance of its publication by the *National Vegetation Classification*, and Professor C. H. Gimingham allowed me to use the categories of heath communities which he summarized in his book *Heathland Ecology*.

I should like to thank the following for supplying photographs: Dr W. Block of Cambridge, both for his own photographs of the Breckland and for those of the late Dr A. S. Watt showing the similar areas in the 1930s; Dr S. B. Chapman, J. R. Cox, Mrs M. Dolton, the Photographic Collection of the Dorset County Museum, B. Pearson and B. P. Pickess.

I am grateful to my wife for preparing a number of the drawings; material has been reproduced with permission from, Dr C. J. Bibby, R. Burden, Dr S. B. Chapman, Dr E. M. Bridges, Professor C. H. Gimingham, Miss B. Kerr, Dr P. Merrett, Bird Study, British Birds, the Bulletin of the British Arachnological Society, Institute of Terrestrial Ecology, Nature Conservancy Council, Journal of Ecology, Journal of Animal Ecology, the New Phytologist, Landscape Design, Geography, the Geographical Association, and Springer-Verlag. The extract from *Winnie-the-Pooh* is reproduced with permission from Methuen Children's Books.

N.R.W.
Stoborough, Dorset.
July, 1985.

'A Waste and Barren Land' CHAPTER I

Purbeck, c. 1899/Dorset County Museum

Heathland is a familiar landscape in several parts of Britain and in some regions of north-west Europe. It is open, with few trees and the sparse, monotonous vegetation which most people recognize as characteristic of poor soils. The *Oxford English Dictionary* defines heathland as 'open, uncultivated ground; a bare, more or less flat tract of land, naturally covered with low herbage and dwarf shrubs, especially heather or ling.' For the naturalist, it is insufficient to define heathland as poor, open land, but this definition does contain two significant points. Firstly, it recognises that the vegetation is dominated by a characteristic group of plants – dwarf shrubs, which to the ecologist is a constant feature of heathlands. Secondly, it considers the heathland to be natural; in fact, it is far from natural and owes its existence to the activities of man over many centuries. We shall consider this aspect in detail later – indeed it is one of the dominant themes of this book – and we shall see that the wild appearance of heathlands is more apparent than real.

In this book, we will confine ourselves to the so-called heathlands of lowland Britain – areas of ericaceous dwarf-shrubs growing at low altitudes, below 250 m (800 ft), in acidic, nutrient-poor, mineral soils – and as we are considering entire communities – will include associated wet heath and valley mires. This type of vegetation is more-or-less confined to the lowlands of southern Britain, although there are areas at sea level elsewhere, especially in Scotland. For the most part, related marginal communities, such as acid grasslands and scrub, will be excluded.

In Britain, as in the remainder of north-west Europe, Common Heather or Ling (*Calluna vulgaris*) is the dominant plant on all heathlands; indeed on many it is almost the only species of plant. Several other commonly-occurring heathland plants also belong to the same family – the Ericaceae, which are all dwarf shrubs adapted to the hostile environment of poor acidic soils – and this imparts character and structure to the vegetation.

Of the many features of heathlands, bleakness and barrenness are those which come most easily to mind, an aspect that many writers, from Shakespeare on, have referred to. Yet the monotony is broken in late summer by the luxuriant purple of Heather in full bloom; then, the heathlands are alive with flowers and insects.

However, it was the desolate quality that caught the attention of the 17th- and 18th-century travellers, who were probably the earliest writers to provide us with a realistic description of Britain's landscape. Daniel Defoe, in his *Tour Through the Whole Island of Great Britain* (1724–1726), said of Bagshot Heath:

'Those that despise Scotland and the northern part of England, for being full of waste and barren land, may take a view of this part of Surrey, and look upon it as a foil to the beauty of the rest of England . . .

'Much of it is a sandy desert, where winds raise the sands . . . This sand indeed is checked by the heath, or heather, which grows in it, and which is the common product of barren land, even in the very highlands of Scotland, but the ground is otherwise so poor and barren, that the product of it feeds no creatures, but some very small sheep, who feed chiefly on the said heather, and but very few of these, nor are there any villages worth remembering, and but few houses, or people for many miles far and wide; this desert lies extended so much that some say, there is not less than a hundred thousand acres of this barren land that lies all together, reaching out every way in the three counties of Surrey, Hampshire and Berkshire.'

Defoe expressed similar views on other heathlands: the New Forest in southern Hampshire . . . 'undoubtedly good and capable of improvement' . . . he crossed 'sandy wild and barren country' to reach Poole; Exmoor was '. . . a vast tract of barren and desolate lands.'

About three-fifths of the Royal Forest of Woolmer lay in the parish of Selborne, and is described by Gilbert White as being

'entirely of sand, covered with heath and fern [fern was the old country name for Bracken (*Pteridium aquilinum*), which is common and widespread on every heathland] . . . diversified with hills and dales, without having one standing tree in the whole extent . . . hungry, sandy, barren waste.'

Because heathland soils are difficult to cultivate, a distinct culture has tended to be linked with them throughout western Europe. The Jydefolk – the inhabitants of Jutland – had a way of life which featured frequently in art and literature, especially in the poems, songs and writings of the famous Danish fairytale writer, Hans Christian Andersen. There were characteristic communities and agricultural practices throughout the north German plains (Gimingham & De Smidt, 1983), and in Britain, among the people of the Breckland, Suffolk Sandlings, and the characters of Thomas Hardy's Wessex novels.

The integration between heathland and its peoples was the subject of Hardy's *The Return of the Native*, one of his 'character and environment' series. Hardy was born on the edge of Egdon Heath (as he later called it) and had an intimate knowledge of both the people and the landscape. *The Return of the Native* was published in 1895 but describes life in the generation before – about 1840–50. He describes many activities which we now

Hardy's 'Egdon Heath'/ N. R. Webb

recognise as essential factors in maintaining the heathland landscape, though he himself was unaware of their significance – the cutting of fern, furze, peat and turf, and the grazing of cattle and a small breed of pony called 'heath-croppers'. But to Hardy, the heaths had always existed as such; he tells us they were mentioned in Domesday and 'The Ishmaelitish thing that Egdon now was it had always been; civilisation was its enemy' – likening the heath to the wilderness into which Ishmael, the son of Abraham, was banished.

Although Hardy cast no role for Man in the past, he saw the quickening pace of change in the late 19th century as an enemy of heathland; in the introduction to *The Return of the Native*, Egdon Heath is 'disguised by intrusive strips and slices brought under the plough with varying dregrees of success, or planted to woodland.' This trend has occurred throughout European heathlands, and today only a small fraction of the original remains (see chapters 4 & 12). But even here, the ancient practices have ceased and, as a consequence, successional change in the vegetation has led to the development of scrub and woodland: the methods needed to conserve open heathland are therefore an important subject for the ecologist and conservationist (see chapter 12).

Throughout almost all of north-west Europe, where languages of Germanic origin prevail, the same vernacular word has been used for what we in Britain call heathland or heath: in old English it is *haethen*, in Saxon *hethin*, and in the old Germanic language *haitha*. Today, in these languages the word persists as *heide* in Germany and *heden* in Scandinavia, both of which indicate a common origin. Correspondingly, the most common plant of these heathlands is Common Heather, or Ling; the name *ling*, which is used in Britain, corresponds with *lyng* or *hedelyng* in Danish and *ljing* in Swedish; yet in Germany the name *Heidekraut* (heath-plant) is used. The term heath has been shown by the early botanist Rubel (1914) to be used in a variety of forms to describe stretches of barren, uncultivated land on acid soils; it alludes much more to the value of the land than to the composition of its vegetation. As it happens, almost all of these poor lands in western Europe were covered in dwarf-shrub vegetation in which Heather (*Calluna*) or other members of the Ericaceae were common, if not dominant constituents of the plant community. Further south, in France, where the language originates from Latin, the word *bruyère* (or one of its many variants, such as *bruère, brière, brouire*, or *bruguière*) is used. In northern Spain, heaths are called *brezales*, and in south-west France, *brandes* or *brandages*, words which owe their origin to the practice of regular burning of dwarf-shrub vegetation. The French also use the word *lande* for heathland; this is of Celtic origin and is related to *lann*, meaning Gorse. These terms are used in Brittany (Noirfalise & Vanesse, 1976).

In many parts of Britain, the words 'heath' and 'moor' are more-or-less interchangeable and both refer to the dwarf-shrub vegetation which grows on acid soils. But frequently a loose distinction is maintained between moorland, which generally occurs on the wetter and more upland soils, and heath, which grows on drier soils. Besides Heather-dominated communities, a heath may be all kinds of poor, acidic grasslands and scrub. In their origins, these words reflect this distinction: *mor* (Germanic) or *myr* (Norse) are used to designate wet, peaty localities where the vegetation is growing in an organic soil, and heath refers to a plant community of Heather growing in a mineral soil, which is generally podsolised. Curiously, the *Oxford English Dictionary* provides a definition for moor which is similar to that for heath – 'a tract of open waste ground especially if covered with heather' – and fails to make the distinction between wet, peaty areas and the drier heathland. However, on both heaths and moors, plants have to contend with similar physiological problems, particularly drought at certain times of the year (Specht, 1979).

In Britain, the distinction between heathland and moorland also reflects a division between the uplands and the lowlands, between north and south, and between organic or peaty soils and sandy, acid soils. Yet in the lowlands, a distinction is drawn between heath and moor; the low-lying valleys which intersect the heathlands are basins lined with peat – called valley mires by botanists – and an investigation of place-names will often show such areas to be called moors, as are other extensive peat deposits such as those in Somerset; the term heath is often reserved for the drier areas which surround these bogs.

Almost all the local names used throughout north-west Europe where a heathland type of vegetation grows refers to the fact that the land is poor and uncultivated, not to the vegetation type. However, since Rubel's early investigations into the etymology of these names, the word heathland has been confined by botanists, ecologists and geographers to the ericaceous dwarf-shrub vegetation which is so typical of many parts of north-west Europe. Subsequently, plant communities with characteristics similar to those of the north European heathlands have been recognized in other parts of the world. The form of the plants and the structure of the vegetation is similar, since the plants are confronted with similar environmental problems, and natural selection has shaped communities which are similar in form, structure and function, but which contain different species.

On a world scale, heathland vegetation is composed of evergreen, sclerophyllous (adapted to dry conditions) plants which are mainly from the Diapensiaceae, Empetriaceae, Epacridaceae, Ericaceae, Grubbiaceae, Pironotaceae and Vaccinaceae families. They are generally referred to as ericoid plants, i.e., dwarf or low, woody plants which are many-branched. The leaves are small with a very small surface area, sunken stomata, and a thick cuticle which contains tannins, resins and oils – all adaptations to dry conditions. The presence of the resins and oils render the vegetation highly inflammable at certain times of the year and, consequently, fire is an important feature of heathland ecology in many parts of the world. Almost all these plants require relatively cool temperatures and fairly high levels of atmospheric moisture; they grow in free-draining, nutrient-poor and acidic soils. Frequently they represent a particular stage in vegetation development, and therefore some factor must be present to restrict the invasion of scrub and trees (Gimingham, 1972; Specht, 1979). These conditions are very similar to those proposed by Beijerinck (1940) for *Calluna* to become dominant in the vegetation.

Gimingham (1972) recognized three circumstances where conditions are suitable for ericaceous shrubs: in oceanic, cool, temperate regions where the growth of woodland and forest is suppressed; in the sub-arctic and sub-antarctic; and on mountains, where the humidity is adequate. It is not within the scope of this book to consider world heathlands, but three main types can be recognised which correspond to the prevalence of the above conditions. The heathlands of northern Europe, with counterparts in North America, exist in areas which are oceanic, cool, temperate regions, where tree and forest growth is checked. The second main type is to be found in sub-arctic and sub-antarctic regions; these circum-polar heathlands occur in northern Canada, Scandinavia and Russia, in the maritime Antarctic, the South Atlantic and South America, and tend to be dominated by the Empetraceae. Extensive heathlands occur in Australia, dominated by members of the Epacridaceae, and in South Africa, where the *fynbos* (fine bush, referring to the structure and appearance of the vegetation) is a form of heathland derived from the large diversity of species of *Erica* to be found in that region. This extensive bush vegetation exists in humid regions of the Cape at altitudes of 900 m (2950 ft). A review of world heaths is provided by various authors in Specht (1979), while Gimingham has provided a more detailed account of European heathlands.

Floristically, heathland vegetation in north-west Europe forms a continuum, and this is reflected in the composition and structure of the plant communities of the heathlands and moors of the British Isles. For this reason Gimingham considers that the term heathlands should be used for all vegetation fitting the description of ericaceous dwarf shrubs, whether or not they grow in mineral or organic soils and at whatever altitude. However we will exclude the upland vegetation of this type which occurs at altitudes over 250–300 m (800–1000 ft), in part because these regions of the British Isles were the subject of an earlier, classic volume in this series – *Mountains and Moorlands*, by the late Professor W. H. Pearsall. However, we will not exclude reference to moorlands and other upland ericaceous communities entirely, since much of the research into the ecology of *Calluna* and related species has been undertaken in these regions, and there is less comparable work from the lowlands.

Confusion sometimes arises because the word heath is used both to describe a type of vegetation and as a name for some members of the Ericaceae. For instance, Cross-leaved Heath (*Erica tetralix*) or Cornish Heath (*Erica vagans*). In this latter name, Cornish refers to the plant and the locality where it is found, and not to the heathlands of Cornwall. To avoid confusion, I have tended, though not exclusively, to call the vegetation heathland. However, this leads one into an unnecessary repetition of *-land*, and where the balance of the words seemed to demand it, I have lapsed, and called heathlands, heaths. After all, this is the most commonly used vernacular word and I hope I have not introduced confusion by so doing. I have retained the word heath for species of the Ericaceae.

Finally, it has become a tradition among heathland ecologists that Heather or Ling – *Calluna vulgaris* – is simply referred to as *Calluna*. This is possible since *Calluna* is a mono-specific genus and no confusion should arise from this laxity. I have adopted this convention throughout this book, since the plant and its ecology are central to an understanding of British heathlands.

The Basic Requirements   CHAPTER 2

Fig. 1
*Distribution of Common Heather (*Calluna vulgaris*) in NW Europe.*
———— *approximate limits of distribution.*
—·—·— *where Heather is invariably dominant on heathland communities.*
———— *optimum habitat.*
(Beijerinck, 1940; modified by Gimingham, 1972)

There are several parts of the world where soils and climate are suitable for the development of dwarf shrub communities, but the type locality for heathland, as we know it, is north-west Europe – the area where this vegetation formation was first described. The autecology of the dominant plant of the European heathlands, Common Heather or Ling (*Calluna vulgaris*), is an important ingredient in our understanding of heathland communities. We shall discuss the ecology of *Calluna* in chapter 8, confining ourselves in this chapter to the physical conditions required for heathland formation.

Dwarf-shrub communities of the type we have defined, both moorland and heathland, occur principally in the lands bordering the North Sea, the English Channel and the Atlantic coasts. This area extends from the north coast of Spain, northwards along the west coast of France, through Brittany and Normandy (where there are extensive and characteristic areas of heathland), continuing into Belgium, through the Netherlands and across the north German plain, where *Lüneberger Heide* is one of the biggest and best-known areas. The heathland zone then extends into Jutland in Denmark, where, up to the 19th century, there were extensive areas, covering almost all of the peninsula; and there were further areas of heathland in the southern provinces of Norway and Sweden (Fig. 2). The whole of the British Isles falls within the zone suitable for heathland formation.

There is a strong association with the distribution of *Calluna* and the distribution of heathland. The range of *Calluna* (Fig. 1) extends from Ireland in the west, to the Urals Mountains in Russia, and from Iceland and Finland in the north, to Spain and Yugoslavia in the south; it then tapers into Russia, and forms a pattern which should be compared with the local climate. There is a smaller area centred particularly on the lands surrounding the North Sea in which *Calluna* is the dominant plant in dwarf-shrub communities. Within this area, the optimum conditions for *Calluna* are found in eastern England, the Netherlands, northern Germany and Jutland (Beijerinck, 1940).

Biejerinck specified that *Calluna* required the following conditions:
1. Soils with small quantities of assimilable plant nutrients (oligotrophy)
2. Soil acidity in the range pH 3.5 to pH 6.7
3. Small seasonal fluctuations in the humidity of the soil and air
4. Protection from low temperatures by snow cover at high altitudes or on mountains
5. Adequate levels of light

These factors fall into two types: those dependent on climate – temperature, humidity and light, and those dependent on soil conditions – the supply of plant nutrients, and acidity. However, open, dwarf-shrub communities only develop where there are factors which prevent the regeneration of woodland; thus, Beijerinck added a further factor to this list to include the activities of Man, grazing, or exposure.

Climate

The distributions of heathland and *Calluna* in north-west Europe coincide with the area which experiences a temperate climate. Sandwiched between a taiga type of climate in northern Europe and Mediterranean types in the south is a wedge of temperate climate, widest at the west and running to a point in eastern Europe (Fig. 2). This zone falls into three parts: the western marginal, central, and eastern marginal zones. The western marginal has the classic temperate climate; it lies in the paths of the mid-latitude westerly winds, which bring a succession of low- and high-pressure systems leading to frequent variations of small amplitude in the weather. In addition, there is a moderating influence from the North Atlantic Drift, keeping the British Isles and parts of the Scandinavian coast free of ice at a latitude where ice readily forms on the eastern seaboard of America. This marginal western temperate climate is characterized as rainy with mild winters. The mean temperature of the coolest month is above 0°C (32°F) but below 8°C (64.4°F) and the mean temperature of the warmest month is above 19°C (50°F) but below 22°C (71.6°F). Rainfall occurs throughout the year and in the driest month is at least 60 mm (2.4 in). This moist climate and small annual range of temperatures is evident from the examples illustrated (Fig. 4) from stations within this climatic zone. On occasions the mean monthly temperature may fall below 6°C (42.8°F), which is generally considered to be the point below which plant growth ceases.

The growth form of ericaceous plants – small, compact, evergreen shrubs, with needle-like leaves often closely pressed to the stems – is well-suited to this type of climate; such plants are sensitive to drought but have thick leaves with protected stomata which enable them to control

THE BASIC REQUIREMENTS

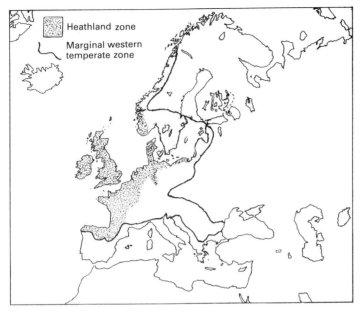

Fig. 2
The Link between the heathland zone of NW Europe and the Marginal Western Temperate Climate

water loss efficiently and, thereby, to tolerate dry conditions (Fig. 3). The evergreen leaves are an adaptation to mild, moist winters (Noirfalise & Vanesse, 1976) but despite this feature, conditions can be too moist – too oceanic – for the optimum formation of heathland, as they are on the western-most coasts of the British Isles. Winter tolerance of frost limits

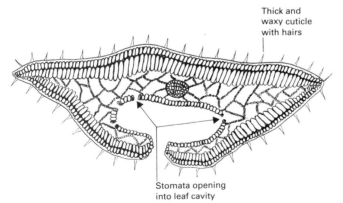

Fig. 3
Cross-section of Erica Leaf

the distribution of heathland eastwards in Europe, where the climate becomes increasingly continental, and at higher altitudes. *Calluna* is intolerant of frosts and Gimingham suggests that the extended autumn which is a feature of the western temperate areas, enables the plants to harden off before winter. The protection that snow cover gives is also important; it was recognized by Beijerinck (1940) as an important factor influencing the dominance of *Calluna* in the vegetation. Frost damage to

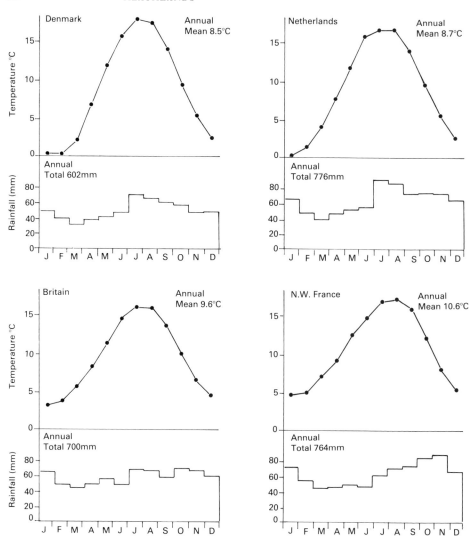

Fig. 4
Uniformity of Temperature and Rainfall throughout Marginal Western Temperate Climate Zone

the plants causes a reddening or browning of the foliage similar to the damage caused by drought, and, in extreme cases, the plants may be killed.

Fig. 2 indicates how closely the distribution of heathland matches those areas of western Europe with a western marginal temperate climate. The distribution of *Calluna* (Fig. 1) is more or less confined to the temperate area of Europe. Temperate climates, very similar to that of north-west Europe, are to be found in other parts of the world: on the north-west coast and in parts of eastern North America, eastern Asia, South America

Snow on heathland – it can provide vital protection to the frost-vulnerable heather/ Nature Photographers, F. V. Blackburn

and Australasia. In all these regions there are vegetation types composed of dwarf shrubs, analogous to the heathlands of north-west Europe.

Soils

Heathland generally forms, as we have seen, in regions where the underlying rock strata result in the formation of poor, acidic and often sandy soils. Beneath most heathlands, soil of the podsolic series are to be found. They have well-defined layers, or horizons, which are indicative of the subtle interactions between rocks, climate and vegetation which constitute the process of soil formation. The soils beneath heathland are, in part, responsible for the spread of heathland vegetation, but, in turn, this vegetation modifies the processes of soil formation.

A vertical section cut through soil will reveal a number of well-marked horizons; the number, structure and depth of these horizons depend on the particular processes involved in the formation of the soil. Pedologists use a system of letters for each horizon to describe and interpret soil profiles. The disposition of the horizons, their structure, and their physical and chemical composition are features used in systems of soil classification.

The uppermost horizon in a soil is called the **A** horizon; this is the more generally recognized topsoil, in which most plant growth occurs and is generally an intimate mixture of minerals and organic matter. The A

Fig. 5
The Sequence of
Development from a
Woodland Soil to a
typical Heathland Soil
(after Mackney). The E
and B horizons develop as
iron and humus are leached
from the upper soil layers

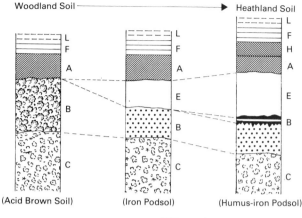

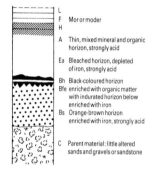

Fig. 6

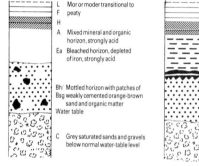

Fig. 7

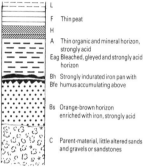

Fig. 8

Fig. 6
Profile of a Humus-iron
Podsol

Fig. 7
Profile of a Ground-water
Podsol

Fig. 8
Profile of a Peaty Gleyed
Podsol

horizon may be overlain by a series of layers of fresh plant litter (the L layer), partly-decomposed plant litter (the F layer) – in which the remains of the plants are still recognizable – and the H layer – in which decomposed plant remains are unrecognizable.

The properties of each layer and the extent to which it is developed enable a simple but familiar system of soil classification to be devised; this recognizes four types – peat, mull, moder and mor. Where there are waterlogged, anaerobic conditions, peat forms, since the accumulating plant remains are prevented from decomposing. In a mull soil there is hardly any accumulation of plant litter since there are good conditions for decomposition. This is the most fertile of the soil types and the organic matter is rapidly incorporated into the A horizon beneath.

In a mor soil, conditions do not favour decomposition; they are generally too acidic and sometimes dry. In addition, the leaf litter which falls is often more resistant to decomposition because of the types of plants, such as heathers and conifers, which grow on such soils. The leaf litter is rich in tannins and resins, acidic and base-deficient; it does not provide a good medium for the organisms which promote decomposition. Decomposition is slow and takes place largely through the agency of micro-organisms, since the large soil invertebrates, particularly earthworms and millipedes, are generally absent. Other soil micro-arthropods, which generally play secondary roles in the decomposition process, such as mites (Acari) and springtails (Collembola), are much less numerous than in richer soils. Because the rate of decomposition is slow, well-developed L, F and H layers develop above the A horizon (Fig. 5).

In a moder soil, the development of these layers reaches a stage which is intermediate between that of mull and mor. Because heathland vegetation generates very acid litter, well-developed mor soils are found beneath this vegetation and, as we shall see later, the changes in microclimate under the canopy of the heather plants, particularly changes in humidity, affect the rates at which litter accumulates and breaks down. Mor soils also form beneath coniferous forests in north temperate regions.

Beneath the A horizon is the E horizon, in which the organic matter content is less and from which bases may be removed by the downward passage of water through the profile. These bases are deposited in the B horizon, which is rich in silica, clay, iron, aluminium and humus. The lower C horizon resembles the parent rock beneath and may contain deposits of carbonates and soluble bases which have been washed from the horizons above (Fig 5).

Soil-formation depends on a variety of factors which include climate, vegetation and fauna, the topography of the area, the parent rocks, and the period of time over which soil-forming processes have been operating. Climate is undoubtedly one of the most important factors; rain falling on the soil and percolating through has an important effect as it transports bases and humus from the upper to the lower horizons. The exact effect depends on the amount of water which evaporated from the soil (an upward movement of water) and that which is transpired by plants. This combined effect, called evapo-transpiration, depends on the temperature and humidity of the atmosphere, and can vary from place to place and from season to season.

Podsols form in regions where rainfall exceeds evapo-transpiration for most of the time. There is an overall downward movement of materials in the soil; fine clay and humus particles are washed down by the movement of water but bases, such as calcium, magnesium, sodium and potassium are leached by chemical processes in which they are replaced by hydrogen ions causing an acidification of the upper soil layers.

The most characteristic feature of a podsol is the ash-grey E horizon which is formed beneath the A horizon by the strong leaching effects. In fact, the name podsol, which is derived from the Russian for ash, refers to the bleached colour of this horizon. Equally characteristic are the hard pan layers which form in the B horizon where humus and iron are redeposited (Fig 5). Formerly, the bleached E horizon was considered to be the diagnostic feature of a podsol, however, recent soil classifications emphasize the existence of the B hard pans layers. In the British soil classification, the B horizon (where deposition occurs) must contain more than 0.3% extractable iron and at least 5% aluminium in the total clay.

It is possible to trace the development of a humus-iron podsol from an acid brown soil through changes in the E and B horizons. In acid brown soils there is a re-distribution of salts and organic matter in the profile but this does not lead to either a bleached horizon or pan layer. Gradually, as oxides of iron are leached from the upper layers and re-deposited as sesquioxides, an incipient **B** horizon forms. This is called an iron podsol (Fig. 6). Further development of the iron-enriched horizon continues, while above it a humus pan begins to form. When this is fully developed this type of soil is called a humus-iron podsol. This type of soil profile is to be found beneath most of the heathlands of north-western Europe. A variant of the podsol exists on dune heathlands, such as those on the Friesian Islands in the Netherlands and Germany, where the E horizon is deficient in iron, and only a humus pan forms.

The process of podsolization is modified in waterlogged conditions and gleyed (clay-like) podsols develop. In the areas where there are high levels of ground-water, the **B** horizon acquires a mottled appearance through the alternation of aerobic and anaerobic conditions. A gleyed podsol will also form if the parent materials are impervious, sometimes with overlying deposits of peat instead of the F and H layers (Figs. 7 & 8) (Mackney, 1961; Bridges, 1970).

In chapter 3, we trace the interaction between the development of podsols and the spread of heathland vegetation in north-west Europe. It is generally thought that the removal of forest cover by Neolithic Man accelerated the rate at which acid brown soils were converted into podsols. There is evidence of acid brown soils or immature podsols in the buried profiles beneath barrows.

Geology

In Britain, the oldest rocks lie to the north and west, with successively younger strata to the south and east. The central mass of chalk (Cretaceous), which extends from Dorset to Yorkshire, forms a convenient division between the younger and older rocks. Igneous rocks, and Devonian and Carboniferous sedimentary deposits form the south-west peninsula, parts of Wales, north-west and north England, and Scotland. East of the chalk lie younger strata, mostly originating in Tertiary times but overlain in places by sands, gravels and clays which have been redistributed by the actions of ice, water or wind. The topography associated with the older rocks is that of upland Britain; although many of these areas are covered by dwarf shrub moorland dominated by *Calluna*, they are at altitudes over 250–300 m (800–1000 ft) and, consequently, outside our definition of heathland. In the south, the younger rocks give rise to more gentle scenery, with a more undulating landscape and, in general, deeper and more fertile soils, which are extensively cultivated. But, in many places, they are thin, sandy, acidic and hungry, and thus suitable for heathland to develop. The range of suitable soils is increased by the complexity of the superficial deposits. It is not possible to generalize in geological terms about the strata which carry heathland vegetation in the various regions of southern Britain: heathland is to be found on soils derived from both the oldest and the youngest rocks.

A Primeval Landscape? CHAPTER 3

Thomas Hardy's assumption that heathland has always existed still prevails to some extent, simply because there is no memory of what was there before. Increasingly, during the last half century, studies of vegetation and land-use history have demonstrated the important role that Man – particularly early Man – has had in shaping the present-day landscape. However, ecologists have been slow to accept this view and inclined to explain the distribution and abundance of plants and animals only by the processes which they see operating in the present. It is now generally accepted that historical processes and events are vital factors in the occurrence and development of modern plant communities. Pollen analysis and historical ecology have both become essential to the study of contemporary ecology: both are required if we are to understand how heathlands came into existence.

Early Views on the Origin of Heathland

In chapter 2 we reviewed the climatic and edaphic (soil) factors required for members of the Ericaceae family, especially *Calluna*, to become dominant in the vegetation. Over most of north-west Europe, where heathlands are found, forest is considered the vegetation climax. That is to say, if factors such as exposure, poor soil, grazing and human activity are slight or absent, the succession of plant communities would eventually lead to mature forest. Without major change in the climatic conditions, it is thought that mature forest would persist indefinitely. With the type of climate we have today, coniferous forest dominated by Scots Pine (*Pinus sylvestris*) would be the climax over the northernmost parts of Britain and Europe; over most of the southern lowlands, the climax vegetation would be deciduous forest composed mostly of oak (*Quercus* spp.) with some Beech (*Fagus sylvatica*). Large expanses of open heathland would not exist because *Calluna* would be shaded by trees. For the most part, heather would grow only beneath the trees in gaps in the forest cover, or on poor soils where the tree cover was thin. As Gimingham (1972) puts it: 'to explain the existence of heathland, we must first explain the lack of trees'.

It was thought at one time, that the decrease in forest cover and the spread of heathland was itself a natural vegetation climax. Graebner (1925) advanced the climax theory of heathland, and suggested that almost all the heathland in north-west Europe, although subject to varying degrees of human influence, was the outcome of forest development on poor soils. His evidence was that on those soils where humus-iron podsol had developed (in the western and more oceanic regions of Europe) and where grazing had ceased, forest regeneration did not take place. In these regions, rainfall was higher – about 700–800 mm (28–32 in) a year – and minerals were leached from these poor soils even where there was forest.

19th-century view of treeless heathland/Dorset County Museum

As the soils deteriorated, so did the forest, to be replaced by dwarf-shrub heathland dominated by *Calluna*. Where the climate was drier, in eastern and more continental parts of Europe, and rainfall was only about 500 mm (20 in) a year, brown forest soils remained, retaining their minerals and enabling the forest to persist; on heathlands, when grazing ceased, trees spread. However, it has been shown that even on the more oceanic, podsolized areas, tree regeneration is possible once grazing has stopped; thus rabbits may at one time have been an important factor preventing the spread of trees (Noirfalise & Vanesse, 1976). More recently, in some parts of north-west Europe, it has been thought that eutrophication caused by the drift of chemicals from surrounding agricultural lands has resulted in more rapid succession to grassland or to woodland.

Tansley (1939) thought open heathland was natural on the western coasts of Europe and on mountain sides up to 610 m (2000 ft), where succession to woodland was checked by exposure or by the pruning effect on the vegetation by salt spray, and that heathland was the climax vegetation. Likewise, where heathland formed part of the primary succession on inland or coastal sand-dunes, it was also considered to be naturally-occurring. In both these examples, an open type of heathland had occurred naturally and it was considered possible that similar factors had operated elsewhere to produce open heathlands and prevented the establishment of trees. Because of this view, it was difficult to accept that the activities of Man had played a part in reducing forest cover. It was acknowledged that Man may have helped heathlands to spread, particularly by grazing, but he was not the primary cause of their existence. This view of the origin of heathlands was held by Beijerinck as late as 1940.

Gradually it became the generally-held view that anthropogenic factors were predominant in the creation and maintenance of heathland. Tansley (1939) recognized that there must be some factors which prevented the establishment of woodland, such as violent winds, recurrent fires, and grazing, and it became evident that where heathlands were not burnt or grazed, trees rapidly invaded. Gimingham (1972) also points out that there is a strong floristic affinity between heathland communities and the lower strata of the vegetation in boreal forests of Scots Pine (*Pinus sylvestris*) or mixed pine/spruce (*Pinus/Abies*), and even beneath oak woodland on acid soils there is a similar heathy type of vegetation. Tansley thought that the lowland heathlands of southern and eastern England were a stage in succession to forest, and that the formation of heathland followed degeneration of oak forest on poor, sandy soils. Some growth of trees was possible on all these heathlands and he regarded them as a subclimax, or deflected succession, to dry oak or beech forest. He proposed the succession

heath → birch → (→ pine) → oak → beech

but also suggested that the soil conditions created beneath beech forest made regeneration impossible, causing a return to heathland – and a cycle would be established.

Gimingham commented on the differences of opinion as to whether heathlands should be regarded as seral or sub-climax communities or derived from the degradation of forest. It was now recognized that most heathland arose in place of forests. There was an increasing trend towards podsolization in these poor soils, but it was not clear whether the deterioration caused the forest to decline or whether the removal of the tree cover hastened podsolization and prevented forest regeneration. Some ecologists, e.g., Pearsall (1950), thought there was a natural trend towards soil acidification in moist oceanic climates. But others, including Dimbleby (1962) and Haskins (1978), considered that leaching and a consequent deterioration of the soil was already in train, accelerated by Man's influence. Dimbleby believed that on the heathlands of southern England, podsolization took place later, the soil profiles taking 1500 to 3000 years to develop, which would suggest that podsolization may have begun in the early Flandrian (see Fig. 10) and that podsols may have been widespread before the Bronze Age. Evidence from buried soil profiles is conflicting: brown forest soils, immature podsols, and well-developed podsols can all be found. It seems likely that the deterioration of these soils had begun by Atlantic times, *before* tree cover had significantly decreased.

The former forests on the heathlands of northern Europe would have been growing on soils derived from poor parent materials; beneath the trees, brown forest soils would have developed. At this time the climate was becoming much wetter (oceanic). These soils, and the forests growing on them, were in a delicate balance. Clearance of the trees, or the prevention of regeneration by, for instance, grazing of the field layer, could easily have initiated changes which would lead to increasing acidity and podsolization. The nutrient capital in these soils was continually in circulation between soil and vegetation. If the vegetation were removed, the cycle would have been broken and the soils would have been unable to retain the nutrients. These would have been leached from the soil, leading to podsolization and preventing the regeneration of the forest. A similar condition exists in the soils of tropical forests today, where felling leads to soil deterioration and prevents re-establishment of the forest.

It is clear we must regard most heathlands to have expanded in areas which were formerly forest. This may have caused soil deterioration (which may, however, have been under way already) and this, together with the influences of Man, helped to maintain open heathland. The detailed sequence of events and the likely causes have been revealed by pollen analysis.

The Evidence of Pollen Analysis

Until the early part of this century, the origin and distribution of British vegetation was deduced from the sequences of geological and climatic changes which were thought to have taken place. The effects of glaciation and the fossil remains of plants provided the main evidence. Then it was realized that it was possible to recover the remains of plants, pollen and spores from the Tertiary and Quaternary deposits, and in many instances, the species of plant from which the pollen had originated could be recognized. The microscopic study of pollen and spore deposits – palynology – developed into a science which enabled, within limits, past vegetation types to be reconstructed. Pollen is often produced in large quantities and may be dispersed over wide areas; it is resistant to decay, especially under anaerobic and acid conditions, and therefore persists in the sediments where it was trapped. The production, dispersal and decay of pollen differs between species, and these factors have to be considered when interpreting pollen diagrams.

Pollen-bearing sediments are usually sampled with a corer, the sequence of sediments providing a chronological series. The grains are extracted by

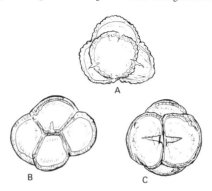

Fig. 9
Microscope Drawings of Pollen Grains

A & B   Common Heather *(Calluna Vulgaris)*
C   Cross-leaved Heath *(Erica tetralix)*

Taking samples for pollen analysis with a peat borer/S. B. Chapman

chemical treatments and then identified and counted under a microscope. Each species of plant has a characteristic type of pollen (Fig. 9). The chronology of the pollen-bearing sediments is calibrated from archaeological features and radio-carbon dating, and is then correlated with geological, climatic and archaeological events or times (Fig. 10).

Counts of the pollen grains for each species from different levels in the profile are expressed in proportions or percentages of either the total pollen count or of the tree pollen count. This means that an increase in the pollen of one species must correspond to a decrease for other species, even if there is no absolute decline of that species. Without care, this way of expressing results can lead to misinterpretation of the significance of vegetation changes. As an alternative, it is sometimes possible to express pollen counts per unit-area of the profile and to estimate absolute, rather than relative, changes in the pollen deposits.

When the ice retreated, temperatures rose and a tundra type of vegetation or grassland, spread in the Post-Allerød period (late Weichselian, about 14,000 BP) (see Fig. 10), but this was rapidly replaced by woodland and forest. The early forest period, about 10,000 BP, is called the Pre-

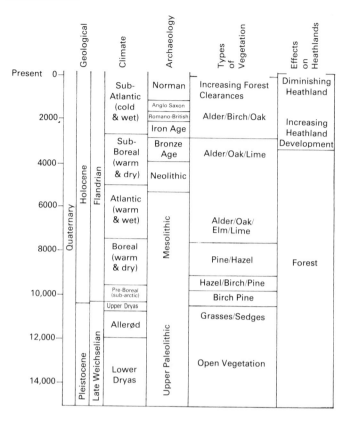

Fig. 10
Geological, Climatic, Archaeological and Vegetational Changes in the Last 14,000 Years – Used for Dating Pollen Deposits

Boreal; temperatures were rising and the ice continuing to melt, and although the sea level rose, the land bridges between Britain and the Continent, and between Britain and Ireland, remained. It was at this time that the Lusitanian elements in the floras of south-west England and southern Ireland were able to migrate northwards along the west European seaboard. The Boreal period saw a continuing increase in warmth-loving species of trees, and the forest, which had been coniferous, gained species such as Oak (*Quercus*), Elm (*Ulmus*) and Hazel (*Corylus*). The gradual changes in the climate led to the establishment of Lime (*Tilia*), the most thermophilous of native British trees. The following Atlantic period is regarded as the climatic optimum and marks the period when warmth-loving trees reached the furthest north. The land bridge between Britain and Europe was probably lost during the transition from Boreal to Atlantic periods, so preventing further significant migration. Pollen diagrams from the Atlantic period are uniform throughout Britain; the forests in the north being coniferous and those in the south being mixed deciduous woodland and forest, predominantly Oak. This type of vegetation can be regarded as the climax. From the Atlantic period, the climate became more oceanic, and an increase in anthropogenic effects can be recognized. Soils, as we have already discussed, began to deteriorate and there was an expansion of heathland and Birch woodland. Both of these indicate a disturbance of the original forest cover.

At the boundary between the Atlantic and Sub-Boreal periods, there is a widespread and dramatic decline in the amount of Elm (*Ulmus*) pollen. This fall in Elm distribution took place throughout north-west Europe and has been radio-carbon-dated to about 3000 BC. The cause was first thought to be due to climatic change, but the decline over the whole region took place at slightly different times; if the cause had been climatic it would have taken place simultaneously throughout.

As an alternative explanation, it was suggested that Elm was used as animal fodder by Neolithic Man. There was still very little grassland and the men cut branches from the trees for stall-kept animals to eat. The repeated cutting of the leafy branches greatly reduced the production of pollen. At first, some doubted that Neolithic farmers of 3000 BC were active enough to have such a drastic effect on the vegetation.

On the evidence pollen studies from a number of Mesolithic sites, Simmonds and Dimbleby (1974) considered that the hunter-gatherer existence may not have been universal, and that some domestic animals may have been kept. Mesolithic Man may also have burnt the vegetation and even have been able to clear it. There is also evidence of the existence of grass, plantain (*Plantago*) and Mugwort (*Artemisia*) pollen, and Bracken spores. It thus seems that Mesolithic Man may have played a role in determining vegetation composition and soil structure in some areas of the British Isles. Hence the changes that would encourage heathland to spread may have started as early as the Boreal period. Haskins (1978) concludes that, if this were the case on the Dorset heathlands, where the inherently poor nature of the parent materials of the soil would have made them susceptible to Mesolithic Man's activities, podsols may have been widespread there before the Bronze Age.

In parts of Britain buried soil profiles from beneath Neolithic burial mounds have been examined. In some cases, they were brown forest earths with typical pollen profiles. In other cases, podsols, or partly-developed (immature) podsols, have been found. At the times the barrows were built, a variety of soil changes was taking place. In some cases, where the original soils were poor and acid and the forest was open, leaching (and hence podsolization) had begun. In other cases, where forest cover was complete, there was no trace of podsolization. Such barrows were probably built in clearings, but although the dates of many barrows coincided with the Sub-Boreal period, others were constructed later (Dimbleby, 1962). The soils beneath these barrows showed that ecological changes mostly caused by Man were taking place in the surrounding landscape. In individual cases it was not always possible to tell whether the spread of *Calluna* preceded or followed the onset of podsolization.

Gradually, however, improved dating of Neolithic artefacts and the pollen-bearing deposits by radio-carbon techniques established a close correlation between the occurrences of Neolithic cultures and the decline of the Elm. In this way, the effect of Man on the vegetation was demonstrated. Besides the evidence of radio-carbon dating and archaeology, there were changes in the composition of the pollen profiles which supported this hypothesis. The pollen of grasses (*Gramineae*), nettles (*Urtica*), Sorrel (*Rumex*), Mugwort (*Artemisia*), Fat Hen (*Chenopodium*) and Ribwort

Plantain (*Plantago lanceolata*) – all plants which are associated with human activity – began to rise.

However, scepticism remained, since Neolithic Man was thought incapable of causing changes of such magnitude. But it is important to remember that tree-clearance was only part of the story – regeneration had to be prevented too. This would have been achieved by the animals grazing beneath the mature trees. Gradually the forest cover would have decreased, and with the more open condition the rate of podsolization would have increased, favouring the expansion of heathland.

An important field experiment at Draved in southern Jutland (Denmark) provided the most convincing piece of evidence. A small group of researchers using primitive implements, were able to clear 500 sq m (600 sq yds) of woodland in four hours. This type of slash-and-burn clearance was called *Landnam*, or land-taking. The area cleared in this way was used to grow crops, the fertility of the soil soon declined, and after about three years another area of forest needed to be cleared. Forest clearances such as these are illustrated in the pollen diagrams, which indicate how trees were cleared in limited areas. Often a charcoal layer can be found in the profile, indicating that burning was used to assist the forest clearance. In a typical *Landnam* sequence, the proportion of tree pollen declines; there is an increase in the pollen of grasses, weeds and herbs, the commonest species being Ribwort Plantain (*Plantago lanceolata*), Sorrel (*Rumex*) and Mugwort (*Artemisia*); and there is often a charcoal layer. Later the proportion of pollen of Ericaceae and grasses begins to rise, representing an intervening stage of heathland or grassland following abandonment, followed by an increase in the proportion of tree pollen as the area reverts to woodland.

The pollen of *Calluna* and other members of the Ericaceae are some of the most abundant and easily-recognized pollens in almost all of the glacial and interglacial stages. The majority of records comes from the late Weichselian period, and represent the types of site from which pollen profiles have been examined. Normally, pollen is best preserved in acidic, peaty deposits, which tend to be naturally surrounded by heathland vegetation types. *Calluna* leaves not only pollen but many sub-fossil remains; the resistant stems of the plant, in particular, are easily recognized. *Calluna* was a constituent of the first tundra type of vegetation, which spread into Britain as the ice retreated. Gradually, as closed woodland developed, suitable conditions for the plant deteriorated, because there was insufficient light beneath a closed forest canopy. At this time, *Calluna* was probably restricted to clearings, forest edges and more open, heathy woodlands on poor soils. The woodland clearances in Neolithic times created the open conditions preferred by *Calluna*.

Heathland Pollen Profiles

To see more clearly the sequence of changes which took place to produce open heathland, we shall examine two examples. One of the earliest was from Hockham Mere, near Thetford, Norfolk (Godwin, 1944). This mere lies at the northern margin of the Breckland, an area which, from time immemorial, has been open and treeless until planted with conifers in the last fifty years. There has always been much speculation on the origins of

A PRIMEVAL LANDSCAPE

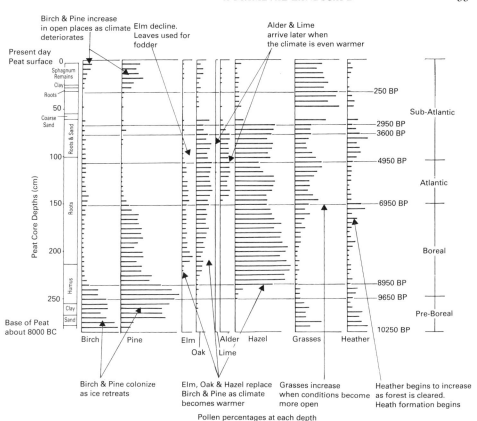

Fig. 11
Pollen Diagram from Dorset (after Haskins, 1978)

this landscape, and grazing was thought to be one of the most important factors (Farrow, 1925).

The pollen profiles from the mere sediments provided a complete sequence from late-Weichselian to post-Tudor times. In the Boreal and Atlantic periods there was complete woodland cover, the proportions of non-tree pollens being very small; between the Atlantic and Sub-Boreal periods, these rose sharply. They were accompanied by similar increases in the pollen of grasses, Ericas (mainly *Calluna*), fern spores, Ribwort Plantain (*Plantago lanceolata*), Sorrel (*Rumex*) and various Compositae. Godwin (1975) concluded that since the Breckland was as densely populated by Neolithic peoples as any part of Britain, and that the great flint mines of Grimes Graves (where radio-carbon dating has shown evidence of flint-mining since at least 4000 BC (Burgess, 1980)) were not far away, the forest cover had been manually destroyed and heathland communities had spread. The pollen diagrams showed that, unlike many areas, open heathland, once established, remained open and treeless.

In south-east Dorset, Haskins has shown (Fig. 11) that the Boreal woodland on the Tertiary deposits surrounding Poole Harbour was not completely closed. It retained an open character which allowed a proportion of heathland vegetation to survive, and which expanded in the Atlantic period. Today, there are podsols here; in Atlantic times there were probably acidic brown forest soils of low fertility and pH value. Because of the more open woodlands, it is not clear whether podsolization commenced before the expansion of the heathlands or after.

Haskins also found a decline in Elm (*Ulmus*) pollen, which was contemporary with the decline over most of north-west Europe. In Britain, the Elm decline is the most extensively radio-carbon-dated horizon (Godwin, 1975), and almost all of the dates fall within the 300 years before 3050 BC. The decline in both Elm and Lime (*Tilia*) pollen was originally thought to be due to climatic changes, but, as we have seen, it is now likely that human activity played an important role. Neolithic peoples are now considered to have been present in the British Isles by 4950 BP (3000 BC). In the Poole Basin at 3600 BP (1650 BC) there is a significant reduction in tree pollens, with declines recorded for *Quercus*, *Alnus* and *Tilia*. The proportions of Hazel (*Corylus*) and Birch (*Betula*) remain constant. There was a considerable Bronze Age occupation of this area, which left a large number of barrows and other remains. The pollen diagrams show that after the initial forest clearances there was extensive development of Hazel scrub. Ericaceous pollen is also well represented at this time. It was unlikely that Bronze Age Man selectively cleared the forest to leave Hazel, so the development of this scrub must have been spontaneous. The buried soil profiles beneath barrows indicate varying degrees of podsolization, and it seems that the Bronze Age clearances simply accelerated a process which was already in train.

Further falls in tree pollen occur later in the Bronze Age, but at these times Hazel pollen also falls. Grass and ericaceous pollen now rise, and chemical analyses of the soil (Haskins, 1978) show that there were increases in magnesium, aluminium and iron, which suggest that the soils were becoming more unstable and that erosion and leaching were taking place at accelerating rates. From this evidence, these heathlands must have become established in the late Bronze Age, 2950 BP (1000 BC).

Pollen records for all members of the Ericaceae are abundant in almost all glacial and interglacial stages. Many palynologists have grouped the pollen of all species together, calling them Ericaceae, ericales or ericoid pollen. Besides *Calluna* and species of *Erica*, this group contains pollen of related species such as *Rhododendron*, *Empetrum* and *Vaccinium*. As techniques have improved, it has become possible to identify genera and species within this family.

From the late Weichselian period, ericoid pollen forms 36–44% of all British pollen zones (Godwin, 1975). Subsequently, this proportion increases markedly. Many of the changes, such as the development of ombrogenous peat, took place in the uplands and are outside the scope of this book. Conditions favoured the spread of Ericaceae in general, and a consequent increase in their pollen records. The pattern is similar for all the species, with scattered records from pre-Flandrian deposits – throughout the Flandrian period there is an increase in the proportion of ericoid pollen, attributable to climatic and soil changes, and anthropogenic effects.

Unlike the Ericaceae, there are few records of gorse (*Ulex* spp.) in the pollen record. Three species occur on the heathlands of southern Britain: *Ulex europaeus* can be found growing almost everywhere, in association with one or other of the dwarf gorses, *Ulex gallii* or *U. minor*. Almost all the records come from Neolithic, Bronze Age, Iron Age and Roman sites. Godwin (1975) considers that forest clearances and pastoral activity created favourable conditions for the spread of gorse. There is a long tradition of Common Gorse or Furze (*Ulex europaeus*) being used for fodder (Lucas, 1960; Tubbs, 1968). In Ireland it was planted for this purpose (Lucas, 1960), which may also have been the case elsewhere. Pollen records suggest a close correlation between the activities of Man and the occurrence of gorse.

Bracken (*Pteridium aquilinum*) is also a widespread, common constituent of heathland today. It is a cosmopolitan species which readily spreads by spores, but its distribution is limited by the sensitivity of its rhizomes to frost. It occurs throughout the British Isles, up to an altitude of 610 m (2000 ft), and in Scandinavia its distribution extends to the Arctic Circle.

There are some scattered records of Bracken in pre-Quaternary deposits, suggesting it is of ancient origin, and from the Quaternary era – approximately the last two million years – there are abundant records. Bracken is usually recognized in pollen deposits as spores, which are easily distinguishable from spores of other fern species. Macroscopic remains, mostly rhizomes, have also been recorded from Bronze Age and Roman sites (Godwin, 1975). Spores and plant remains occur in all the temperate stages of the Quaternary era. Bracken is thought to have been a component of the herb layers in deciduous woodlands, since at the same time tree pollen counts are high and the country was still covered with climax woodland.

After the Atlantic-Sub-Boreal transition, the proportion of Bracken in pollen diagrams increases from less than 2% of tree pollen in early Atlantic times to 50–80% in the Sub-Atlantic period. As we have already seen, this was when forest clearances commenced. The varying proportion of bracken spores from site to site emphasize the transient nature of the man-made clearings. These temporary clearings would lead to a local abundance, which would then decline when the clearing was abandoned and tree cover re-established (Rymer, 1976). The pollen diagrams from Hockham Mere (Godwin, 1944) show increases in Bracken, but the levels remain high – another indication that in the Breckland forest did not regenerate. Elsewhere Bracken would have been checked, because it was only as the woodlands became more open or were cleared that it was able to spread and sporulate more freely (Conway, 1957). But as tree cover was re-established, Bracken declined in abundance and became a component of the herb layer once more. The subsequent history of Bracken, in common with most other heathland species was closely associated with the activities of Man; and was subsequently confined to the poorer soils since regular cultivation kept the better soils free of the plant (Rymer, 1976).

CHAPTER 4 **The Influence of Man**

From the Iron Age and Roman times, history and pre-history merge; we need no longer rely on palynology and archaeology to reconstruct the past for there are written sources. From Roman times until the Middle Ages, both palynology and historical sources can be used to interpret vegetation changes, but from the Middle Ages, changes in the composition and distribution of vegetation took place too rapidly for the reliable interpretation of pollen diagrams. So historical sources become much more important, particularly from the 19th century, when agricultural changes and improvements were very rapid indeed. In the last twenty years, historical ecology has developed as a distinct discipline within the science of ecology. The source materials for the historical ecologist are documents, publications, maps, deeds, manor court rolls, wills, and so on.

After the Middle Ages, the number of documentary and similar sources increases. This large body of written evidence relates to the use of the land and its apportionment between different landlords and tenants. The types of land changes described can be interpreted by an ecologist (who recognizes the conditions under which certain species and communities exist) to give a picture of the vegetation at that time, based on his knowledge and experience of present-day species and communities.

There is considerable regional variation in the quality and abundance of sources, and the extent to which they can be interpreted. The earliest sources are probably Anglo-Saxon charters. There are many hundreds of these surviving which describe Old English estates. Often they provide us with no more information than the boundaries, or perambulations, of the estates, many of which were drawn to prominent landmarks, woods, hedges, streams, roads, ditches, rocks and especially trees. Rackham (1976) notes that when reading these today, one is struck by how little England has changed in the millenium since they were written. Woods and forests are undoubtedly the best candidates for study because of their permanence in the landscape. The uses of woodland were under the strict control of their owners; so their location, type, and area were important, and therefore recorded. Hedges have also proved fruitful for studies of a similar type and are fully described in the *New Naturalist* volume *Hedges*, by Pollard, Hooper and Moore (1974). Besides presenting much biological information on hedges, the study provides a useful introduction to the methods of historical ecology.

For the Lizard, an extensive area of heathland in southern Cornwall, a number of 10th-century documents survive in Exeter Cathedral library. They show that in certain parts, the distribution of enclosed and unenclosed heathland was similar to that of today; indeed, it seems that the Lizard may have been even more open then than now, since some of the landmarks recorded in the Saxon perambulations lie amid scrub today (Hopkins, 1983).

Further forest clearances probably occurred during the Viking period. The work of Iversen (1964 and 1969) in Denmark suggested that some heathland areas were established in Viking times, and fire horizons in the peat layers indicate the role of burning in both their establishment and maintenance. Most of the Viking records concentrate on archaeological, cultural and mercantile activities and contain relatively little information on agricultural activities (e.g. Brønsted, 1965; Wilson, 1980). There were stable farming communities, which grew cereals and bred cattle, but although forest was cleared (often assisted by burning), this was probably not extensive. In some areas, such as the Suffolk Sandlings, both the Saxon and Viking immigrants in the period 780–1070 AD cleared the forest and so initiated changes which eventually led to the development of heathland (Chadwick, 1982).

In Britain, the pattern of forest clearance continued up to 1200 AD, by which time much of the modern landscape was established. Rackham considers that the proportions of farmland, woodland and moorland were not very different from those of today. There was a gradual development of arable farming, and it has generally been thought that scrub and woodland regenerated in places after the Romans left, but this view has been challenged (Taylor, 1970; Rackham, 1976). Both authors consider that although there may have been some decline and change, it was nowhere near as extensive as was previously thought. Forest clearances stabilized, and woods were managed by what Rackham termed 'woodmanship' (as distinct from forestry) to provide a continuous supply of different types of timber and fuel. A pattern of arable and grazing land was thus established to meet the needs of the inhabitants, and further change and expansion were unnecessary.

The Domesday Survey of 1086 gives us a reasonably accurate description of the early Medieval landscape, and the geography of England at this time has frequently been reconstructed. The Survey emphasizes assets, productive farmland, plough teams, buildings, agricultural machinery, mills, woods and numbers of people; there is no more than allusion to pastures, meadows and wastes . . . or heathland. The only reference to heathland is for the village of Boveridge, on Cranborne Chase, Dorset (Darby & Welldon-Finn, 1967). Here, St Mary's Church at Cranborne, a priory established by Tewkesbury Abbey, held heathland 'two leagues long and wide (*Bruaria ii longa et lata*), together with nine-and-a-half furlongs of pasture and a woodland one league by a half'.

Some inference regarding heathland can be drawn from examining the pattern of woodland and farmland, especially in settlements where the underlying rocks caused poor soils to develop. The general picture is much the same for all the heathland areas: settlement is confined to the better soils and there are almost none on open heathland, because the effort and expense of establishing them were too great. In the New Forest there is, as with almost all heathlands, abundant evidence of Mesolithic occupation; by the Bronze and Iron Ages the open heathland was used for hunting and was not settled (Tubbs, 1968). Since the Iron Age, these areas have been regarded as waste, suitable only for free grazing. But not all of the New Forest lies on poor soils: the modern pattern of settlement probably originated in Saxon times – communities developed on the better soils, the remainder being exploited for grazing and timber. The pattern is

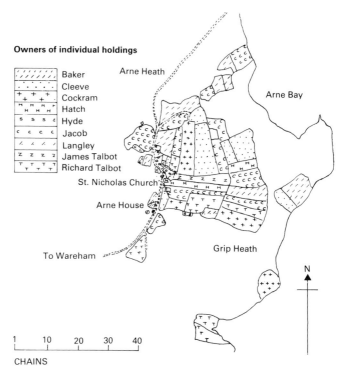

Fig. 12
Cultivated area of Arne Manor, Dorset, c. 1750, Showing Distribution of Individual Holdings (Kerr, 1968)

similar elsewhere: in few of the heathland areas are there parishes which are entirely heathland; the boundaries of most are drawn to include areas of better soil. This pattern is particularly evident in Dorset, where the heathlands are intersected by several river valleys with richer alluvial soils. Here, and on the fringing Reading Beds and London Clays, was a pattern of settlement that hardly changed from Roman times until the middle of the 18th century (Haskins, 1978). Even within a parish, fertile land was shared among the farmers. Fig. 12 shows how, in the parish of Arne on the Dorset heathlands, fields on the better soils were distributed among the landholders, while the heathland was used for rough grazing (Kerr, 1968).

At the time of the Domesday Survey there was very little woodland remaining in the Breckland of East Anglia. In the Middle Ages the Breckland was probably the largest heathland area in lowland England, occupying about 1000 square km (247,000 acres). Thetford was the Saxon capital of East Anglia, and the pattern of settlement on the better soils and adjacent to the rivers was similar to other heathland areas. The undulating landscape is crossed by four principal rivers and the soils are formed from superficial deposits of chalky, glacial till and sands which overlie the chalk. There is a wide range of depths and acidity which create a diversity of soil and vegetation types. The whole area has been strongly influenced by Man since the forests were cleared, the nature of the soils leading to the development of a special kind of shifting cultivation. Portions, called *brecks*, were ploughed up from time to time and crops grown. When this land was exhausted, it was abandoned and a new piece ploughed. This traditional practice created the characteristic Breckland landscape, which remained intact until some fifty years ago. Later in the Middle Ages, extensive sheepwalks were to be found. As well as sheep, goats and cattle were kept, and later rabbits, whose warrens became a distinctive feature of the Breckland (Sheail, 1971 & 1979; Chadwick, 1980). The manors of the Breckland typically had large and permanently-cultivated fields with outlying stretches of heath and common.

This pattern of land-use was typical of most of the heathland areas of England. Cultivation and settlement were on the seams of good soils which intersected almost all of the heathland. The heathland itself was not cultivated, except in the Breckland, but was used to support farming on the good soils by providing rough grazing, fuel and turf. We can envisage this pattern of use persisting until the influence of the improvers of the 18th century began to be felt. Until then it would have been very difficult to survive on a purely heathland holding.

Thomas Hardy, in *The Return of the Native*, remarks how a man could, with considerable effort, gradually win a small area from the heath, but his successors would be unlikely to be able to maintain it for more than two generations after, and the heath would reassert itself. A similar picture was sketched by Charles Vancouver in 1813, when reporting on the state of agriculture in Hampshire; he described the New Forest dweller who,

'from time to time, has encroached a few perches from the forest, and at which at lengths amounting to two or three acres, constitutes what he conceives a sort of independence to himself and family. Upon this he pretends to grow as much grass and hay as will suffice to bait his working horse, or horses night and morning; a few potatoes; and some bread corn for his family. His principal exertions are directed to the cutting, rearing and carting of peat-fuel, and of procuring or removing any other combustible matter to the neighbouring towns and villages. In the winter, he jobs at wood-cart and in carrying stones or gravel for highways; and thus with raising a forest colt or two, provincially called heath-croppers, and one or two of equally inferior species of meat cattle, is found to get on easily, and in some respects independently, through life.'

This type of existence must have been typical for the heathland inhabitants in lowland England.

Rackham (1976) describes the changes which affected Thorpe Wood and Mousehold (or Mushold) Heath on the outskirts of Norwich. The changes are typical of what happened to a Domesday pannage wood and which lead to the establishment of a treeless common. At the time of the Domesday Survey, Thorpe Wood was one of the largest in Norfolk. Later documents show that in 1140 it covered both the steep slopes above the River Wensum and the area of the present-day Mousehold Heath. Thorpe Wood was used both as a source of timber and fuel and as wood pasture (pannage) for pigs. These uses conflicted, since the pigs prevented the regeneration of trees and an area of open heathland was created, which was recorded in documents from 1236. From this time onwards there is clear evidence that woodland persisted only on the slopes above the river, and heathland was established on the gravel plateau. Later enclosures have reduced the area of heathland still more and today it is a relict common, largely unmanaged as heathland.

'Man could, with considerable effort, gradually win a small area from the heath'/ Dorset County Museum

Until the 17th century, little more than documents and statistical accounts could be used as sources by the historical ecologist, but after this two other important sources are available: the increasing production of maps and plans, and the published accounts of the growing number of travellers through Britain.

Cartography developed during the 16th century, when it played an important part in the development of agriculture which had started to take place. Agricultural improvements and the organization and management of estates required evidence for the best layout for fields, arable land and woods. The Napoleonic Wars of the late 18th century led to the creation of the Ordnance Survey, whose first series of maps appeared between 1810 and 1817, although their planning began as early as 1792. These maps and their subsequent editions enable detailed chronologies of parts of the landscape to be built up. From about 1840, maps from the *Tithe Commutation Survey* are also an important source. Later, in the 1930s, there was a *Land Utilisation Survey*, although the maps from this need to be interpreted cautiously because of the criteria used to define land categories.

The written accounts of the 17th-, 18th- and early 19th-century travellers often provide us with an insight into the countryside and the way of its inhabitants. But, again, their comments must be interpreted with caution since they were often influenced by the ideas prevailing at that time – their accounts tell us as much about the writers as of the countryside itself. The increased zest for improvement, for economic and social progress, and for a spirit of enquiry, which characterized post-Restoration England, is evident in almost all of these writings. In the countryside, agriculture ceased to meet the needs of the local population; it looked for wider markets, and gradually farming became a business. It was assisted by the spirit of enquiry, which led to the discovery of soil improvement methods that enabled waste and marginal land to be brought into cultivation. As we have seen, much of this type of land had, through past use, become heathland; now it was to become farmland, woodland, or even built on, to meet the needs of the expanding towns. The agricultural changes led to a more organized countryside, and open lands and wastes were enclosed with increasing frequency.

In 1771, Arthur Young published his letters as *A Farmer's Tour Through the East of England*, describing 'vast tracts of waste land that call aloud for improvements . . . What fortunes are here to be made by spirited improvers.' In 1830, William Cobbett published *Rural Rides*, reminiscences peppered with personal views and political comments. Even here, we are still left with the feeling that he, too, saw nothing when crossing the heaths but waste land with potential for improvement.

These accounts take us from the late 17th century, when agricultural improvements had just begun, from a time when pastoral farming – particularly sheep and wool – had started to decline, to a period when arable farming began to increase and open commons and wastes were enclosed. Then came decline, and by the early 19th century, villages had become depopulated, farmland neglected, and the rural population was invariably poor. Cobbett saw a very depressed countryside during his rides in 1820, but he was at the turning-point between the open-field system's subsistence farming and the prosperity of the middle decades of the 19th century, which he was not to see. All these changes intimately affected the status of the heathland of lowland England.

For many centuries, the way in which land had been divided among its holders and cultivators prevented any improvements. Most of the produce from the land would have been for the holder's own consumption. It was not possible to improve the yield from the open fields, in the first place, because they were too large (covering hundreds of acres) and more importantly, because their management was not in the hands of a single person. Each farmer held a number of strips, which were seldom adjacent to one another, and this – perhaps more than anything – deterred initiative. The geometry of these open fields made cultivation difficult. But gradually the view spread that cultivation could provide a profit as well as sustenance, and with it came a slow change in the distribution of land. Enclosure, both of the open fields and of wastes, became increasingly common, and no attempt was made to discourage it. As the wool trade declined, farmers turned more attention to improvements of arable land; proper manuring, crop rotation and weed control became much more systematic than in the past. Gradually, soil and the crop cultivation became more of a science. This was assisted by the prevailing interest in the natural world and its underlying processes, which had its roots in the 17th century. During this and the following century, a variety of treatises and textbooks appeared, concerned with geology, soil science, husbandry and agricultural chemistry. It became possible to turn what had been waste land into reasonably pro-

*Arne, Dorset, c. 1899/
Dorset County Museum*

ductive farmland. The processes which led to the considerable reduction of heathland area in southern England had begun.

Arthur Young may have commented, in his *Farmer's Tour*, on the wastes covered with furze and fern which he saw in Dorset, but he was complimentary when he saw new and effective agricultural methods. He obtained much information from Mr Humphrey Sturt of Crichel, an improving landlord who experimented with sainfoin, lucerne and buckwheat, and attempted to control rabbits. From our point of view, the most profound change he made was the reclamation of some 365 ha (900 acres) of fern, furze and ling on Brownsea Island in Poole Harbour, by forestry and sowing clover. After burning the heath and adding fertilizer based on ash from London soap factories he managed to grow other crops, too. Likewise, at Moreton in Dorset – the seat of Mr William Frampton – waste land was brought under cultivation. Frampton grubbed out furze, collecting and burning the clods, ploughing and harrowing several times, and then proceeded to an ordinary course of cropping. His success was emulated by one of his tenants, who raised himself from day labourer to farmer controlling some 50 ha (120 acres), sixteen of which he enclosed from the heath and reclaimed by methods similar to Frampton's (Fussell, 1952).

In Hampshire we see the contrast between areas such as the New Forest, which were subject to Forest Law and protection of the Rights of Common, and other heathlands which were gradually enclosed and reclaimed. The technique was very often paring, followed by burning. A labourer used a breast plough which turned a sod about $25 \times 38 \times 914$ mm (1 in $\times$ $1\frac{1}{2}$ in $\times 3$ ft), which was later burnt. Remaining scrub and vegetation was also burnt (Hazel, 1983). Similar changes must have affected the heathlands in many other parts of the country. Enclosure was a prelude to reclamation for agriculture. Much of Ashdown Forest was enclosed in 1693, leaving about 2590 ha (6400 acres), much of which remains today (Yates, 1972). In Hampshire, areas which were not royal hunting forests were enclosed with increasing frequency during the 17th and 18th centuries (Hazel, 1983), as was the case in Dorset (Haskins, 1978). Elsewhere, heathland had been completely enclosed by the mid-18th century. For instance, on the Lizard, by 1748, most of the land forming the Meneage, and that on the more fertile soils of schists, granites and gabbro, were enclosed, thus establishing the present-day landscape (Hopkins, 1983). But where the laws governing Rights of Common and hunting in the royal forests persisted, as in the New Forest and Woolmer Forest in Hampshire, the heathland remained open. In the Breckland of East Anglia, the pattern of land-use changed little until this century.

The Cartographic Evidence

The systematic improvements in farming and estate management which have been described were frequently accompanied by detailed plans. These, together with maps, including various O.S. editions, tithe maps and the maps produced by the *Land Utilisation Survey*, have enabled considerably more detail to be added to the picture of heathland decline in lowland England. It can be seen, for example, that the extent of Dorset heathlands and their pattern of settlement changed little from Roman times until the mid-18th century (Haskins, 1978). Elsewhere, the changes were similar, although in some places they occurred much later.

The first attempt to map the decrease in heathland was for Dorset, in what is now a classic example of this procedure (Moore, 1962). The area of heathland was reconstructed from the first and second editions of the O.S. maps from 1811 and 1896, respectively. Moore was able to draw a similar map from those produced by the *Land Utilisation Survey* of 1934, and, finally, drew a map from his own field survey in 1960. Webb and Haskins (1980) revised and added to this work, after making a detailed field survey in 1978, which not only mapped the extent of the heathlands, but recorded the proportions of different types of vegetation and the individual area of each of the remaining fragments. They also reconstructed the extent of the heathlands in the mid-18th century (which was some fifty years earlier than the earliest map used by Moore) from the maps of Hampshire and Dorset drawn by Isaac Taylor in 1759 and 1765. From the various maps, the changes in the coverage of the Dorset heathlands has been traced over the last two centuries (Fig. 13).

44 HEATHLANDS

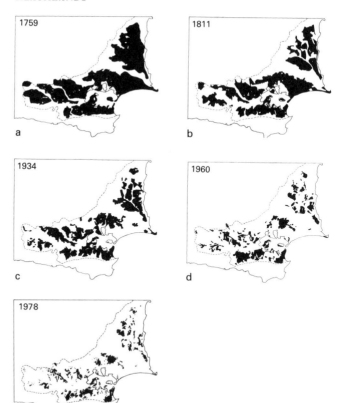

Fig. 13
Changes in the Extent of
Heathland in the Poole
Basin
a) *1759*, taken from the
maps of Isaac Taylor
(after Haskins, *1978*)
b) *1811*, from the first
Ordnance Survey edition
c) *1934*, redrawn from
Land Utilisation Survey
maps (after Haskins,
1978)
d) *1960*, redrawn from
Moore's map of *1962*
e) *1978*, Webb &
Haskins, *1980*
-------- approximate
extent of Tertiary deposits
in the Poole Basin

Webb and Haskins estimated that in the mid-18th century some 40,000 ha (98,400 acres), or about 60% of the land area, of the soils on the Tertiary deposits in the Poole Basin were heathland. Claridge (1793), an 18th-century agriculturalist, estimated there to be 14,670 ha (36,088 acres) of heathland out of a total land area in Dorset of 755,000 ha (1.85 million acres). By the time of the first O.S. map, this area had been reduced to 30,400 ha (74,784 acres), and to 22,672 ha (55,773 acres) by the time of the second 1896 edition. The losses had mostly been caused agricultral reclamation and afforestation. By 1896, urban development had begun on the heathland in the east of the county and in Hampshire, as the newly-founded resort of Bournemouth began to expand. By 1934 the area had declined to 18,220 ha (44,821 acres) and in 1960 Moore estimated there to be 10,000 ha (24,600 acres) remaining. The most recent estimate, which is for heather-dominated communities only, is 5832 ha (14,350 acres) by Webb and Haskins.

Similar reconstructions are available for several other heathland areas. Armstrong (1973) figures a series of maps (Fig. 14) which illustrate the decreases on the Suffolk Sandlings from 1793 to 1931–32, and to 1965. Using a similar range of sources, Hopkins (1983) mapped the losses on the

Lizard Peninsula, where the changes have been less, large areas still remaining intact. Yates (1972) provides some limited information on the changes in use in Ashdown Forest.

Looking at any of these maps one notices not only the overall decrease in the area of heathlands but the considerable fragmentation which has occurred. At the time of Isaac Taylor (mid-18th century), the Dorset heathlands were formed from eight large blocks separated by only the river valleys (Webb & Haskins, 1980). Moore (1962) showed that by 1960, these heathlands had become fragmented into over 100 pieces. In 1978, Webb and Haskins, using a precise definition of a fragment, estimated there to be almost 800 separate pieces of heathland in Dorset (Fig. 13). The biological consequences of this fragmentation are difficult to assess.

Great care must be taken when interpreting maps and measurements of areas in the types of study described here. Criteria for recognizing heathland and for defining a fragment differ from one survey to another. When using old maps, it is not possible to define heathland precisely. They may include not only the open, heather-clad areas but also associated plant communities, such as bracken stands, gorse and birch scrub and acid grasslands. Because such maps do not plot heathland itself but include fields, woods and so on, the heathland area has to be estimated by difference. For this reason, it is impossible to isolate small fragments. The 1960 survey adopted an explicit definition of heathland: the areas mapped not only included areas dominated by *Calluna* and *Erica* but also valley bogs, pine heath, thickets of *Ulex*, and *Agrostis curtisii* and *Molinia* grasslands. It was the intention in the maps and acreage figures to give a reliable picture of the broad patterns and relationships and large-scale trends (Moore, 1962). Moore strongly emphasized that the maps were not

Fig. 14
Changes in the Extent of Heathland in the Suffolk Sandlings
a) *1889, from the second Ordnance Survey edition*
b) *1966, Armstrong 1973*

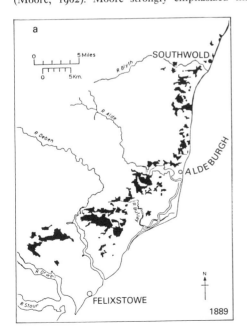
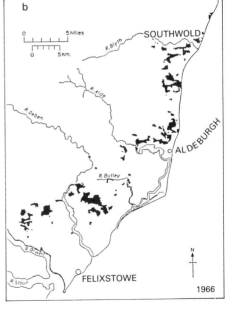

accurate in detail and should not be used as evidence that any particular small area was or was not heath.

Similar constraints apply to the maps of Webb and Haskins (1980), who adopted a precise definition of what they recognized as heathland. They recorded only dry heath, humid heath, wet heath and peatland. This is a much stricter botanical definition and excludes many areas which would be included in a wider definition of heathland. If a wider definition, similar to Moore's, had been used, the estimate for the total area of Dorset heathland is likely to have been 7000–8000 ha (17,200–19,700 acres) instead of the 5832 ha (14,350 acres) that they estimated. It is wrong, therefore, to compare exactly the survey from 1960 with that of 1978, as this would exaggerate heathland loss. Likewise, no real comparison of the extent of fragmentation is possible since, again, Webb and Haskins adopted strict criteria which resulted in the recording of a large number of fragments. Too frequently, results from such surveys are compared without a real understanding of the criteria used, leading to misinterpretation and wrong conclusions.

The Profitable Use of Heathlands

Up to the 18th century, it was not possible for men to reclaim heathland and then use the land profitably. No technology existed to alter heathlands significantly, so they were used as they were to supplement rural life. Many practices developed which utilized heathland and its plants, so helping to perpetuate it; grazing and burning, for example, helped to check scrub invasion and the ultimate development of woodland. Fuel-gathering of various kinds helped to keep the nutrient content of the soil low, and created conditions unfavourable to woodland regeneration.

Grazing

Almost all heathland areas in southern England have extensive records relating to grazing – how it was apportioned, the number of animals to be grazed, and the settlement of disputes among graziers. Many field names on the Suffolk Sandlings refer to their use as sheep walks and in some places the practices extended unbroken into this century (Chadwick, 1982). There seems to be good evidence that the sheep were grazed on the heath in the daytime, but folded at night on arable land, thereby increasing its fertility with their dung. Cattle were also grazed on the heaths at times. Up to the beginning of the century, the Breckland was the most extensive area of heathland in lowland Britain, and grazed vast flocks of sheep (which were also admitted to arable land after the crops had been harvested). The lands of the Breckland were managed on a four-course system and sheep were used to manure land before enclosure, after which it was ploughed and cultivated regularly. The commons of Ashdown Forest were subject to rights governing grazing by commoners, who could graze all the cattle and pigs they could keep on their own lands except for five weeks in autumn between the feasts of St Michael and St Martin 'for the preservation of bushes and maste' (Yates, 1972). When William Cobbett visited Romney Marsh in Sussex, he saw cattle which were of the same Sussex breed he discovered in Ashdown and St Leonard's Forests. He remarked 'How curious is the natural economy of a country'. The cattle he described were calved in the spring, spent their first two years on the rough grazing of the forests, and were then moved to the marsh or elsewhere to be fattened.

The present-day grazing of the New Forest indicates how the centuries-old grazing rights have been preserved. Cattle, horses, pigs and sheep have all figured in these at various times and are described in detail by Tubbs (1968). Although rights have been exercised at various times for sheep, they do not seem to have occupied a prominent position in the local pastoral history. The grazing of pigs was closely associated with the related rights of mast and pannage. Ponies and cattle tended to be the most important beasts, and there is a large body of evidence right up to the present, of official enquiries and court sittings which attempted to regulate the common rights to graze there. In many instances, animals which grazed in the Forest were removed to be fattened on better pastures. The existence today of New Forest ponies is a relict of a practice which was typical of many heathlands: most had their own local breeds of ponies, or heathcroppers, and Exmoor, Dorset and Sussex all developed their own breeds of small, sturdy ponies, which were able to survive on the sparse diet obtained from the heathlands.

In Dorset the pattern was similar. Sheep and cattle were frequently grazed, although heathland sheep were less important than the vast flocks pastured on the chalk downs; heathland grazings merely supplemented those of the downs. Cattle were raised in much the same way. They were held on the rough heath grazings and then fattened on the better land nearby. The contrast between farming on heath and on chalk is illustrated by an analysis of probate inventories for Dorset farmers between 1573 and 1670: on the heathlands the average proportion of a farmer's wealth represented by his livestock was 44%, whereas on the chalk downs a farmer derived only 35% from his livestock (Betty & Wilde, 1977). Finally, in Cornwall, there is evidence that the heathlands were grazed. On the Lizard, the few details that exist suggest that cattle were most common (Hopkins, 1983).

Traditional heathland grazing practices were in decline by the middle of the 19th century, and in the early years of this century, only a few places were grazed. The ancient common rights for the New Forest, which still exist and under which much of the Forest is still managed, are unique and are a valuable retrospect of the ways in which heathland was used. Grazing animals helped to maintain open heathland; they prevented the regeneration of woodland, and clearly still do in parts of the New Forest. They helped to maintain the low nutrient status of the soils, as nutrients were taken from the heathland in their carcasses and manure and usually deposited on other land.

Finally, the composition of the vegetation was probably different from that which today we consider typical of heathland – regular grazing would have resulted in a vegetation which was much richer in the proportion of grasses. It may be that the large areas of even-aged *Calluna* with few associated species, like many lowland heathlands today, are not representative of the heathland of former times. Related to this point are two other extensive practices which are usually associated with the use of heathland for grazing: the cutting of gorse for fodder, and the rotational burning of the heather.

Gorse, or furze, is widespread on almost all lowland heathlands. In the New Forest, gorse-cutting was common, although it never assumed the status of a right. Furze tops were cut and allowed to wilt, for animal fodder, and this practice is still prevalent (Tubbs, 1968, and personal communication). Tubbs and Jones (1964) were unable to find any reference to the deliberate cultivation of gorse, although it was grown elsewhere in England* and in Ireland (Lucas, 1960) for this purpose.

The regular burning of heather has, somehow, always been regarded as part of traditional heathland management, yet there is relatively little evidence for this in lowland Britain. Today, heathlands are frequently burnt for a variety of reasons; the ecological effects and the succession following these fires are discussed in chapter 7. Fire may well have formed part of the process by which Bronze Age Man cleared the land and, because heathland vegetation is very inflammable at certain times of the year, it is likely that fires occurred naturally from time to time. The use of fire to manage the heathlands of northern England and Scotland dates from about 1800 (Gimingham, 1972), providing a supply of young, more succulent grass and encouraging the growth of young heather shoots, which are more palatable and nutritious for sheep and grouse. When sheep production was at its height, there was less need to burn, but when it declined, it seems that the sheep alone were not sufficient to keep the moor in a productive condition and prevent the invasion of woody species; hence the increasing use of burning (Gimingham, 1972). Whether this was the case in the lowlands is not clear. Ecologists often describe grazing and burning as the main factors perpetuating lowland heath, but it may be that regular burning was introduced as late as the 19th century, following the example set in the uplands. There seem to be relatively few references in earlier sources to burning, although Gilbert White comments on the fires in Woolmer Forest in 1689:

'to burn any waste, between Candlemas and Midsummer, any grig, ling, heath and furze, goss or fern, is punishable with whipping and confinement in the house of correction yet, in this forest, about March or April, according to the dryness of the season, such vast heath-fires are lighted up, that they often get to a masterless head, and, catching the hedges, have sometimes been communicated to the underwoods, woods and coppices, where great damage has ensued. The plea for these burnings is, that when the old coat of heath, etc., is consumed, young will sprout up, and afford much tender browse for the cattle.'

This is no more than a century before the practice was well established in the uplands, but provides a clue as to whether it had been traditional – fire may have been less important in maintaining heathland than was previously thought; grazing, turf- and peat-cutting, and fuel-gathering may have been sufficient to maintain an open plant community and resist the invasion of woody species.

Fuel-gathering

Until the improved transport systems of the 19th century brought a supply of coal to almost every part of England, the rural population had to

---

* See Thomas Page, 'On the culture of furze, *Annals of Agriculture* 9, 1788, 215–217. Elly Sandham, 'On the preparation of gorse as food for cattle', *J. Roy. Agric. Soc. England*, 1st Series, 6, 1846, 523–428.

Turf-cutting experiment to assess the affects on vegetation/N. R. Webb

rely on whatever fuel could be gathered locally. The amount of forest and woodland on or near any of the major lowland heath was small, and where it occurred it was valued for timber. Because of this, the rights and practices of turf- and peat-cutting (Right of Turbary) and gathering gorse (furze) and scrub for fuel were widespread. On the Lizard, the cutting of peat and turf has been established from the earliest times and described in a considerable amount of documentary evidence from the medieval period.

Peat was cut not only for domestic use but also in connection with the important tin-smelting industry which flourished at that time. For this purpose, peat charcoal was made, and it seems that archaeological features called turf huts were in fact associated with the process of making peat charcoal (Hopkins, 1980). Hopkins (1983) was unable to distinguish between peat and turf, but he considers it likely that some turf was also converted to charcoal. On the Lizard, turf-cutting for domestic use continued until the 19th century, and even into this century in some places, but industrial use ceased by the 17th century. Peat and furze were generally cut in the summer, over a period which would amount to about fifteen man-days work each year. The turves would be stacked to dry and then carted to a storage rick near the farmhouse. Hopkins considers that almost all of the surface soil horizon was removed from the Lizard heathlands during the Middle Ages, and that these areas were subsequently cut repeatedly – an activity which would have had a profound effect on the composition of the vegetation. Although little evidence can be found on the ground today to show where cutting took place, linear patterns can be discerned from air photographs.

On Dorset heathland, cutting of turf and peat for fuel is evident from the earliest times. Cutting for domestic use was common and many of the rights were defined during the Middle Ages; these years coincided with a period of cold weather – the coldest since the late-Devonian (Lamb, 1965) – and Haskins (1978) suggests that the origin of these rights may be connected with a climatic change. In the late 16th century there was a demand for peat fuel for the copperas (ferrous sulphate) and alum works on the shores of Poole Harbour. These 'great furnaces' were recorded by Celia Fiennes during her travels. Various disputes arose between industrial interests and domestic requirements. For almost all the heathlands in this area there is abundant documentary evidence relating to peat- and turf-cutting, much of which specifies the numbers of turves to be cut each year. There has been no detailed analysis of the extent of these rights, but, as on the Lizard, we may speculate that almost all of the area was cut, and undoubtedly affected the composition of the vegetation.

In the New Forest, the rights of turbary are well documented – up to half a million turves were cut annually. A single turbary right averaged about 4000 turves annually (Tubbs, 1968). Turf was cut in a traditional way which preserved the grazing and aided the regeneration of the vegetation; for every turf cut, two were left (Pigott 1960, Passmore 1969).

Similar evidence of turbary exists for almost all of the other heathland in Britain. As in Dorset, the rights often mention peat and turf separately, although we cannot be certain of the distinction between the two. Peat is undoubtedly the deposits of *Sphagnum* which accumulate in the valley mires. But to interpret turf is more difficult: it may well refer to the upper layers of soil corresponding to the A horizon of wet and humid heaths. It seems unlikely that this horizon of dry heath would have been useful as fuel as it was probably not easily cut.

The ecological consequences of peat- and turf-cutting on this scale must have been considerable. Not only would the composition of the vegetation be modified, but the low base status of the soils would be maintained, since nutrient accumulation was prevented. It is well known that in the Netherlands and northwards into Jutland there was an extensive and well-established practice of turf-cutting combined with sheep-grazing on the heathlands, called *plaggen*. This practice is generally considered to be the most important factor in maintaining these open heathlands for 1000 years until it ceased in the early years of this century (Gimingham & De Smidt, 1983). Such organized agricultural practice was not evident in Britain, although turf-cutting was.

Gorse, or furze, was also gathered from heathland for fuel. This was a widespread practice, and because gorse was so abundant, there seems to have been no need to regulate the practice with common rights: it remained a custom. The species most widely cut was the common gorse (*Ulex europaeus*), for the more prostrate forms (*U. minor* and *U. gallii*) would have been difficult to gather. On the Lizard the poorest peasants may have been compelled to gather *U. gallii* because they were prevented from gathering *U. europaeus* by the more wealthy (Hopkins, 1983). Gorse was used for both domestic and industrial uses. Bread ovens and pottery kilns were fired using faggots of gorse. It was used in thatching to provide a structure equivalent to the rafters of a cottage, over which thatch was woven. It was used for land drains, where a trench would be filled with

Fuel-gathering in the late 19th century/Dorset County Museum

gorse and then covered with earth. Gorse was cut, when time was available from other farming activities, in the summer on the Lizard (Hopkins, 1983), or by specialist furze-cutters, who figured in Hardy's *Return of the Native*. The furze was bundled into faggots and tied with a briar. These faggots were often stored in highly inflammable stacks in the yards of houses and many accidental fires occurred. An indication of the importance of gorse as fuel is evident from the inventories made of resources which were compiled in preparation for the Napoleonic Wars, when the amount of gorse and its value was estimated (Minchinton, 1955).

The Uses of Bracken

Bracken (*Pteridium aquilinum*), or fern, as it was called, is a widespread and common plant on all heathlands. Today it is generally regarded as a pernicious weed, but in former times it was gathered for a variety of different purposes, an activity which undoubtedly affected its distribution and abundance. There are numerous accounts of gathering bracken for use as animal bedding (Tubbs, 1968 or Haskins, 1978). It was also used as a domestic fuel, probably supplementing gorse and wood. It is light and burns quickly, but despite this there is some documentary evidence of its use for firing brick kilns (Rymer, 1976). It was also used, from Neolithic times, for compost, (but there seems to be no evidence for stable bedding being used as compost), and for thatching, although this seems to have been more common in Scotland.

The high potassium content of the ash from burnt bracken was a way of obtaining the potash required for industrial uses, and there are many accounts which describe the best methods of burning to get the greatest yield. The potash was subsequently used in glass- and soap-making, and bleaching (Rymer, 1976).

A Redundant Landscape?

Where heathland remains today, it is unused. In the past, poor transport meant that heathland dwellers had to rely on local resources. Fuel, animal bedding, compost, thatching materials, etc., were all obtained from the heath. The heath itself was used for rough grazing. All these activities maintained open conditions, prevented the encroachment of scrub and woodland, and (perhaps most important of all) the low base status of the soils, making any woodland regeneration more difficult. In the 19th century, when transport improved, it became possible to obtain fuel, timber, animal feed and fertilizers from elsewhere, and the use of the heaths began to decline. In most areas this happened before the First World War. Since then, heathlands have been neglected, scrub and bracken have invaded, and the vegetation composition has changed. We cannot really speculate on the composition of the former vegetation but it is likely that the monoculture of *Calluna* on many heathlands was not typical. Since heathlands were used in a way which maintained their openness, we must reassess the role that fire may have played. It is generally thought that fire was part of grazing practice, but with so many other activities which would check regeneration, it may not have been necessary to burn heathlands frequently. Burning may have increased, following the example in the uplands, as other uses declined, in an attempt to maintain the quality of the grazing. The fact that heathlands were so extensively used in the past has important implications for the development of management programmes today, particularly in the areas of nature conservation and amenity (see chapter 12).

British Lowland Heaths CHAPTER 5

Lowland heaths are scattered across most of southern England, from Cornwall to East Anglia and from Sussex to Yorkshire. Similar communities occur in parts of west Wales, the Midlands, Cumbria and in parts of Scotland. There are about sixty sites of national importance, with a total area of 20,000 ha (49,200 acres) on a wide range of soils (Farrell, 1983; Ratcliffe, 1977). Relatively few large heaths remain – the main exception being the New Forest in Hampshire. Almost everywhere else heathlands have been fragmented through reclamation for farming, forestry, urban development, mineral extraction, military training and public recreation. On many, almost all of the traditional heathland uses have ceased; they are no longer rotationally burnt or grazed; turves, furze and bracken are no longer cut. Without these activities, vegetation succession proceeds, the nutrient status of the soils increases, and the heaths are invaded by scrub and woodland. Although many heathlands in southern England are nature reserves, their management is often insufficient to maintain them in top condition.

There is a gradient in the composition of the heathland flora and fauna across England, depending on climate and soil types. On the Lizard, the soils developed from the Serpentine rocks are ultra-basic and lack essential plant nutrients, and so their flora is characteristic. The Tertiary soils of the Hampshire and London Basins are highly acidic and of very low base status compared with the soils derived from the Lower Greensands. The complex soils of the Breckland and those formed from glacial outwashes in other parts of eastern England also have characteristic features, particularly in their grassland communities. Variations in plant species composition are related also to climatic differences: the heathlands of eastern England are the driest and least maritime and are typically continental in character; but westwards, oceanic influences increase, rainfall is higher, and there is less seasonal variation in temperature – and all these affect the composition of the flora. These physical gradients have been recognized in the schemes to classify heathland vegetation (chapter 6).

The Isles of Scilly and Cornish Coasts

The south-west peninsula contains some of the oldest rocks in Britain and has sequences from pre-Cambrian to Lias, almost all of which produce very base-poor soils. The area has an extremely mild and humid oceanic climate; under these conditions, on the Isles of Scilly and on the coasts of Cornwall, a sub-maritime dwarf-shrub community develops which can probably be regarded as the climax vegetation, since exposure to Atlantic winds prevents tree growth.

The Isles of Scilly, of which there are about 140, are flat-topped granite masses eroded by wind. The soils, which are frequently podsolized, are

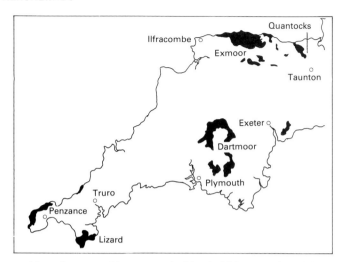

Heathland areas on the SW Peninsula

Wind-stunted Heather on Tresco

very thin and peaty and interspersed with wind-blown sands and Pleistocene deposits. The heathland plant communities are unusual: *Calluna* and Bell Heather grow in an association in which the plants are stunted and compact because of wind and salt spray; this gives the vegetation a peculiar, waved appearance, the plants being largely dead on their windward sides but growing actively on their sheltered sides, in much the same manner as heather grows on exposed mountain tops. Other typical

heathland species which grow in this association are Common Gorse (*Ulex europaeus*), Western Gorse (*U. gallii*), Bracken (*Pteridium aquilinum*) and Sheep's Fescue (*Festuca ovina*). It is interesting that Cross-leaved Heath (*Erica tetralix*), Purple Moor Grass (*Molinia caerulea*) and Bristle Bent (*Agrostis curtisii*) – the latter a characteristic species of the south-west heaths – are all absent from the Isles of Scilly (Ratcliffe, 1977). Maritime species, such as Thrift (*Armeria maritima*) may also occur.

The south-west tip of Cornwall (Penwith) is also granite, but northwards there are successive outcrops of slates, grits, sandy and silty shales of the Middle Devonian, and Old Red Sandstones until north of Boscastle, where the coast is formed from Carboniferous Culm Measures. Maritime heathland occurs in many places along this coast, and is also maintained by the action of wind and salt spray. Some of the best examples occur at Chapel Porth and St Agnes Head. These heathlands consist of an association of *Calluna*, Bell Heather and Western Gorse, the Gorse growing profusely at some locations. Generally, the soils are better than in the far west and on the Isles of Scilly. Bristle Bent and Sheep's Fescue are the main grasses, the latter growing in patches of slightly better soil. The maritime influence is seen in the presence of species such as Thrift, Buck's-horn and Sea Plantain (*Plantago coronopus* and *P. maritima*).

The Lizard

The Lizard is Cornwall's most important heathland area, with a landscape and flora unique in Britain. The attention of botanists was first drawn to the area by John Ray, who visited the Lizard in 1662, when he first described *Erica vagans* – the Cornish Heath – which he found growing over a large part of the plateau. The subsequent interest which botanists have shown in this area stems from the large number of rare species which grows there, and for the unusual heathland plant communities, which have no other counterpart in Britain. Collectively known as the Lizard rarities, the most interesting species are Cornish Heath, Fringed Rupturewort (*Herniaria ciliata*), Quillwort (*Isoetes histrix*), two species of Rush (*Juncus capitatus* and *J. pygmaeus*) and three species of Clover (Twin-flowered Clover, *Trifolium bocconei*; Long-headed Clover, *T. molineri*; and Upright Clover, *T. strictum*). Three other rare species (Sea Knotgrass, *Polygonium maritimum*, Slender Birds-foot Trefoil, *Lotus angustissimus* and Four-leaved Allseed, *Polycarpon tetraphyllum*) formerly grew on the Lizard but are now thought to be extinct. The *Red Data Book for British Plants* (Perring & Farrell, 1977) lists seventeen threatened species in this area.

The Lizard, which is the most southerly part of England, is a broad peninsula about 100 m (328 ft) above sea level with a total area of about 100 sq km (24,700 acres), separated from the mainland of Cornwall by a series of river valleys draining into the Helford River and Looe Pool. There is a geological boundary running from Polurrion Cove in the west, to Porth Hallow in the east; to the north are sedimentary rocks and more fertile soils, which form an area called the Meneage; this is now largely agricultural. To the south is a complex of metamorphic and igneous pre-Cambrian rocks, dominated by the famous Lizard Serpentine, with deposits of gabbro, hornblende schists, loess, Crousa gravels and calcareous shell sands. Serpentine is a crystalline rock containing large amounts of magnesium, chromium and nickel but little calcium, potassium and phosphorus. The soils are mostly surface water gleys with a pH of 5.5 to 7.5, and, although containing bases, lack those essential for plant growth. Therefore, the vegetation is poor and typical of acid soils. Similar soils are formed from gabbro; they are also ultra-basic, with a low phosphorus content, but contain slightly less magnesium, nickel and chromium and have slightly more calcium than Serpentine soils.

The distinctive series of heathland plant communities were first described by Coombe and Frost (1956, a and b), and subsequent work (e.g. Malloch, 1971; Hopkins, 1983) has confirmed their descriptions of four plant communities, with variants depending on the age of the heathland since it was last burnt, and the transitional soils between one rock and another. Ericaceous dwarf shrubs are dominant, co-dominant or important components in all the heathland associations. Ten species of plants, which occur in different proportions in each association, form the basis of the community descriptions:

Bristle Bent (*Agrostis curtisii*)
Ling (*Calluna vulgaris*)
Bell Heather (*Erica cinerea*)
Cross-leaved Heath (*Erica tetralix*)
Cornish Heath (*Erica vagans*)
Sheep's Fescue (*Festuca ovina*)
Purple Moor Grass (*Molinia caerulea*)
Black Bog Rush (*Schoenus nigricans*)
Gorse (*Ulex europeaeus*)
Western Gorse (*Ulex gallii*)

Rock heath (*Festuca ovina–Calluna* heath), dominated by Sheep's Fescue and Ling, with seventy-three other species, occurs in the shallow pockets of soil (pH 6–7) which cover the Serpentine. The plants experience severe exposure and there may be patches of bare ground colonized by the lichens *Ramalina scoparium* and *Xanthoria parietinum*.

Mixed heath (*Erica vagans–Ulex europaeus* heath) is dominated by Cornish Heath and Common Gorse and has seventy-four associated species. This association occurs on the well-drained, brown earth soils with a pH 6–7. There is a wide variation in depth, composition, and exposure of these soils which, combined with the different ages of heath caused by burning, induces considerable variation. Coombe and Frost recognized four variants, two of which depended on the age of the heath.

Tall heath (*Erica vagans–Schoenus* heath), containing forty-three species, is dominated by Cornish Heath, with Black Bog Rush and Purple Moor Grass as co-dominants; this vegetation occupies the shallow depressions over the main area of the Lizard Plateau. The soils may be gleyed and seasonally waterlogged and are slightly more acidic than those beneath the other types of heath.

Short heath (*Agrostic curtisii* heath), with twenty-four associated species, contains Bristle Bent, Ling, Bell Heather, Cross-leaved Heath, Purple Moor Grass and Western Dwarf Gorse as co-dominants. Most level parts of the plateau with granitic loess soils are covered by this type of vegetation, which differs from all the other types by the absence of Cornish Heath and the presence of a greater number of species characteristic of basic soils. These soils are fine and silty with pH in the range 4.5–7. They mostly overlay the Serpentine rocks and may be podsolized.

The Lizard heathlands are unsuitable for agriculture, and frequently burnt; Coombe and Frost considered that the composition of the vegetation was determined more by differences in soil type than by the effects of post-fire succession. There has been much speculation on this subject, but Marrs and Proctor (1978), from chemical analyses of the soils, have confirmed this view.

The occurrence of such a large number of rare and restricted species on the Lizard is less easily explained than the principal types of heathland. Many of the species are warmth-loving and in this part of southern England reach the northern limits of Mediterranean or continental ranges. The strongly maritime climate and the variety of soil types have been put forward as explanations, but despite much speculation, there is no really satisfactory explanation. Elsewhere in Europe, base-rich soils formed from Serpentine rocks often have a rich flora of endemic species.

There are no peat deposits on the Lizard from which an adequate pollen profile can be obtained; thus, the post-glacial history of the area cannot be reconstructed. It seems likely that the area would have been covered with scrub and carr dominated by Grey Willow (*Salix cinerea*) with small areas of woodland, since extensive woodland development would have been prevented by exposure (Hopkins, 1983). Hopkins considers that this vegetation would have persisted in the absence of Man and his animals, and today, where grazing and fire are absent, this community regenerates. The Lizard was open heathland by Anglo Saxon times and may have been more open than it is today. There was a decline in use during the Middle Ages (13th–14th centuries), and agriculture did not recover until the 16th century. The present landscape features were probably established by the 18th century. Hopkins reconstructed changes in the areas covered by these heathlands from documentary sources from 1813 to the present. Over this period, 64% of the losses have been due to agriculture, 13% to military uses, 10% to afforestation and 9% to telecommunications installations. Today, up to 600 ha (1475 acres) are protected by the National Trust, the Nature Conservancy Council and the Cornish Naturalists' Trust.

Granite Areas of Devon and Cornwall

Granite underlies the moors of Dartmoor, Bodmin, St Austell and Carnmenellis, besides Land's End and the Isles of Scilly. All these areas have heathland types of vegetation although, strictly, since parts of Dartmoor and Bodmin Moor exceed 250–300 m (800–1000 ft), they are outside our definition of heathland. But in all these areas considerable heathland areas lie below this altitude. Blanket bog covers the highest parts of Dartmoor, which rises to 610 m (2000 ft), where the vegetation is dominated by *Calluna*, Cotton Grass (*Eriophorum vaginatum*) and a mixture of species of *Sphagnum* (Bog Mosses) – *S. papillosum*, *S. recurvum* and *S. capillifolium*. Other species which occur include Bog Asphodel (*Narthecium ossifragum*), Cotton Grass (*Eriophorum angustifolium*) and Purple Moor Grass (*Molinia caerulea*). At lower levels on these moors, the vegetation is more grassy, with mixed communities containing Heather, the Bents (*Agrostis curtisii* and *A. tenuis*), Sheep's Fescue (*Festuca ovina*), Bracken (*Pteridium aquilinum*), Mat Grass (*Nardus stricta*) and Purple Moor Grass.

Besides the heathlands on soils derived from granite, there are many

Cornish coastal heath at Chapel Porth, Cornwall/ S. B. Chapman

scattered fragments of heathland on acid soil derived from shales, slates and on the Culm Measures of Devon.

East Devon Commons

The most extensive areas of lowland heathland in Devon are in the east, between the Exe Estuary and the River Otter, north of Budleigh Salterton. Here there are about 1000 ha (2460 acres) of varied heathland on the commons of Bicton, Collaton Raleigh, Woodbury, Aylesbeare and Venn Ottery, which has developed on soils derived from Keuper and Bunter sandstones and pebble beds (Triassic deposits). There is considerable topographic variation on these commons: the dry heath is typical of that of south-west England, and is a species-poor community containing *Calluna*, Bell Heather (*Erica cinerea*), Bristle Bent (*Agrostis curtissii*) and Western Gorse (*Ulex gallii*). In the wetter parts, Cross-leaved Heath (*Erica tetralix*) grows with Purple Moor Grass (*Molinia caerulea*), Deer Grass (*Scirpus cespitosus*) and *Sphagnum compactum*. Species present in the bog communities include Cotton Grass (*Eriophorum angustifolium*), Bog Asphodel (*Narthecium ossifragum*) and *Sphagnum papillosum*. The plant communities on the drier parts of the commons may be dominated by Bracken or scrub. In the wetter areas there are species-rich Purple Moor Grass communities containing Devils-bit Scabious (*Succisa pratensis*), Meadow Thistle (*Cirsium dissectum*) and Tawny Sedge (*Carex hostiana*). In parts, there are calcium-rich wet flushes in which the Black Bog Rush (*Schoenus nigricans*) predominates. Both this community and the species-rich Purple Moor Grass community reflect the local variations in soil nutrient content, which is characteristic of these commons. A community analysis of the vegetation has shown that dry heath, Bracken and scrub communities are well defined, but the remaining communities of wet heath, bog, wet flushes and species-rich Purple Moor Grass intergrade with one another (Ivimey-Cook, Proctor & Rowland, 1975).

Devon and Somerset

Exmoor, which straddles the border between north Devon and Somerset, lies on a plateau at about 300 m (984 ft), but rising to a height of 518 m (1700 ft) on Dunkery Beacon. At this altitude, much of the moor lies just above our limit for lowland heath, but the vegetation shows many transitional features. The moorland is formed on soils (mostly podsols), gleys and peats, derived from Old Red Sandstone (Devonian sandstones). Exmoor was hardly affected by glaciation and, because of this, there is a greater range of soil types and fewer peat deposits than on the granite moors further west. The vegetation can be divided into five categories (Sinclair, 1970): coastal heaths dominated by *Calluna*, with the associates Bell Heather (*Erica cinerea*) and Western Gorse (*Ulex gallii*); the northern heather moors, where *Calluna* is also dominant, but where there is much less Western Gorse; the central grass moors, where there is little heather and the vegetation consists almost entirely of Purple Moor Grass (*Molinia caerulea*); southern heather moors, which have a similar vegetation to that of the coastal heaths but with a greater proportion of Purple Moor Grass; and the Brendon heaths, which have a similar vegetation but with slightly more Bracken.

The main area of open moorland is dominated by *Calluna* and Bilberry (*Vaccinium myrtillus*), growing in association with Western Gorse (*Ulex gallii*), Bristle Bent (*Agrostis curtisii*), Wavy-hair Grass (*Deschampsia flexuosa*), Cross-leaved Heath (*Erica tetralix*), Mat Grass (*Nardus stricta*), Purple Moor Grass (*Molinia caerulea*), Deer Grass (*Scirpus cespitosus*) and the Cotton Grasses *Eriophorum angustifolium* and *E. vaginatum*. The Gorse does not grow above 400 m (1300 ft), and above this altitude Crowberry (*Empetrum nigrum*) forms part of the *Calluna* community. A number of upland species, which mostly have northerly distributions, grow on both Exmoor and Dartmoor. Among these species are the Fir Clubmoss (*Lycopodium selago*) and Cowberry (*V. vitis-idea*). A glacial relict also present on Exmoor and Dartmoor is the Grey Mountain Carpet Moth (*Entephria caesiata*), and birds include Black Grouse, Merlin, and Hen and Montagu Harriers.

The granite island of Lundy, off the north Devon coast, is covered with heathland vegetation which has maritime species, such as Thrift (*Armeria maritima*) growing amongst it; Broom (*Cytisus scoparius*) is also present. The invertebrates living in pioneer heath communities on Lundy were studied by Delany (1956).

The heathlands of Devon and Cornwall are all on poor, acid soils derived from some of the oldest rocks from the Palaeozoic Era, the Granites and other intrusive rocks, Devonian and Old Red Sandstone or Millstone Grits and Culm Measures. The heathland lying further east in southern England are all on younger strata from the Mesozoic Era.

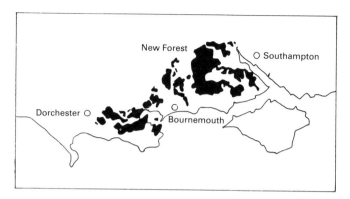

Dorset Heathland

Dorset

The Dorset heathlands are on sandy, acid soils derived from deposits of the Tertiary period. These heathlands form the hinterland of Poole Harbour, which has been called the Poole Basin (Good, 1948). The Poole Basin is western extension of the Hampshire Basin, which includes the New Forest. In this area, Bagshot Sands (Tertiary deposits) overlay the chalk which forms the margin of the Poole Basin. This is fringed by Reading Beds and London Clays, where the soils are brown earths and surface-water gleys. These soils are more fertile than the podsols formed from the sand and gravel deposits of the Bagshot Beds, and the beds have extensive seams of pipe clay. In a few places, younger Bracklesham Beds overlay the Bagshot. Well-developed humus-iron podsols are found throughout the whole Basin, but in places where clay deposits impede drainage, gleyed soils result, and in the valley bogs there are extensive peat deposits.

The Dorset heathlands form an important transitional area between the more oceanic heathland of the south-west peninsula and the continental heathlands in eastern England. The distribution of many species of both plants and animals reflects this transition. Throughout the Basin, the dry heath is dominated by *Calluna* growing in association with Bell Heather (*Erica cinerea*) and one of the Dwarf Gorse species (either *Ulex gallii* or *U. minor*). The dominant grass is Bristle Bent (*Agrostis curtisii*). In the damper areas (on humid and wet heaths), Cross-leaved Heath (*Erica tetralix*) and Purple Moor Grass (*Molinia caerulea*) occur, and in some wet heath areas the Dorset Heath (*Erica ciliaris*) grows. It is the mixture of species at the limits of their geographical distribution which produces the variety and interest of the Dorset heathland. Bristle Bent (*Agrostis curtisii*) is nearing its eastern limit; the Marsh Gentian (*Gentiana pneumonanthe*), although widespread in Britain, is nowhere common except in Dorset, where in some of the wet heath areas there are dense populations; Brown Beak Sedge (*Rhynchospora fusca*) grows abundantly in some wet heaths and bogs in the Poole Basin, and the New Forest, but in general has a northerly distribution in Britain. The Mossy Stonecrop (*Crassula tillea*) is well established on these heathlands, although it is diminishing in its other main localities of the New Forest and East Anglia.

The distribution of Dwarf Gorse in the Poole Basin is particularly

Urban encroachment on Canford Heath, Dorset / N. R. Webb

interesting. In Britain as a whole, *Ulex gallii* has a western distribution and *U. minor* an eastern, with the exception that in Suffolk and Norfolk there is a small area of *U. gallii* (Fig. 35). In the Poole Basin both species occur. The central heaths have *U. gallii* and the outer, both east and west, have *U. minor*. There are very few places where both species occur together. The reasons for this curious distribution are not known.

The Dorset Heath (*Erica ciliaris*) has its British stronghold in the Poole Basin, where there are many acres of the plant on the heaths south of Poole Harbour. It occurs at various scattered localities in Devon and Cornwall, but is never very common. More details on its ecology and distribution are given in chapter 8.

The fauna of the Dorset heathlands is as interesting as the flora, with evident transitional features. The heathlands are renowned for their reptiles: all British species occur here, but the specialities are the Sand Lizard (*Lacerta agilis*) and the Smooth Snake (*Coronella austriaca*). With the New Forest, this is the main area where the Dartford Warbler (*Sylvia undata*) is found. The insect life is also very rich. The Heath Grasshopper (*Chorthippus vagans*) and the Large Marsh Grasshopper (*Stethophyma grossum*), a number of species of dragonflies and damselflies, several species of Lepidoptera (e.g. the Speckled Footman, *Coccinia cribraria*) all feature. Almost all these species are continental in their distribution and reach the northern limits of their European range here.

The ecology of the Dorset heathlands has been studied in detail for many years. The pioneer work was by Captain Cyril Diver (later to become the first Director-General of the Nature Conservancy) on Studland Heath in the decade before the Second World War. There has been much subsequent research, the latest summary is Chapman and Webb (1978). Many aspects of these works feature in other sections of this book.

The New Forest

The New Forest is the largest tract of lowland heath in Britain. This has been brought about by a unique form of land use which has preserved the landscape since Norman times. The ancient forest law is upheld within a Perambulation of 37,636 ha (93,000 acres), of which 7954 ha (19,656 acres) are Statutory Enclosures. Of the remaining unenclosed land, 3642 ha (9000 acres) are woodland and 14,369 ha (35,505 acres) are heathland. Geologically, the New Forest lies on similar formations to the Dorset heathlands. But whereas in Dorset the strata are almost entirely Bagshot Beds, in the New Forest they are more complex.

The Hampshire Basin consists of a series of sand and clay deposits from the Eocene and Oligocene (Tertiary) periods in a downfold of Chalk. Subsequent denudation left the oldest deposits at the periphery of the Basin and the youngest in the centre. The marginal Reading Beds (laid down under freshwater conditions) and London Clays (laid down under marine conditions) which fringe the Dorset heathlands, are absent in the New Forest. Extensive deposits of Bagshot Beds are also absent, except in the very north. The main, central area of the Forest is on Bracklesham Beds (both freshwater and marine deposits), Barton Sands and Barton Clays (both marine). These deposits are Eocene and are overlain in places by Oligocene strata of Headen Beds. These deposits vary widely in quality and, in general, give rise to better soils – the loams and clays of the southern Forest. Over many parts of the Forest there are superficial plateau and valley gravels, all of Pleistocene origin. This greater diversity of soil types, and a less oceanic climate than the Dorset heathlands, is reflected in the composition of the flora and fauna. The highest point of 127 m (418 ft) lies in the north, and there is a gentle slope southwards to areas which are about 60 m (200 ft) above sea level. The topography in the north is of high ridges with steep-sided valleys, and in the south there are plateaux with gentle slopes and valleys with, in places, fairly deep accumulations of peat. The heathlands are found on the deposits of Plateau Gravel, Bracklesham Beds, Bagshot and Barton Sands.

The soils beneath the heathlands are humus-iron podsols, but they are not as deficient in nutrients as those in Dorset, and, in the absence of grazing or burning, are colonized by a wider range of woody species, such as Oak (*Quercus* spp.), Holly (*Ilex aquifolium*), Hawthorn (*Crataegus monogyna*), in addition to Birch and Pine. The presence of Holly in the understorey is a feature of the New Forest; it seems to have occupied this position in the succession since the Bronze Age, though previously, as on the Dorset heathlands, Hazel (*Corylus avellana*) was the predominant understorey shrub (Tubbs, 1968).

The dry New Forest heathland is a community of *Calluna*, Dwarf Gorse (*Ulex minor*) and Bristle Bent (*Agrostis curtisii*). In many places there are extensive areas of Common Gorse (*U. europaeus*), the distribution of which can largely be attributed to past land use (Tubbs & Jones, 1964). The humid, and wet heath are similar in composition to those in Dorset, con-

BRITISH LOWLAND HEATHS

sisting of *Calluna*, Cross-leaved Heath (*Erica tetralix*) and *Sphagnum compactum*. Species which grow in many of the damper areas include Bog Myrtle (*Myrica gale*), Black Bog Rush (*Schoenus nigricans*), Purple Moor Grass (*Molinia caerulea*), species of Sundew (*Drosera* spp.), Bog Asphodel (*Narthecium ossifragum*), Cotton Grass (*Eriophorum angustifolium*) and White Beak Sedge (*Rhynchospora alba*).

Of the rare heathland plants, Marsh Gentian (*Gentiana pneumonanthe*), Yellow Centaury (*Cicendia filiformis*), Bog Orchid (*Malaxis paludosa*), Hampshire Purslane (*Ludwigia palustris*), Coral Necklace (*Illecebrum verticillatum*) and Slender Marsh Bedstraw (*Galium degile*) all occur, but the most notable is the Wild Gladiolus (*Gladiolus illyricus*), which grows amongst dense bracken in one or two places.

There are several species of dragonfly which inhabit the wetter parts. The Scarce Ischnura (*Ischnura pumilio*) and the Small Red Damselfly (*Ceriagrion tenellum*), which are both Mediterranean species, have decreased in numbers because of drainage of many wet areas. The southern heathlands, particularly those in the New Forest, are now the most important localities for these species.

In the past, so large an uninhabited area as the New Forest was important for breeding birds of prey. There were populations of Kite, Honey Buzzard, Common Buzzard, Montagu's Harrier, Hobby and several more common species. Persecution from the middle of the last century has depleted these populations and the Kite is now extinct. Black Grouse occurred in the Forest until the Second World War, but had been sustained

'Heath-croppers' in the New Forest/Nature Photographers, S. C. Bisserot

HEATHLANDS

by several introductions. Today, the Forest is important for breeding colonies of Red-backed Shrike (whose distribution in Europe has altered), Nightjar, and Dartford Warbler. Like Dorset, the New Forest is also important for two rare reptiles: the Sand Lizard and the Smooth Snake.

The maintenance of the characteristic landscape of the New Forest depends on its unique form of agriculture and institutions (Tubbs, 1968). The legal status as a Royal Forest, and the lack of enforcement of Forest law, has helped to maintain open heathland. The various Rights of Common (estovers, turbary, grazing, and so on) have been jealously guarded by the Commoners and Verderers. There have been, and continue to be, disputes over the use of the Forest, with nature conservation interests also having a say today. The operation of the Forest institutions is complex and their history fascinating; the reader is referred to the excellent account by Tubbs (1968).

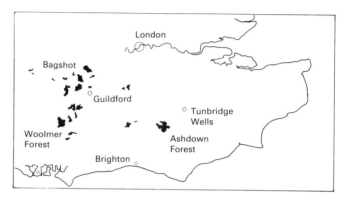

Heathlands on the Greensands

Heathlands on the Greensands

The various outcrops of rocks and sediments in south and south-east England have a continuity throughout Hampshire (north), Surrey and Sussex. It is, therefore, simpler to group these heathlands geologically and not geographically. North of the Hampshire Basin (Tertiary deposits) lies an extensive area of Chalk; eastwards, this divides into two arms – the North and South Downs, which enclose the Weald. Surrounding the Weald is a strip of Lower Greensand and the related deposits of Hythe and Folkestone Beds. On these formations is a series of heath extending from Leith Hill in Surrey westwards to Blackdown, Woolmer Forest, and around Frensham. In Hampshire there are about a dozen heaths remaining on these Wealden deposits, amounting to some 842 ha (2070 acres); the largest areas are Woolmer Forest 241 ha (600 acres) and Bramshott and Ludshott near Liphook 378 ha (930 acres) (Hazel, 1983). In Surrey, the most important area is some 728 ha (1790 acres) comprising Thursley and Hankley heaths. Further south, on the same formations, is a series of heaths between Petersfield, Rogate and Midhurst, the most important of which are Iping and Ambersham Commons. These heathlands show more continental characteristics than the more oceanic heaths of Dorset and the New Forest. Bristle Bent (*Agrostis curtisii*) is no longer the principal grass in the community, and in fact is rare on these heaths, its place being taken by Sheep's Fescue (*Festuca oxina*) or other species of Bent. The dry heath is dominated by *Calluna* and Bell Heather (*Erica cinerea*) and *Ulex minor* is the dwarf gorse in this community.

On almost all these heaths, scrub and birch woodland has developed since cessation of rabbit-grazing in the mid-1950s; this now causes serious conservation problems.

Woolmer Forest was formerly an extensive area of heathland and bog communities, known to the 18th-century naturalist, Gilbert White. There were extensive wet communities near Woolmer Pool. Today, however, parts have been afforested, others dominated by scrub and birch wood, and much of the area used for military training. Woolmer Pond and its associated communities have decreased in extent, and Marsh Club Moss (*Lycopodiella inundata*) and Greater Bladderwort (*Utricularia australis*) are now very scarce, but Cranberry (*Vaccinium oxycoccus*), which is rare and local in the south and east of England, occurs here, as well as on Thursley Common. Woolmer Forest is noted for its reptiles and amphibia, and is probably the only locality where all twelve British species are found. Its jewel is the Natterjack Toad, and the populations which breed in pools in the sandy areas form the largest heathland population. The insect fauna of the damp areas is diverse and contains important species of aquatic Coleoptera.

Thursley and Hankley Commons form one of the largest and best tracts

Invading bracken on Surrey heathland/Nature Photographers, F. V. Blackburn

of heathland in this series, with extensive areas of dry heath dominated by *Calluna*, growing in association with *Ulex minor*. There are important wet heath and *Sphagnum*-dominated communities at Pudmore Pond which contain Great Sundew (*Drosera anglica*), Bog Orchid (*Malaxis paludosa*) and Brown Beak Sedge (*Rhynchospora fusca*). Both heaths are noted localities for the rare heathland vertebrates, particularly the Sand Lizard and the Dartford Warbler, although the latter has been scarce since the severe winter in 1962/63. Thursley is noted for its rich dragonfly fauna, and besides having the rare heathland species, the Small Red Damselfly (*Ceriagrion tenellum*), is one of the few localities in southern England for the White-faced Dragonfly (*Leucorrhinia dubia*).

Iping and Ambersham in West Sussex are typical of the Lower Greensand heaths; both contain good dry and wet heath communities which correspond closely with the heaths of northern France (Harrison, 1970), and are considered important for the richness of their invertebrate faunas. It is thought that ericaceous vegetation became established on these heaths in Mesolithic times, about 8000 BP (Dimbleby, 1976), which is earlier than elsewhere.

The Lower Greensand extends into Kent, where there is a single remaining heathland, Hothfield Common, which contains a complete range of communities from dry heath to bog, with a central flush of more nutrient-rich water, giving a wide range of communities somewhat similar to Roydon Common in Norfolk.

The London Basin

North of the Hog's Back – a chalk ridge with almost vertical bedding planes – lies the London Basin, an area of Tertiary deposits similar to the Hampshire Basin. The entire basin is bounded by chalk – the North Downs and the Hog's Back in the south and the Chiltern Hills in the north. Overlying the chalk in the London Basin is a variety of Eocene beds known as the London Tertiaries; then comes a deposit of London Clays overlain by Bagshot and Bracklesham Beds. The soils of this area are typical heathland podsols. The extensive areas of heathland around Bagshot, now mostly lost to urban development, have long been a famous feature of the landscape and, in the past, were an obstacle to the traveller southwards from the capital. This area extends from Aldershot, Farnborough and Fleet in the west, and northwards to around Windsor and into Berkshire. Chobham Common now remains one of the most extensive areas; much of the remainder has been lost or is used as military training areas.

The association of plants on the dry heath is of *Calluna* with Dwarf Gorse (*Ulex minor*) and Bristle Bent (*Agrostis curtisii*). The presence of Bristle Bent, at its northernmost limit, makes these heathlands very similar to those of the Hampshire Basin, but different from the nearby Greensand heaths south of the Hog's Back. This similarity is reflected in the fauna, particularly the invertebrates, which are very similar to those of the New Forest, but, again, different from Greensand heaths such as Thursley (Ratcliffe, 1977). Chobham Common has long been famous among entomologists, partly because it was easily reached by train in the Victorian times; it has counterparts in Beaulieu Road in the New Forest and Parley Common in Dorset, both of which could be reached in this way, and all of which are renowned for the numerous rare species that have been found there. The damp heath and valley bogs of this area are similar to those in the Hampshire Basin and contain such species as the Marsh Gentian (*Gentiana pneumonanthe*) and Marsh Clubmoss (*Lycopodiella inundata*).

In former times, there were heathlands scattered eastwards south of the Thames around Dartford, Bexley, and Blackheath but, except for scattered fragments, almost all have been built over. Likewise, north-east of the Thames, there are isolated fragments, mostly used as public open spaces. However, there was probably much less heathland there than to the south-west of the London Basin since, although the London Clays extend towards Ipswich, the overlying Bagshor deposits are thin and scattered.

Ashdown Forest.

'Through copse and spinney marched Bear; down open slopes of gorse and heather, over rocky beds of streams, up steep banks of sandstone into the heather again . . .'
Winnie the Pooh – A. A. Milne

Ashdown Forest is the precious habitat of that rare species of bear, Winnie the Pooh. Christopher Robin's map gives a good representation of Ashdown Forest itself, . . . and Eeyore's 'gloomy place' is a typical heathland valley bog.

Apart from its literary connections, much of the interest of Ashdown lies, like the New Forest, in its large area and in the management of the land through the operation of common rights (Yates, 1972; Burnham, 1983) (see chapter 4). It is the largest tract of heathland in south-east England and is part of the former royal hunting forest of Wealdon. The Forest rises to 200 m (650 ft) and covers some 2500 ha (6150 acres). The whole area is underlain by Cretaceous deposits made up of Hastings Beds and Ashdown Sands, which are a series of clays and sands. Opinions differ on the effects of glaciation on this part of Britain; the soils are predominantly podsols, with gleyed podsols in some places.

Heathland seems to have spread later in Ashdown Forest than elsewhere. Woodland was cleared from the Middle Ages, but in the 15th century, blast furnaces for smelting iron, which required enormous quantities of wood, were established on the periphery. As a result, the woods, like those on Cannock Chase, were soon cleared away and, by the 18th century, the area was open, treeless heathland on which stock grazed and heather, bracken and turves were cut. Ashdown Forest is a relatively high area and drained by a series of valleys; this topography results in a mosaic of vegetation types not present on most other lowland heaths, and, unlike the heathlands on other geological formations (especially on the Greensands and Bagshot Beds), those of Ashdown Forest tend to have, even on the dry heath, a much greater proportion of Purple Moor Grass (*Molinia caerulea*) in the community (Rose, 1976). Much of the higher ground is covered with typical *Calluna*-dominated dry heath with Bell Heather (*Erica cinerea*), Dwarf Gorse (*Ulex minor*) and Bracken (*Pteridium aquilinum*). The principal grasses are fescues and bents, but in some places Heath Grass (*Danthonia decumbens*) grows. Associated species include Needle Furze (*Genista anglica*) and Sawwort (*Serratula tinctoria*).

In the valleys, oligotrophic to weakly-mesotrophic mires have developed

HEATHLANDS

(Ratcliffe, 1977) and there are extensive areas of humid and wet heath with patches of bog vegetation. The damp heath contains Cross-leaved Heath (*Erica tetralix*) with much Purple Moor Grass, Marsh Gentian (*Gentiana pneumonanthe*), White-beaked Sedge (*Rhynchospora alba*) and Marsh Club Moss (*Lycopodiella inundata*). The wet areas are the habitat of two rare dragonflies, the Small Red Damselfly (*Ceriagrion tenellum*) and Brilliant Emerald (*Somatochlora metallica*).

The present open heaths and commons of Ashdown are a relict of more extensive areas that were used for grazing and fuel-gathering, but past enclosures reduced this area; so, too, has the encroachment of scrub and Bracken. Birch and Pine have regenerated in the absence of grazing, Bracken is no longer cut, and an increase in fires through greater recreational pressure has encouraged a larger proportion of Purple Moor Grass in the vegetation. The management of the Forest is under the control of the Conservators of Ashdown Forest who attempt to maintain the heathlands in the face of these pressures.

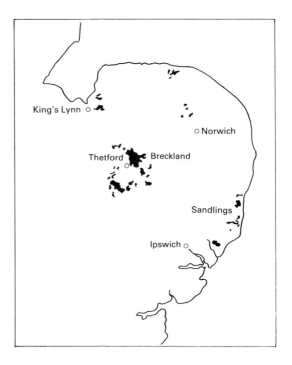

East Anglian Heaths

East Anglia and Breckland

The geology and soils of East Anglia have been complicated by the effects of successive glaciations, which have left a great variety of superficial deposits over the area. Earlier glaciation spread clays and loams and, ultimately boulder clays, over Norfolk and Suffolk. From these deposits, the light, sandy soils of the Breckland were formed by leaching. Later glaciations were less extensive and are represented by sands and gravels in terminal moraines near Cromer (which bears heathland), and sands and gravels in the outwashes near Lowestoft. The Breckland is noted for the solifluction patterns in its soils caused by glaciation. Where the ground is level, soil polygons have formed, but on slopes the differential sorting of soil particles by repeated thawing and freezing has produced 'stone stripes'. One of the best examples is to be seen on Thetford Heath, where the stripes carry alternate bands of grassland and heathland corresponding respectively to the coarse and fine particles (Duffey, 1976). The Breckland heaths form one of the most important and extensive areas of its kind in Britain, supporting a unique mixture of dwarf shrub heathlands, grass heath, Sand Sedge, and sparse woodland. They cover some 1000 sq kms (247,000 acres) in Norfolk and Suffolk, from Swaffham in the north, southwards to Bury St Edmunds, and from Lakenheath in the west, eastwards to East Harling, and are traversed from west to east by the rivers Thet, Little Ouse, Lark and Wissey. The average rainfall of 558 mm (22 in) is among the lowest in Britain, leading to a semi-continental climate which, together with the traditional pattern of land use, has created a steppe-like landscape.

The Breckland has always been renowned for its traditional land use based on sheep and rye, whereby the heathland, or 'breaks', mostly used for grazing, were ploughed and sown in more prosperous times, only to revert when the soil was exhausted or prices fell. There has been much speculation on the origin of the open landscape, but it is evident from the pollen record of Hockham Mere that forest clearances commenced in Neolithic times, about 4000 BC (Godwin, 1944). Forest regeneration was prevented by sheep- and rabbit-grazing. Sheep were present in the Breckland in Roman times and were of major importance until this century. The grazing pattern involved the few tracts of arable land, the meadows along the shallow valleys and the grass heaths. In the winter, the sheep were grazed in the meadows but at other times they were folded on the arable lands unless these were under cultivation, when the extensive heaths were used as sheep walks (Sheail, 1979). This procedure ensured a transfer of nutrients from the heaths and grasslands to the arable lands which, together with the erosion caused by over-grazing, perpetuated the open heathland landscape (Fig. 23). This practice was similar to that on the Suffolk Sandlings, as well as on the continent. In the Middle Ages, rabbit warrens were established and by the 15th century extended over 4000–6100 ha (9850–15,000 acres) on the Suffolk Brecklands. The rabbits maintained a closely-cropped sward and added to the erosion.

Extensive areas of inland dunes were a well-known feature of the Breckland, together with their accompanying sand storms. Lakenheath Warren, which remained one of the largest tracts until this century, contained an extensive dune system which was estimated to be 280 ha (690 acres) in 1835. These were largely destroyed when the airfield was constructed in 1942, and the only dune to survive is Wangford Warren. The vegetation changes associated with a large blow-out on the dunes of Lakenheath Warren have been described by Watt (1937). Improving agriculture and forestry have changed the landscape of the Breckland, especially in the present century; so, too, has the loss of rabbits through myxomatosis. Heathland losses have been estimated to be some 70% since 1880, when there were some 22,000 ha (54,120 acres) to 2,700 ha (6650

Inland sand-dunes – a well-known feature of Breckland heath/A. S. Watt, c. 1930

acres) in 1968, largely due to afforestation (Duffey, 1976).

The combination of shifting cultivation, intensive grazing by sheep and rabbits, and the wide variation in soils are responsible for the diversity of the Breckland vegetation. The complex series of grass- and heathlands have been the subject of detailed (and now classic) ecological research by Dr A. S. Watt of Cambridge. These communities he named grasslands A to E: Grassland A grows on shallow 15–18 cm (6–7 in), highly-calcareous soils (pH 8.0) and has approximately equal proportions of bare ground and Sheep's Fescue (*Festuca ovina*) sward, and there are about fifty associated plant species, most of which are calcicoles. The soils of Grassland B are deeper 33 cm (13 in) and contain less calcium. The sward of Sheep's Fescue is continuous, and this is the richest community with about eighty species of plants, many of them calcicoles. Grassland C has a depth of 46 cm (18 in) and has acidic surface layers; there are about sixty species of plant present, but the calcicoles have declined in number, and calcifuge species, such as Heath Bedstraw (*Galium saxatile*) and the moss (*Pleurozium schreberi*) appear. In Grassland D, the sward is a mixture of *Festuca* and *Agrostis*, the soils are deeper still (81 cm (32 in)) and acidic (pH 4.4) with leached upper horizons. The plant community contains typical calcifuge species such as Sheep's Sorrel (*Rumex acetosella*), Shepherd's Cress (*Teesdalia nudicaulis*) and Field Wood Rush (*Lazula campestris*); this community of thirty-eight species forms a mosaic with lichens sominated by *Cladonia arbuscula*. Grassland E is the most acidic (pH 3.6–4.0); it is a heavy podsol with a well-developed humus pan and little or no free calcium. The flora is an almost continuous carpet of *Cladonia arbuscula*, with about twenty plant species (Duffey, 1976).

On the acidic podsols, heathlands dominated by *Calluna* develop; areas of Bracken grow where the soils are deeper but acidic, and a community dominated by Sand Sedge is typical of the eroded areas of blown sand. This Sand Sedge community is unique to the Breckland, but the dwarf shrub communities are similar to those on the heaths of southern England (Ratcliffe, 1977). The lack of grazing has resulted in many areas becoming invaded by Birch and Pine.

Group 1 Ungrazed Turf Species	Heath Sedge Sickle Medick Purple-stemmed Cat's-tail	*Carex ericetorum* *Medicago falcata* *Phleum phleoides*
Group 2 Perennial Species	Breckland (or Spanish) Catchfly Spiked Speedwell Grape Hyacinth Field Southernwood	*Silene otites* *Veronica spicata*, ssp. *spicata* *Muscari atlanticum* *Artemisia campestris*
Group 3 Poor Competitors	Dense Silky-bent Mossy Stonecrop Wall Bedstraw Glabrous Rupturewort Small Medick (Bur) Striated (Sand) Catchfly Breckland Speedwell Fingered Speedwell Spring Speedwell Perennial Knawlweed Wild Thyme	*Apera interrupta* *Crassula tillaea* *Galium parisiense*, ssp. *anglicum* *Herniaria glabra* *Medicago minima* *Silene conica* *Veronica praecox* *V. triphyllos* *V. verna* *Scleranthus perennis*, spp. *prostratus* *Thymus serpyllum*, ssp. *serpyllum*

Fig. 15
Rare Plants of the Breckland

The Breckland, like the Lizard in Cornwall, has a flora noted for its phytogeographical interest. Creeping Ladies Tresses (*Goodyera repens*) and the moss *Rhytidium rugosum* grow at the southern limits of their British ranges; Ground Pine (*Ajuga chamaepitys*) reaches its northern limit; Sand Sedge (*Carex arenaria*), Grey Hair Grass (*Corynephros canescens*), Sand Cat's-tail (*Phleum arenarium*), Wild Pansy (*Viola tricolor*, ssp. *curtisii*) and the mosses *Pleurochaete squarrosa* and *Tortula ruraliformis* are coastal species. Grey Hair Grass, although regarded as a coastal species in Britain, is a regular component of the dry heath vegetation from the Netherlands to Jutland. Two species, Spear-leaved Skull Cap (*Scutellaria hastifolia*) and the moss *Eurhynchium pulchellum*, var. *praecox*, are confined to the Breckland. Up to twenty other species (Fig. 15) are only found infrequently outside the grass heaths of the Breckland (Watt, 1971b).

Watt examined factors such as soil nutrients, rabbit-grazing and competition, which affect the distribution of eighteen rare Breckland species (most are confined to the less acid grasslands). He recognized three groups: first, three species which persist in ungrazed turf dominated by grasses, and all of which are capable of vegetative reproduction; second, four perennial species which establish on bare soils or in short turf and which persist until dominated by grasses; lastly, eleven annuals or perennials with low competitive powers, which require open or short vegetation on suitable soils. Many of these eleven have declined as the grass heaths have become overgrown since the disappearance of rabbits. Their future depends on manipulating the balance of competition in the grass sward

Dr A. S. Watt's 1930s photograph of Lakenheath Warren – and (below) as it is today, showing the effects of decreased rabbit grazing (the fenced area is one of Dr Watt's experimental quadrats/W. Block

and the creation of open patches of bare soil or short vegetation – characteristics of the Breckland vegetation which arose from the shifting cultivation and intensive grazing of past times.

The Stone Curlew is the most important Breckland bird, with the largest breeding concentration in Britain. Other species, some of which no longer breed there, include the Red-backed Shrike, Hobby, Tree Pipit, Nightjar, Woodlark and Wheatear, and the Great Bustard. The invertebrate animals, although less well known, are as interesting as the flora, and

similarly dependent on the diversity of habitats. There is an important element which is coastal in origin, depending on open, bare, sandy areas and dunes; among these are species of ground beetles and spiders. There is also a group of insects rare in Britain, although fairly common in the Breckland. They feed on common plants characteristic of disturbed ground, wasteland and abandoned fields. A further group of insects feeds on the rare Breckland plants – such as the Viper's Bugloss Moth (*Hadena irregularis*), the larvae of which feed on the seed capsules of the Spanish Catchfly (*Silene otites*).

Many of the remaining pieces of grass and dwarf shrub heathlands in the Breckland are nature reserves; other areas are used for military training, especially around Stanford – and this is now a prime example of grass heath. The main localities where dwarf shrub heaths, dominated by *Calluna*, grow on highly acid soils are Cavenham, Tuddenham, Lakenheath Warren, Berners, Horn, Weather and Thetford (with solifluctuation patterns). Less extensive areas of *Calluna*-heathland occur on many of the other main heaths, such as Foxhole, Stanford and Wangford. For more detailed accounts of the ecology and diversity of the plant communities of the Brecklands, see Duffey (1976) and Ratcliffe (1977), and the long series of papers by Watt.

East Anglia Heathlands

Bordering the Suffolk coast is a band of heathland, about 15 km (10 m) wide, known as the Suffolk Sandlings, which extends from the River Orwell northwards to Lowestoft and includes the heaths of Walberswick, Westleton, Minsmere, Lieston Common, Snape Warren and Hollesley Common. This mosaic of heath and arable land is on a low plateau of Pleiocene and Pleistocene deposits called Crag. In this part of eastern England, the central band of Chalk dips eastwards; south of Ipswich it is overlain by London Clays but northwards there are deposits of Norwich, Red and Corallian Crag, which are unique in Britain. These are fairly hard, sandy rocks of marine origin which were laid down in Quaternary times, about two to five million years ago. The soils are leached, acidic and sandy, with well-developed podsols.

Originally, there were about 95 sq km (23,370 acres) of heathlands on the Sandlings, which were used extensively for sheepwalks and muchburrowed by rabbits, both activities which would have maintained open heathland. Today this area has dwindled to 22 sq km (5412 acres) of widely-separated fragments (Armstrong, 1973). The dry heaths are a typical mixture of *Calluna* and Bracken, but there is an unexplained outpost of the Gorse *Ulex gallii*, which is normally predominant in western Britain (Fig. 36). The grasslands associated with the heaths are composed of Sheep's Fescue (*Festuca ovina*) and Bents (*Agrostis capillaris*). Wet heath and mire communities are less common and much of the heathland is invaded by Birch scrub. Here also, are important sites for heathland birds, such as the Nightjar (Berry, 1979) and the Woodlark.

In the north of East Anglia, the Chalk is bounded on its western edge by Sandringham Sands, Snettisham Clay and Carstone, the latter corresponding to the Lower Greensand. Formerly, there were heathlands on

HEATHLANDS

these deposits, from King's Lynn southwards, but today the most extensive areas remain on Sandringham Warren, Roydon Common and at Shouldenham; Massingham Heath, a little to the east, is on glacial sands. Roydon Common is a fine example of a valley mire, noted for its flora, with surrounding *Calluna*-dominated dry heath communities, and Sand Sedge (*Carex arenaria*) growing in the bare areas. The mire is similar to those in the New Forest, but with floristic differences due to its geographical position. The zonation of its vegetation has been found to be correlated with the patterns of physical and chemical variation (Daniels & Pearson, 1974).

Scattered heathlands occur around Holt, and include Holt Lowes, Salthouse Heath and Kelling Heath. These heaths are on soils derived from glacial sands and have *Calluna*-dominated communities in which Western Gorse (*Ulex gallii*) is an associated species. Similar plant communities are to be found on the fragments of heath, also on glacial sands, which remain to the north of Norwich at Buxton, Horsford and Newton Heaths, together with scattered fragments towards Fakenham.

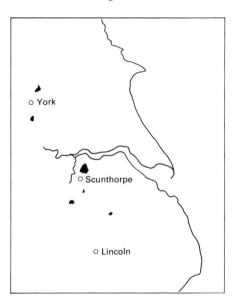

Heathland in Lincolnshire and Yorkshire

Lincolnshire and Yorkshire

Superficial sand deposits, similar to those of the Breckland, are found in Lincolnshire (where they are known as the cover sands) overlying oolitic limestone. Elsewhere, especially around the head of the Humber estuary, there has been deposition and redistribution of similar sands as deltaic deposits. Little heathland remains in Lincolnshire, save scattered fragments from Wood Hall Spa, north and east to Market Rasen and Scunthorpe, including Meassingham Heath and Scotton Common. Risby Warren, near Scunthorpe, is the most extensive tract remaining; here the sandy deposits vary in thickness and produce a diversity of soils and vege-

*Suffolk heathland/
Nature Photographers,
D. Washington*

tation comparable with that of the Breckland, showing transitions from calcareous soils (grass heath with *Calluna*) to acidic podsols; in parts, the mobile sand is fixed by Marram Grass (*Ammophila arenaria*).

Glaciation has also produced a complex series of superficial deposits in the Vale of York, once a flat-bottomed lake in a moraine area; the Vale has a topography of hummocks and depressions, with sands and clays of varying depths. Formerly there were extensive heathlands in this area, but today only scattered fragments remain; of these, Skipwith Common is the largest heathland in the north of England. Although there are areas of dry heath dominated by *Calluna*, much the greater part of the Common is made up of humid and wet heath communities with Cross-leaved Heath and associated species, together with important bog communities. This area, now a nature reserve, is noted for its birds and insects. South of York lies Strensall Common, a similar area, but with a greater proportion of dry heath communities, much of which has been invaded by Birch. The morainic topography has created local conditions where bogs have formed, typified by those at Askham and Allerthorp; although predominantly bog communities, these may be fringed by areas of wet and dry heath.

Midlands

North and west of the Jurassic rock outcrop running from the south, north-eastwards across England, is a series of Triassic deposits forming the Midland Plain and running from the Severn north-eastwards to Yorkshire, with a western branch extending to the Lancashire coast. The Plain is largely covered by drift but there are outcrops of acid and more sandy deposits in the form of Bunter Pebble Beds and Sands. In places, there are outcrops of older and igneous rocks; these, too, provide poor soils, but throughout this area where the Bunter sands are fairly coarse, poor, hungry soils result, on which there were heathlands in former times. Good examples are Sherwood Forest and Cannock Chase; in the former there is now little heathland remaining, but on Cannock Chase there are extensive areas of Heather.

Formerly a Norman forest, heathland spread on the Chase from the middle of the 16th century, when there was extensive tree-felling to meet the needs of iron-making. Sheep-grazing also increased, allowing the spread of heathland, until by the early 19th century there was a large area south from Cannock covering about 10.4 sq km (25,600 acres), growing on thin podsols derived from Bunter Pebble Beds. The vegetation is an association of *Calluna* and Bracken (Bell Heather (*Erica cinerea*) is scarce) with Bilberry (*Vaccinium myrtillus*), Cowberry (*V. vitis-idea*) and, in a few places, Crowberry (*Empetrum nigrum*). The last two species indicate the intermediate position of these heathlands between the northern moorlands and the southern heaths. The grasses present include Wavy-hair Grass (*Deschampsia flexuosa*), bents (*Agrostis* spp.) and fescues (*Festuca* spp.), Purple Moor Grass (*Molinia caerulea*) and Mat Grass (*Nardus stricta*). Much of the Chase has become dominated by Bracken and there have been extensive trials to control it, together with other heathland management experiments (Daniels, 1983). The multiple use of the Chase for nature conservation, amenity and recreation has also been the subject of much enquiry.

Wales

In Wales, much of the vegetation dominated by dwarf shrubs falls into our definition of upland moorland as it occurs at higher altitudes, but there are areas of lowland heath, such as those west of Mynydd Prescelly in western Pembrokeshire, and in Cardiganshire, where there is a lowland heath on Ordovician deposits. Otherwise, there is little true heathland until the coastal heaths of the Lleyn Peninsula and on Anglesey, where heathland has developed on sandy, Pre-Cambrian deposits similar to those beneath the Long Mynd in Shropshire.

Scotland

Although there are many thousands of acres of dwarf shrub vegetation in Scotland, little of it falls within our definition of heathland. The best and most interesting area is the Sands of Forvie on the east coast near Aberdeen. The sands forming these dunes are non-calcareous, and the vegetation shows transition from unstable to stable dune communities and wetter areas. Crowberry (*Empetrum nigrum*) is an important constituent of the plant community and, in the earlier stages of heathland formation, grows in association with lichens, *Calluna*, Marram Grass and Sand Sedge; as conditions become more stable, the community acquires more grasses, *Empetrum* is less abundant, and *Calluna* dominates. This type of dune heath is similar to that on the North European coast.

CHAPTER 6 **Heathland Plant Communities**

European Heath Classification

In chapter 2 we discussed the physical conditions, especially soils and climate, which favour the growth and dominance of dwarf shrubs. In general, heathland plant communities are poor in species. The dominance of *Calluna* with only a few associated species gives the impression that there is relatively little variation in the species composition of European heathlands. But if the lower plants, particularly mosses and lichens, are counted, richness increases and shows distinct regional and local variations. Over the entire range of European heathlands there is a discernible pattern of which British heathlands form a distinct part. In Britain, there is an overall pattern which varies according to altitude, climate and soil; and on any single heath, there is often a further distinct pattern in vegetation composition and structure, which depends on differences in the nutrient and moisture contents of the soil and effects of management, such as burning and grazing. One of the most difficult problems with heathlands is the continuous variation in species composition; one type merges into another, and it is difficult to draw the boundaries of regional (phytogeographical) units.

One of the earliest and most significant contributions to understanding the phytogeography and classification of heathland communities was by the Danish botanist, T. W. Bøcher (1943), who looked upon dry and wet heaths, as well as dwarf shrub bogs, as one very large vegetational unit, yet

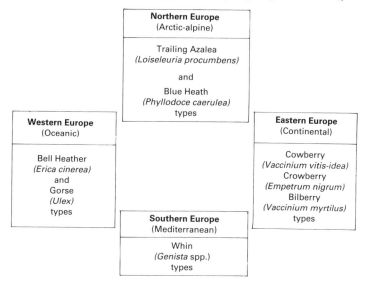

Fig. 16
Bøcher's 'Euoceanic' Heaths

recognized that the great number of small vegetation types within this larger unit were never separated by sharp boundaries. He first recognized two major divisions: dry heath communities, and wet heath and bog communities. Each of these was divided into a number of series, based on the frequency of occurrence of certain species. His regional distribution of main heathland types is evident from Fig. 16 and reflects geographical trends in the species composition of the communities. Most of the communities in which we shall be interested fall in Bøcher's Euoceanic series, which contains the heaths of the Faroes, west Norway, the British Isles and northern France. These are subdivided by the occurrence of species of Gorse (*Ulex*) into a northernmost type, the *Erica cinerea* (Bell Heather) group, and a southern type, the *Ulex gallii-europaeus* (Common and Western Gorse) group. The southernmost alliance is distinguished by the presence of *Erica scoparia* (Besom Heather), which does not occur in Britain, but a variant of this alliance, *Erica vagans* (Cornish Heather), does. Bøcher divided wet heath and bog communities into three series: the Atlantic, sub-Atlantic-sub-continental series, and a continental series, which are more clearly defined geographically than the dry heath communities.

Bøcher's work has continued to influence subsequent classifications. An analysis of the species composition of sixty stands selected from the heathlands of Norway, southern Sweden, Denmark, north Germany, the Netherlands and Great Britain (Gimingham, 1961) revealed four groupings: stands with *Calluna* and Bell Heather; *Calluna* with *Vaccinium* species; *Calluna* with *Empetrum nigrum*; and *Calluna* with *Genista* species. Statistical analysis of these stands showed that the trend from *Vaccinium*-rich to *Genista* heaths corresponded with the north–south transition from Arctic-alpine to Mediterranean heaths of Bøcher, and reflects a climatic trend.

The second axis of Gimingham's analysis was an east–west one from a continental type of heathland to the oceanic one of Britain, and was reflected in the distribution of Bell Heather, Cross-leaved Heath, Crowberry (*Empetrum nigrum*) and Bilberry (*Vaccinium myrtillus*). Subsequent work has confirmed this view of European heathland phytogeography, adding edaphic variation to the list of principal factors governing the patterns within the communities. This has been summarized by De Smidt (1967) as water economy, the mineral content of the soil, and human influence. Gimingham (1972) concluded that approaches such as Bøcher's, which correlate floristic variation with geographical location, could obscure other important factors, and although certain groupings might generally occur within a certain region, examples might be found elsewhere. For instance, types characteristic of high latitudes may occur at lower ones, but at higher altitudes.

There have been numerous attempts to erect a classification system for European heaths, following the principles of the various schools of phytosociology; it is outside the scope of this text to consider them in detail since the criteria and the nomenclature which they adopt are unique. For the reader who is interested in this subject, Gimingham (1972) provides an excellent comparative assessment of the hierarchies proposed. He notes always that it is difficult to represent multivariate systems in a few dimensions, when there is a continuous range of variation within floristic composition which may not be simply related to individual environmental features but to combinations of them. He provides a synthesis in the form of a list representing the important features of the variation which, although not offered as a definitive scheme, is a practical one. His main categories are:

A. **Mountain heaths**
Divided into six sub-categories which, since they fall outside the scope of this book, will not be described in detail.

B. **Dry heaths**
These occur on both the lowlands and the uplands but do not extend to high altitudes; they are divided into three groups containing a total of twelve sub-categories:

1. *Calluna*–Crowberry (*Empetrum hermaphroditum*) heaths. Northern and oceanic, occurring at low altitudes in the Faroes and Shetland Islands.

2. *Calluna*–Bell Heather (*Erica cinerea*) heaths. Bear Berry (*Arctostaphylos uva-ursi*) often present. Generally in localities with a strong maritime influence, on soils of relatively high nutrient content, often herb-rich. Species with northern affinities generally well represented; Highlands of Scotland.

3. *Calluna*–Western Gorse (*Ulex gallii*) heaths. The type of lowland heath typical of the western regions from Ireland and Wales and the south-west of England (Cornwall, Devon and west Dorset, and parts of Hampshire) and north-western France.

4. *Calluna*–Dwarf Gorse (*Ulex minor*) heaths. Comparable with the previous type but typical of eastern England and therefore less oceanic. There is an overlap in these two types on the Dorset–Hampshire borders. Also present in some parts of northern France.

5. Cornish Heath (*Erica vagans*) heath. A highly oceanic type, occurring only in the extreme south-west of England, especially on the Lizard Peninsula; also in parts of western France.

6. *Calluna*–Spring Squill (*Scilla verna*) heath. An exclusively maritime heath of the cliffs of south-western England.

7. *Calluna*–Bilberry (*Vaccinium*) heath. *Calluna* growing on peaty podsols or peat in association with one or more of Bilberry (*V. myrtillus*), Cowberry (*V. vitis-idea*) and Crowberry (*Empetrum nigrum*). The mosses *Hylocomium splendens*, *Pleurozium schreberi* and *Hypnum cupressiforme* are common. A widespread heath type in southern Norway, south-west Sweden and northern Britain.

8. *Calluna*–Bearberry (*Arcostaphylos uva-ursi*) heath. A sub-continental type, occurring in a transitional position in Denmark and south-west Swedeff.

9. *Calluna*–Alpine Bearberry (*Arctostaphylos uva-ursi*) heath. This community contains species with continental distribution patterns as well as some with southern affinities and therefore occupies a

transitional position. Although it contains Alpine Bearberry it differs from community B2. It occurs in Denmark and south-west Sweden (Halland).

10. *Calluna*–Heath Grass (*Danthonia decumbens*) heath. A herb-rich, transitional community from the Netherlands and Belgium.

11. *Calluna*–Whin (*Genista* spp.) heath. Generally on deep, well-formed podsols. The main species is Hairy Greenweed (*G. pilosa*) but also Petty Whin (*G. anglica*). Generally lichen-rich; occurs, mainly in northern Germany and eastwards.

12. Besom Heather (*Erica scoparia*) heath. Very oceanic and southern type, with species related to Mediterranean types of vegetation, such as Tree Heather (*Erica arborea*) and Mediterranean Heather (*E. mediterranea*). Occurs in south-west France and northern Spain.

C. Humid and wet heaths

1. *Calluna*–Cross-leaved Heath (*Erica tetralix*) humid heaths. In habitats of intermediate moisture status. Species of bog moss (*Sphagnum* spp.) generally not well represented. A widespread community in the more oceanic parts of the heathland region.

2. *Calluna*–Dorset Heath (*Erica ciliaris*) humid heath. Very similar to the previous type but Dorset Heath replaces Cross-leaved Heath. Occurs in Dorset, rarely in Cornwall, and also in north-west France.

3. *Calluna*–Cross-leaved Heath (*Erica tetralix*) wet heath. On permanently wet soils; characteristic species include *Sphagnum compactum*, *S. tenellum* and some other species of bog moss, Heath Rush (*Juncus squarrosus*), Sharp-flowered Rush (*J. acutiflorus*), Purple Moor Grass (*Molinia caerulea*), Deer Grass (*Scirpus cespitosus*) and Bog Asphodel (*Narthecium ossifragum*). A widespread heath type in the more oceanic parts of the heath region.

4. *Calluna*–Cottongrass (*Eriophorum vaginatum*) wet heath. Occurs on the peat, forming tussocks of *E. vaginatum* and bushes of *Calluna*. Crowberry, Deer Sedge and the moss *Polytrichum commune* may be present. A more northern type.

5. *Calluna*–Cottongrass (*Eriophorum vaginatum*) upland wet heath. On hill peat in the northern parts of the region. The Cloudberry (*Rubus chamaemorus*) is a characteristic species.

Of the twelve types of dry heath listed above, five are not represented, or only poorly so, in Britain. *Calluna*–Bilberry heath is not common in the lowlands but occurs occasionally in association with acid woodlands and at slightly higher altitudes in the transition zones to upland moorland communities. Neither of the southern sub-categories of dry heath are really represented in Britain. Variants of the humid and wet heath categories are all to be found under various conditions in Britain.

From Gimingham's categories, we will make a further breakdown based on the range of heathlands dealt with in this book. From the dry heath category we will consider *Calluna*–Western Gorse, *Calluna*–Dwarf

Gorse, Cornish Heath and *Calluna*–Spring Squill heaths; from humid heath, *Calluna*–Cross-leaved Heath and *Calluna*–Dorset Heath; from wet heath, *Calluna*–Cross-leaved Heath. These are the main associations to be found in the British lowlands but may also occur at more northerly locations; all the other types are predominantly upland and northern in distribution.

British Heath Classification

Variation in the composition of vegetation depends mainly on soil moisture conditions, which in turn depend on topography. Where soils are free-draining, or drier than field capacity, and where the water table remains well below the soil surface at all times, dry heath vegetation develops. Where drainage is impeded, the soils are more-or-less at field capacity, and the water table is near the surface (or at times above it) wet or mesophilous heath develops. Humid heath is an intermediate form between dry and wet heaths where, although drainage may be impeded, the soils are drier. Where drainage is impeded at all times, and the water table is more-or-less at the surface, valley mire communities develop and peat accumulates.

The system description and classification of Britain's vegetation has never been fully compatible with those used by continental botanists, and this has made comparisons difficult. In recent years, there has been an attempt to correct this through the *National Vegetation Classification*. So far as heathlands are concerned, the work is incomplete, particularly with regard to the transitional communities between lowland heathland and upland moorland. Nevertheless, it is possible to provide a preliminary summary of the main types of vegetation recognized for lowland heaths. This is the most recent formal classification of British vegetation and recognizes nine major heath types from the British lowlands. They are described from variations in the occurrence of *Calluna*, Bell Heather (*Erica cinerea*), Cross-leaved Heath (*E. tetralix*), Dwarf Gorse (*Ulex minor*), Western Gorse (*Ulex gallii*), Purple Moor Grass (*Molinia caerulea*) and Bristle Bent (*Agrostis curtisii*). Additional sub-communities are recognized which contain Dorset Heath (*Erica ciliaris*) and Cornish Heath (*E. vagans*). Many heathland communities can become modified, particularly as a result of draining, over-grazing and burning, all of which lead to impoverishment. In these cases, the vegetation becomes extremely species-poor and, in some instances, consists almost entirely of *Calluna*. These communities can be very difficult to assess since it is not always possible to recognize from which of the nine types they were derived.

The nine major types recognized from the lowlands are given below.

Dry heath types

1. *Calluna vulgaris–Festuca ovina*

    A species-poor community, centred on the sands of the Breckland and East Anglian coast, running a little into Lincolnshire and southwards into the Home Counties. The constant species are *Calluna*, Sheep's Fescue (*Festuca ovina*) and the mosses *Dicranum scoparium* and *Hypnum cupressiforme*. Both typical and lichen-rich communities can be recognized, as well as a form in which Sand Sedge (*Carex arenaria*) becomes

Typical dry heath community/ N. R. Webb

dominant, tending to suppress Sheep's Fescue and *D. scoparium*. This subcommunity readily degrades into a type of dune vegetation dominated by Sand Sedge, while the typical form degrades into a type of vegetation consisting almost entirely of *Calluna*.

2. *Erica cinerea–Ulex minor*
   Occurs from Kent to East Dorset and characterized by the presence of *Calluna*, Bell Heather and Dwarf Gorse (*Ulex minor*). Wavy Hair Grass (*Deschampsia flexuosa*) replaces Fescue as the commonest grass, but there is little Bristle Bent (*Agrostis curtisii*). It becomes more abundant westwards and is represented in the next type. Besides the typical form, there is an ungrazed type with *Vaccinium* and numerous tree seedlings, and a type containing Purple Moor Grass and Cross-leaved Heath, which has affinities with types occurring further westwards.

3. *Ulex minor–Agrostis curtisii*
   Similar to the previous one, containing as constant species *Calluna*, Dwarf Gorse, Bell Heather, Bristle Bent (*Agrostis curtisii*) and Purple Moor Grass. On occasions, Dorset Heath (*E. ciliaris*) replaces Cross-leaved Heath (*E. tetralix*). There are typical, lichen-rich and *Agrostis*-rich subcommunities recognized from Dorset and the New Forest.

4. *Ulex gallii–Agrostis curtisii*
   Much the same as the previous one in general floristics, except that Western Gorse (*Ulex gallii*) replaces Dwarf Gorse (*U. minor*). This

community occurs from West Dorset right down the south-west peninsula and into South Wales. Like the previous type, there is an *Agrostis*-rich type in which Cross-leaved Heath (*Erica tetralix*) is much reduced and stands where Dorset Heath (*Erica ciliaris*) accompanies or replaces other species of *Erica*. In this type, the most important internal division is between the type represented by the central six species and, on the one hand, much grassier vegetation (with Sheep's Fescue (*Festuca ovina*), Heath Grass (*Danthonia decumbens*), Heath Bedstraw (*Galium saxatile*) and a little *Vaccinium* (upland grass heath remnants)) and, on the other, *Trichophorum*-rich samples, which represent a transition to valley mire wet heath; Bell Heather (*Erica cinerea*) is much reduced in this latter kind.

5. *Ulex gallii–Erica cinerea*
Geographically, this type takes over from the last, running in an arc from the south-west peninsula up through Wales to the Isle of Man, across Derbyshire and down again onto the East Anglian coast. Western Gorse (*Ulex gallii*), Bell Heather (*Erica cinerea*) and *Calluna* are the only constant species throughout and, in lower altitude samples, they are very much the predominant species. As in the previous type, there is a grassier form containing Heath Grass (*Danthonia decumbens*), Sheep's Fescue (*Festuca ovina*), Common Bent (*Agrostis capillaris*), Sweet Vernal Grass (*Anthoxanthum odoratum*), Red Fescue (*Festuca rubra*) and sometimes a little *Vaccinium*. In coastal, but not strongly maritime, areas, there is a distinct type in which Spring Squill (*Scilla verna*), Wild Thyme (*Thymus praecox*), Sea Plantain (*Plantago maritima*), Bird's-foot Trefoil (*Lotus corniculatus*) and Common Cat's-ear (*Hypochoeris radicata*) become predominant.

6. *Erica vagans*
Occurs on the Lizard in Cornwall and has been described by Coombe and Frost (1956a); a description of this community appears in chapter 5.

7. *Calluna vulgaris–Deschampsia flexuosa*
A species-poor type of heath containing *Calluna*, Wavy Hair Grass (*Deschampsia flexuosa*) and the moss *Pholia nutans*. It is centred on the polluted Pennine foothills around the northern industrial areas, and also in the North Yorkshire Moors and parts of the West Midlands. Somewhat more bryophyte- and lichen-rich types can be recognized as well as transitions to drained mire remnants and sub-montane acid grasslands.

8. *Calluna vulgaris–Scilla verna*
A maritime type containing the rare species Spring Squill (*Scilla verna*). It occurs on the coasts of western Britain, on the south-west peninsula, west Wales, Cumbria, western Scotland and the Isles, and the coasts of north and east Scotland; it is absent from the eastern and south-eastern coasts from Durham to Dorset. The constant species are *Calluna*, Bell Heather (*Erica cinerea*), Sheep's Fescue (*Festuca ovina*), Spring Squill (*Scilla verna*), Bird's-foot Trefoil (*Lotus corniculatus*), Wild Thyme (*Thymus praecox*), Sea Plantain (*Plantago maritima*),

Tormentil (*Potentilla erecta*), Common Cat's-ear (*Hypochoeris radicata*) and Yorkshire Fog (*Holcus lanatus*). Six sub-associations are recognized (Malloch, 1972).

Wet or mesophilous heath types

9. *Erica tetralix–Sphagnum compactum*
Widespread, occurring in all the major heath areas of southern England, where the topography is suitable and where there are gley-podsols or peaty gleys with at least seasonal waterlogging. This type becomes more local in distribution northwards. The constant species are *Calluna*, Cross-leaved Heath (*Erica tetralix*), Purple Moor Grass (*Molinia caerulea*), *Sphagnum compactum*, *Sphagnum tenellum* and, locally, Deer Grass (*Scirpus cespitosus*). Rarities occurring in this type include Marsh Clubmoss (*Lycopodiella inundata*), Marsh Gentian (*Gentiana pneumonanthe*), Brown Beak Sedge (*Rhynchospora fusca*) and, in parts, Dorset Heath (*Erica ciliaris*). Four sub-associations are recognized: a typical form, a *Rhynchospora alba–Lycopodiella inundata* form, a form growing under more base-rich conditions and containing Heath Spotted Orchid (*Dactylorhiza maculata*), Devil's Bit Scabious (*Succisa pratensis*), Meadow Thistle (*Cirsium dissectum*), Tawny Sedge (*Carex hostiana*) and Flea Sedge (*C. pulicaris*). Frequent, uncontrolled burning can lead to a related community becoming established – *Molinia caerulea–Erica tetralix–Calluna vulgaris* – which is characteristic of damp and wet heaths and common on marginal, disturbed heathland throughout southern England. The proportions of the principal constituent species may vary but, in general, burning favours Purple Moor Grass at the expense of the heathers.

Besides the heathland communities of acid, mixed soils and peats, chalk and limestone heaths have been recognized. This is a community containing the usual grassland species but in which *Calluna* and Bell Heather may be present. In this community there is an intimate mixture of calcifuges with calcicoles. The origin and persistence of these communities has provoked much discussion (Grubb et al., 1969; Etherington, 1981). The *National Vegetation Classification* does not recognize them as distinct communities but as a mosaic of either *Ulex gallii–Agrostis curtisii* heath, *Ulex gallii–Erica cinerea* heath and *Calluna vulgaris–Scilla verna* heath with the calcicolous grassland characteristics of the particular area or site.

CHAPTER 7 **The Dynamics of Heathland Vegetation**

There is a process of natural change which occurs in heathland vegetation and this is checked or modified by factors such as grazing or burning. All vegetation is dynamic: it is a mosaic of species and individuals which differ in age and structure. If we closely follow a patch of heathland vegetation over a number of years, we can see these changes; plants grow from seedlings, become larger and more woody, occupy more space, cover a larger surface area, and show changes in their aerial structure. Not only do individual plants change throughout their life cycles but there are changes in the spaces between the plants as they grow and die. Other species colonize these patches, each of which in turn, shows a similar sequence of changes in space and time. By understanding all these patterns of change and how they interrelate, we can manage and conserve heathland more effectively in the future.

Throughout their life cycles, individual plants vary in the amount of green matter they produce, in the amount of their litter which falls to the ground, in the quantity of nutrients they take up – and in the amount released into the soil by decomposition. These complex patterns of change are evident in all vegetation, but particularly so on heathland, where the changes take place over the relatively short period of some 40–50 years, compared with many decades for similar changes in a forest.

Accompanying these vegetation changes are complementary changes in the fauna. Some invertebrates are characteristic of the young stages, when there are open spaces; others are monophagous – eating only a single species of plant – and thus, can only occur in the same stage of the succession as their host plant. Other animals depend on the structural changes in the vegetation or the consequential changes in the microclimate. These important vegetational changes in time are of two types – successional and cyclical.

Successional change occurs as one type of vegetation is gradually replaced by another, in a directional change leading to a community with a stable composition called the climax. With cyclical change, there is a repeating pattern of vegetation – although there may be an overall appearance of stability. The sequence of changes and their underlying processes have always caused controversy amongst ecologists; they have been unable to agree on the extent to which succession is directed – whether it inevitably leads to a climax vegetation of the same composition, or to different climaxes in which the composition varies in response to local differences in topography, soil moisture, nutrients and the effects of animals.

Succession may be either primary or secondary. Primary succession takes place on newly-created soil surfaces, which have been previously unvegetated. One of the best examples is dune heath, such as Studland Heath in Dorset or the Sands of Forvie in east Scotland. At Studland, the dune ridges have been formed from re-deposited Bagshot Sands, and are acidic (many sand dunes are formed from marine sands and therefore are calcareous). The dunes at Studland have developed during the last 300 years (Diver, 1933); the oldest ridges now have a vegetation similar to the surrounding heathland, but the most seaward ridges have dune vegetation dominated by Marram Grass (*Ammophila arenaria*), Lyme Grass (*Leymus arenarius*) and Sand Sedge (*Carex arenaria*). Similar examples of this type of primary succession may be found on the inland dunes of the East Anglian Breckland (e.g. Wangford Warren), where, although Sand Sedge is present, the other maritime species are not.

More frequently, succession on heathland is secondary and follows the destruction of the vegetation by fire. A new and similar type of vegetation regenerates in which the succession passes through pioneer to degenerate phases of heathland development, but, if there is no fire again, continues to scrub and woodland. Usually in lowland Britain, the heathland is burnt before secondary succession proceeds so far; the succession is checked and re-set, repeating a similar sequence of changes time after time. At the climax, the composition of the vegetation is stable; it is in equilibrium and self-perpetuating. The reader is referred to standard texts on ecology, or to that of Miles (1979).

It is sometimes difficult on heathland to distinguish between cyclical and successional processes. Where there is a constant pressure from factors such as grazing or exposure which maintain open heathland, cyclical processes operate; here the vegetation acquires a mixed age structure and its composition and spatial pattern constantly change even though the heathland, as a whole, appears unchanged. Generally, true examples of heathland showing cyclical phenomena are rare, but may occur at high altitudes above the tree line or on exposed coasts (Gimingham *et al.*, 1979).

Cyclical change is very well documented for the Breckland heaths. Here, Watt (1955) showed that under constant grazing pressure, which prevented succession, the composition and structure of the vegetation changed from a *Calluna*-dominated phase to a Bracken-dominated phase, and then returned to a *Calluna* phase. In other places, the change may be from *Calluna*-dominated heath to grass heath, with Wavy Hair Grass (*Deschampsia flexuosa*) as the dominant, and then back to dominant *Calluna*. This alteration of balance in the competition between species results from changes in the growth and age structure of the plant populations.

Such a community, which had probably existed in this form since the early 19th century, was described by Barclay-Estrup & Gimingham (1969). Permanent quadrats, each of 1 m^2, were laid out in patches of vegetation representing the four phases. The changes in vegetation cover and composition were mapped for three years. In this way, it was possible to examine the changes which would take place in a single quadrant over a period of some thirty years. *Calluna* was dominant in all the age classes represented; in the pioneer phase its cover was 4%, in the building phase 22%, in the mature phase 42%, and in the degenerate phase 32%. The figures show how the spatial pattern changes during the cycle; small *Calluna* plants grow into bushes and increase in cover (Fig. 17), while old plants die, making spaces in the vegetation canopy and opening the soil surface for seedling regeneration. The individual plants of the dominant species (*Calluna*) pass through a sequence of growth phases which, because the whole heathland has a mixed age structure, appear as a cycle.

HEATHLANDS

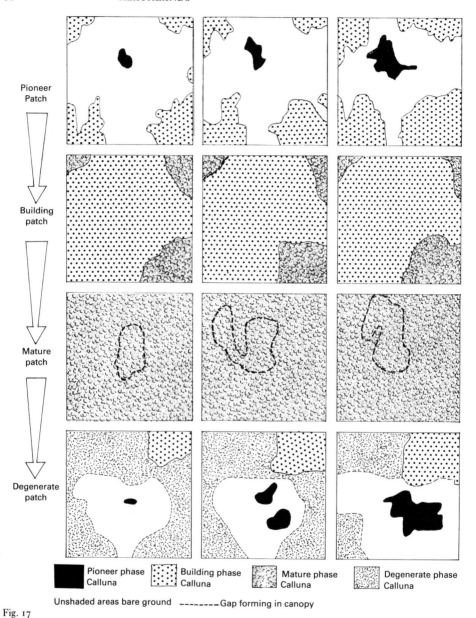

Fig. 17
Cover Changes on Different-Aged Heaths
Four 1m sq quadrats – each one dominated by a different phase of Calluna – were studied over a period of three years

In the pioneer phase, *Calluna* cover is small and other species of vascular plants reach their greatest abundance; in the next phase – the building phase – *Calluna* excludes all other species; by the mature phase, bryophytes colonize the soil surface, since the humidity beneath the closed canopy has increased considerably, but still *Calluna* remains dominant. Bryophytes reach their maximum abundance in the degenerate phase and, as the canopy becomes more open, other species of vascular plants and *Calluna* seedlings are able to establish. This important study described in detail the types of cyclical change which can occur in heathland vegetation under certain circumstances and which had been previously described by Watt (1947, 1955). It must be added that heathlands in which such a cycle of change is recognizable are relatively rare in lowland Britain.

A certain amount of confusion may arise in the terminology used to describe the various processes on heathland. Individual plants may represent one of the four growth phases described in the previous chapter. These phases – pioneer, building, mature, degenerate – in the life cycle of *Calluna* are defined arbitrarily from the morphology and behaviour of the plants (Watt, 1955; Gimingham, 1960). In old, unmanaged heathland, where succession is checked, a mixed age structure develops and plants representing all phases are distributed throughout the vegetation. If a small sample of this heathland is examined, it will appear to be of one phase, although the heathland as a whole represents no phase. Fires create large, homogeneous areas of vegetation where all of the plants belong to one of the phases and have the same age and structure. The application of this terminology depends on the scale at which the vegetation is examined. There is a third type, although not characteristic of lowland heathland, where the stems of *Calluna* are continually being buried by accumulating peat (Forrest, 1971; Forrest & Smith, 1975) or sand (Wallen, 1980), into which they root. The age structure of this heath does not change with time and the *Calluna* can be considered immortal. On these heaths, the above-ground biomass is in a steady state where input equals loss (Forrest, 1971; Wallen, 1980), but in the other types of heath, the input to the above-ground biomass varies throughout the phases.

Microclimate

The structural changes which occur in heathland vegetation undergoing cyclical or successional change profoundly affect the climate near the ground. In turn, the occurrence and distribution of many species of animal may be affected, and so may the germination and establishment of seedlings beneath the canopy. Early work on this topic by Delany (1953) in pioneer communities on the Pebble Bed heathlands in south-east Devon, by Stoutjesdijk (1959) in the Netherlands, and by Gimingham (1964) in Scotland, showed that temperatures were lower and humidity was higher beneath the canopy of the heather plants than in the air above the plants, and on sunny days this difference was greater than on dull days. The canopy restricted air movement, thereby enabling differences in humidity and temperature to build up, but, on windy days, these differences were less, due to a greater mixing of the air within the vegetation. The canopy reduced the light reaching the soil surface by 80%, making germination and seedling establishment almost impossible. These early studies were made using thermometers, thermistors and cobalt thiocyanate humidity papers; all are rather crude methods since the successful interpretation of microclimatic measurements depends on the estimation of parameters at locations which are of biological significance. (For instance, it is very difficult to record the microclimate in the places where small invertebrates live.)

	Pioneer	Building	Mature	Degenerate
Age (years)	3–10	7–13	12–28	16–29
Percentage of over-storey	10	85	75	35
Illumination at ground level	high	reduced to 2% of ambient	Increased to 20% of ambient	Up to 75% of ambient
Surface max.	highest	intermediate	lowest	second highest
Surface min.	intermediate	second highest	highest	lowest
Soil max.	high	lowest	intermediate	highest
Soil min.	low	lowest	highest	intermediate
Saturation deficit	high	low	low	Increasing (high on warm clays)
Air movement	maximal	negligible	restricted	much greater
Throughfall	at a maximum	at a minimum	still at a low level	much greater, approaching that of pioneer phase

Fig. 18
Characteristics of the Microclimate Beneath the Vegetation in the Different Growth Phases of a Calluna Heath in Scotland
(Barclay-Estrup, 1971)

On the same Scottish heathland from which the cyclical processes in the community were described and interpreted, Barclay-Estrup (1971) made a detailed study of the microclimate beneath representative *Calluna* bushes from the four morphological phases. Maximum and minimum thermometers and mercury-in-steel thermometers were used to measure surface and soil temperatures, and thermocouples to describe the temperature profile in the canopy. Comparative estimates of the illumination above and beneath the canopy were made with a photometer, and atmospheric moisture and throughfall of precipitation were also measured.

In the pioneer phase, the microclimate was characterized by extremes (Fig. 18). At ground level, illumination was high and temperatures were high on days when there was strong insolation (sunlight). In the winter, night temperatures were often low. High saturation deficits were often reached and both air movement and throughfall of precipitation were at a maximum. The closed, dense canopy of the building phase profoundly modified this pattern (Fig. 18). Illumination at ground level was reduced to as much as 2% of the outside, temperatures were generally lower than in any of the other phases, saturation deficits were always low, air movement was negligible and very little precipitation reached the ground level. Changes in the structure of the *Calluna* canopy were mainly responsible for differences between the building and mature phases; in this latter phase, illumination at the soil surface increased to 20%; temperatures were both higher and lower than in the building phases, but the saturation deficit was still low; the canopy was still sufficient to considerably restrict air movement and intercepted most precipitation.

The degenerate phase was somewhat similar to the pioneer in its micro-

THE DYNAMICS OF HEATHLAND VEGETATION 91

climate characteristics. The microclimate became increasingly extreme, sometimes even exceeding that in the pioneer phase. Illumination increased up to 57%, the range of temperatures was much greater than in either the building or mature phases, saturation deficits were higher, air movement much more, and the amount of precipitation reaching the ground was similar to that in the pioneer phase. Soil temperatures showed much less range between the phases, but the highest maxima occurred in the degenerate and pioneer phases; the minima had a very small range with their lowest values in the first and last phases.

Delany (1953) undertook his study in pioneer heathland in order to interpret the occurrence of the bristle-tail *Dilta littoralis*, but despite the recognition by animal ecologists of the influence that microclimate plays in the distribution of animals, little attempt has been made to correlate the occurrence of heathland invertebrates, particularly those characteristic of the different phases, with the corresponding changes in the microclimate beneath the plants. Nor is there any information on the differences in microclimate in even-aged stands representing the different phases.

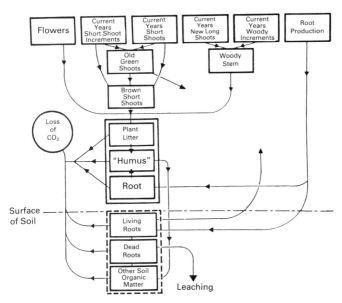

A Flowers
B Current year's green short shoots
C Current year's green short shoot increments
D Old green short shoots
E Brown short shoots
F Current year's long shoots
G Wood matter
   Current year's green production = B + C
   Total green material = B + C + D

Fig. 19
The Relationships between Production of Different Components of Calluna, *the Transfer of Organic Matter, and the Accumulation of Litter and Soil Organic Matter*

Vegetation Production and Decomposition

Green plants make use of sunlight and through the medium of their green pigment (chlorophyll), are able to combine carbon dioxide from the air and water from the soils into energy-rich organic compounds: they are thus said to be autotrophic – manufacturing their own food. This process is called primary production and the quantity of organic matter produced is called gross primary production. Part of this production is used by the plants for maintenance and is oxidized during respiration; the remainder, called net primary production, may be added to the plants as new tissue during growth. The quantity of plant material in a unit area at a fixed time is called the standing crop; the difference in the standing crop over an interval is a measure of net primary production. This is only true if no parts of the plant, such as flowers, leaves, bud scales, have been shed during the interval observed. When this is the case, these quantities must be added to the standing crop difference to estimate primary production.

The productivity of heathland vegetation has been measured in a variety of ways to meet a variety of aims, and most measurements have been made on upland communities; Miller (1979) and Miller and Watson (1978) estimated Heather productivity in relation to the food supply of the Red Grouse on Scottish moors, and Grant (1971) and Grant and Hunter (1966) have estimated it in relation to sheep-grazing. The International Biological Programme (IBP) provided a stimulus to compare productivity in a number of upland dwarf shrub communities (see Forest, 1971; Forest & Smith, 1975; Grace & Marks, 1978; Grace & Woolhouse, 1974; Summers, 1978). Most studies in Britain and elsewhere in Western Europe have been on younger stands of Heather, generally less than 20 years old, where productivity has been calculated from changes in standing crop, but this is variable and, although most stands show a uniformity up to 15 years, discrepancies appear between the older stands (Gimingham, Chapman & Webb, 1979). Barclay-Estrup (1970) concentrated on small-scale change in sample plots which corresponded to more-or-less individual plants representing each phase, whereas much of the work on southern heathlands (Chapman, 1967; Chapman *et al.*, 1975a; Chapman & Webb, 1978) has involved large stands of uniform age, where all the plants represented one of the growth phases. Because the definition of growth phases is arbitrary, Chapman *et al.* (1975a) correlated changes in productivity with the age of the plants, using data derived from plants up to 42 years old. The mode and pattern of *Calluna* growth (Mohamed & Gimingham, 1970) (see chapter 8) make the estimation of standing crop difficult, and this was separated into seven constituents by Chapman *et al.* (Fig. 19). The separation into these constituents enables the flow of organic matter to be represented.

The standing crop of *Calluna* increases over 40 years; at first it builds up to about 1800 gm per sq m* until the plants are about 25 years old (Fig. 20); thereafter, the rate of increase is much less and reaches a maximum of about 2500 gm per sq m. After initial very rapid growth, the rate at which the standing crop increases is slower, but builds up to about

---

* 1 cwt per acre = 125.5 kg per ha.
  1 ton per acre = 2.47 tonnes per ha.

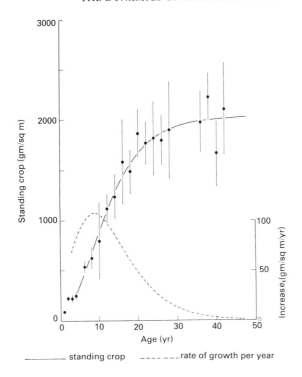

Fig. 20
Heather Growth
following Burning

100 gm per sq m per year at 10 years, then declines to almost nothing at 40 years. The very rapid growth of the first two years may be a result of nutrients derived from the fire ash, or from the translocation of food reserves in the roots (Chapman et al., 1975a). This rapid growth is a feature of heathlands regenerating from the stem bases following a fire and is not present where regeneration is from seed; it has been called the post-burn phase (Chapman & Webb, 1978).

These results are typical for lowland heaths and are comparable with those obtained for other British and European heaths, where regional differences in soils and climate may affect the productivity of the vegetation (Gimingham, Chapman & Webb, 1979). Statistical analysis (Principal Components) based on the mean April–August temperature, mean annual rainfall and of five principal plant nutrients from the root zone, has revealed three main groupings in Britain: southern lowland heaths, characterized by high temperatures, low rainfall and low nutrient status; upland heaths with lower temperatures, higher rainfall and soils with a higher nutrient status; and a group of residual sites where soil nutrients, particularly calcium and magnesium, are higher (Chapman & Clarke, 1980).

The root system of *Calluna* is finely branched and there is often adventitious rooting from buried stems. Ninety-two percent of the total root system is concentrated in the top 20 cm (8 in); the soil profile and the root content of heathland soils is comparable with that from many woodlands

(Chapman, 1970). There are many practical difficulties in the estimation of root crop and production. The weight of organic matter in the root zone on southern heathlands is in the order of 140×10^3 kg per ha, of which about half is probably roots. The standing crop of roots is about three times that of the organic matter in the above-ground crop on older heathlands, and the ratio of extractable root to above-ground vegetation varies from about eight in the youngest stands to three in the older ones. There is little variation in the standing crop of roots beneath heathlands of different ages, and this can be attributed to past histories of management by burning, whereby the root system remained fairly constant (Chapman, 1970).

Root production has been estimated by washing out roots from the soil and by assuming a constant ratio between root production and above-ground production. Soil respiration – the rate of evolution of carbon dioxide from soil – has been used to estimate both root production and decomposition rates of litter. Macfadyen (1971) suggested that in poor heathland soils, soil respiration might be a more reliable guide to decomposition than in other soils, especially woodlands. Chapman (1970), however, showed that root respiration in a southern heath can account for up to 70% of the total soil respiration, and Brown & Macfadyen (1969) found that in a Danish *Calluna* heath, soil respiration was ten times that which could be accounted for by litter production. Carbon dioxide evolved from the soil is related to the root biomass, the weight of humus in the root and sub-root zones; its output from these sources may be modified by temperature (Chapman, 1979). From measurements of soil respiration on a southern heath, root production has been estimated to be 400 gm per sq m per year, and when this figure is combined with estimates for above-ground production by *Calluna* (Chapman *et al.*, 1975a), an estimate of annual total net production of about 700 gm per sq m is obtained – a figure comparable with woodland communities on similar soils (Chapman, 1979).

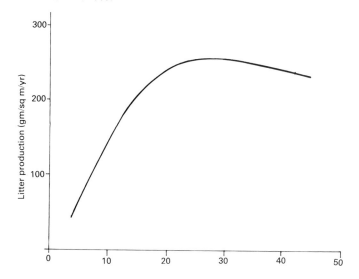

Fig. 21
Rate of Litter Production over 50 Years

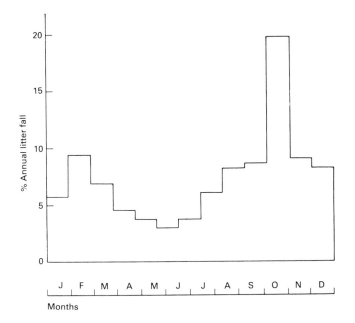

Fig. 22
Yearly Pattern of Litter Fall on Calluna *Heathland*

Calluna litter has four main components: woody material, long shoots, short shoots and flowers (which also include seed capsules). Litter is shed from the plants all through the year with peaks in October and November, when the short shoots are lost, and in February, when most of the seed capsules are shed (Fig. 22) (Cormack & Gimingham, 1964; Chapman *et al.*, 1975b). Up to 80% of the organic matter contained in these green shoots is re-absorbed by the plants before the leaves and shoots are shed as litter (Chapman *et al.*, 1975a). Litter-fall from young plants is negligible until the third or fourth growing season, but then increases to rates of 200 to 250 gm per sq m per year at about 20 years of age (Fig. 21). The composition of the litter also changes; at first, it is mostly short shoots, flowers and seed capsules, but during the building and degenerate phases, the woody component increases.

Much of the litter shed from the plants in the early years does not accumulate, but is blown away by the wind; it is not until the building phase, when the canopy has closed and airflow in the vegetation is reduced, that accumulation begins. This accumulation is the interaction between litter production and litter loss. Losses may be due to physical removal by wind or animals, or through decomposition. Litter accumulation may be measured directly, by taking samples from the soil surface from time to time, but this method can never be accurate as the lower litter layers are turning into humus and becoming incorporated in the upper soil layers, and there may also be adventitious rooting from the stems. But accumulation may be predicted from the rates of litter production and what is assumed to be the rate of litter decomposition. This calculation has been made on the Dorset heathlands (Chapman *et al.*, 1975b), assuming both a constant rate of litter decomposition and a rate which increases linearly

COLOUR

1. Dry Heath, Studland, Dorset *N. R. Webb*

2. Bell Heather *N. R. Webb*

3. Western Gorse *N. R. Webb*

with the age of the heathland. Field measurements show that litter builds up to about 2500–3000 gm per sq m over about 25 years.

Litter breakdown describes the physical loss of litter from the soil surface by the action of wind, water and frost, or by removal or comminution by animals. Litter decomposition, on the other hand, is the chemical degradation of the litter, caused through the metabolic activity of soil organisms, which results in the release of nutrients and energy. Some chemical changes occur before the litter is shed from the plants, and some organic compounds, particularly soluble carbohydrates, may be withdrawn by the plant or leached from the foliage.

The commonest way of estimating litter decomposition is by using special net bags which are filled with small quantities of litter, placed in the field, and the changes in dry weight of their contents measured. There has been a number of studies of this type in both upland and lowland heaths (reviewed by Gimingham *et al.*, 1978); results suggest that from 15–20% of the dry weight loss occurs in the first year – much less than deciduous woodland, where up to 70% may be lost in the same length of time. Litter bag data are notoriously difficult to interpret because the presence of the bag in the litter modifies the micro-environment, and on heathland there may be an invasion of the litter bags by the fine rooting system of the *Calluna* plants. On southern heathland up to 15% roots have been recorded in the litter in the bags after 2½ years. This root invasion may have been stimulated by humidity changes or by the release of nutrients from the decaying litter. About 60% of the potassium and magnesium is lost from the litter after 4 years, and 40% of the sodium, but there is hardly any loss of calcium and phosphorous. Over the first year, there is hardly any loss of soluble carbohydrates since these are mostly lost before litter fall, but there is a decrease of 10–15% in both holocellulose and α-cellulose, and less than 10% in soluble tannins. The litter has a high tannin and polyphenol content, which is not reduced by weathering or decomposition, and this is probably responsible for the low palatability of *Calluna* litter to so many soil animals.

On heathlands, the contribution of the soil fauna to decomposition is small, mainly because the large species – earthworms and millipedes – are absent due to the soil acidity. Densities of animal populations are generally very much smaller than in woodlands, where the large invertebrate animals contribute significantly to litter decay. It has been estimated that on a southern heath the soil mites consume less than 1% of the annual litter fall (Chapman & Webb, 1978), and on heathlands most of the plant litter decays through the action of micro-organisms. There have been few studies of the microflora associations on lowland *Calluna*-heath, although these associations in peat beneath *Calluna* have been studied extensively in the uplands (Heal & Perkins, 1976). *In vitro* studies have shown that leaves of all members of the Ericaceae offer similar substrates to micro-organisms, but the succession on *Calluna* leaves was poorer than that associated with typical herbaceous species. Peptone- and pectin-decompositing yeasts have been shown to be important in the decomposition of *Calluna* litter (Mangenot, 1966).

1 △   2 ▽   3 ▽

4 △   5 △   6 ▽

7 △

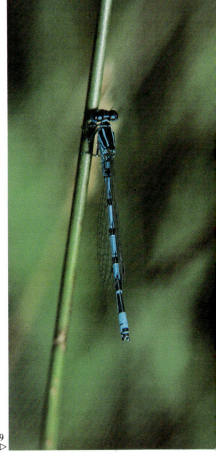

9 ▷

8 △

4. Marsh Gentian *N. R. Webb*

5. Pale Butterwort *B. Pearson*

6. Common Sundew *J. A. Thomas*

7. Scarce Ischnura Damselfly *Nature Photographers – S.-C. Bisserot*

8. Small Red Damselfly *Nature Photographers – D. Sewell*

9. Southern Damselfly *B. P. Pickess*

10. Grayling *Nature Photographers – P. Sterry*

11. Silver-Studded Blue *N. R. Webb*

12. Green Hairstreak *N. R. Webb*

13. Emperor Moth *Nature Photographers – H. Clark*

14. Crab Spider *M. Dolton*

15. Emperor Moth Caterpillar *Nature Photographers – A Wharton*

10 △

11 △ 12 ▽

13 △ 14 ▽ 15 ▽

16 △   17 ▽   18 ▽

19 ▽   20 △

16. Heathland Bog Pool
Nature Photographers – D. Hawes

17. Large Marsh Grasshopper *Nature Photographers – P. Sterry*

18. Raft Spider
B. P. Pickess

19. Natterjack Toad
Nature Photographers – P. Sterry

20. Sand Lizard
M. Dolton

21 △

22 △

23 ▽

Nutrients

Essential plant nutrients are in short supply on heathlands, and in the past, have been depleted through grazing, cutting, burning and turf-cutting. This lack tended to perpetuate heathland vegetation by limiting plant production. To plan present-day management, it is important to understand nutrient cycling. The main nutrient inputs are from weathering, water movement in the soil, rainfall and airborne particles. The plants take up nutrients from the soil and return them when litter falls to the soil, where they are released by decomposition processes. Herbivorous animals take off some of the nutrients, part of which may be returned as dung, frass or dead bodies, but in the case of grazing vertebrates, nutrients may be lost from the system in animal carcasses or when dung is voided by animals removed from the heathland grazing areas.

Substantial nutrient losses may occur during heather-burning; up to 80% of the nitrogen in the vegetation may be lost in the smoke and, above 600°C, appreciable quantities of phosphorus, potassium and iron, too (Allen, 1964; Evans & Allen, 1971). In simulated fires on a southern heath, 28% sodium, 21% potassium, 26% calcium, 23% magnesium, 26% phosphorus and 95% nitrogen were lost (Chapman, 1967). Nutrients deposited in the ash may be lost through leaching, but in organic soils this may be reduced (Allen et al., 1969); however, most lowland heaths have free-draining mineral soils in which leaching may be expected to be maximal.

Chapman (1967) prepared a nutrient budget for dry heathland by measuring the standing crop nutrient content of above-ground vegetation, of the litter, and of the root zone of the soil. He calculated the rate of nutrient release during decomposition and simulated fires, and the input from rainfall. The nutrient balance sheet (Fig. 23) indicates that, through

COLOUR

21. Dartford Warbler
RSPB – M. W. Richards

22. Stonechat
B. Pearson

23. Nightjar B. Pearson

		Sodium	Potassium	Calcium	Magnesium	Phosphorus	Nitrogen
12-year stand	Vegetation	4.7	34.3	33.0	13.4	4.1	107.7
	Litter	0.7	5.0	15.2	3.8	4.2	74.5
	Total	5.4	39.3	48.2	17.2	8.3	182.2
	Soil 0–20 cm*	84	288	229	236	37	2210
% crop and litter lost on burning		28%	21%	26%	23%	26%	95%
leaving		3.9	31.0	35.7	13.2	6.1	9.1
and losing directly		1.5	8.3	12.5	4.0	2.2	173.1
Nutrient content of 1 year's rainfall		25.4	1.2	4.7	5.6	0.01	5.2
∴ 12 years (approx.)		305	14	56	67	0.12	62
Nutrient balance (gains – losses)		+303	+5.7	+43.5	+63	–2.08	–111

Expressed as Kg per ha

Fig. 23
Nutrient Balance Sheet for an Area of Lowland Heath (expressed as kg per ha)

burning, losses of sodium, potassium, calcium and magnesium can be replenished by precipitation within a few years, but the losses of phosphorus and nitrogen cannot be made good through precipitation alone. In the older stands, the accumulation rates of nutrients are lower than their input to the litter layer (Chapman & Webb, 1978). The data for phosphorus (and most other nutrients show a similar pattern) illustrate that when the heathland reaches an age of about 20 years, the accumulation rate decreases and phosphorus is lost.

The relative activity of the root system in mature and degenerate dry heath (when there may be adventitious rooting into the litter layer) may be important. If phosphorus input were a little higher, then losses could be made good in 10 years, but for nitrogen the picture is less clear and losses cannot be made good over a burning cycle. Additional inputs may occur through insects breeding in wet heath and bog, and dying over the dry heath (Chapman, 1967), or through the nitrogen-fixing properties of root nodules of the dwarf gorses (Chapman & Webb, 1978).

No entirely satisfactory synthesis of nutrient data for southern heathlands has been achieved, despite detailed studies of plant production. Computer modelling has been attempted, particularly for nitrogen and phosphorus; but to account for insufficient amounts of soil phosphorus, additional inputs (which may be little more than the annual atmospheric inputs) have to be built into the models (Chapman, 1984). Further refinements include temperature and rainfall, since these can regulate the availability of soil phosphorus (Chapman & Clarke, 1980). The resulting model can predict: the magnitude of phosphorus loss at different stages in the fire cycle; concentrations of available phosphorus in different-aged stands; the effects of leaching; and simulate the effects of management such as mowing and ploughing (Chapman, 1984). Attempts to model nitrogen and phosphorus turnover in Dutch heathlands following heather-burning produced similar results, and phosphorus equilibrium may be restored after 30 years (De Jong & Klinkhamer, 1983). These models do not always match field conditions and are not substitutes for field data, but their discrepancies may reveal where the process of nutrient cycling is insufficiently understood.

Some changes in vegetation composition may be attributable to changes in nutrient status. For instance, in the Netherlands, *Calluna*-dominated communities have been replaced by grasslands dominated by Wavy Hair Grass (*Deschampsia flexuosa*) or Purple Moor Grass (*Molinia caerulea*). Experiments in which nitrogen was added at a rate of 28 kg/ha/year caused *Calluna* heath to be replaced by grass, although additions of phosphorus produced little effect. The level of nitrogen was similar to that caused by an infestation of Heather Beetle (*Lochmaea suturalis*) – an event that might induce vegetation changes (Heil & Diemont, 1983). Similarly, burning old stands may initiate vegetation change because the plants' declining vigour affects their ability to regenerate. Generally, in southern Britain, the most frequent change is into *Molinia*-dominated communities after burning, which may be due to changes in nutrient status. In other instances, the decline of agricultural practice, which have left many heathlands unmanaged for many years, or atmospheric pollution might alter the nutrient status and consequently the composition of the vegetation.

The Effect of Fire

The periodic burning of heathland has two important effects: it modifies the structure of the vegetation and it ensures that the nutrient status remains low. In addition, the intensity of the fire may influence the succession which follows – and heathland fires vary – depending on the wind strength, direction and force, and on the age and moisture content of the vegetation. When a fire runs with the wind, only the plant canopy is burnt, but in controlled burning, when the fire is 'back-burnt' against the wind, conditions are much hotter and all of the above-ground vegetation is burnt. Because a heathland fire can vary in so many ways, it is difficult to predict the consequences of individual fires.

Clearly, the most important step in understanding the role of fire is to examine the course of the fire itself, and in particular the temperatures reached. Whittaker (1961), in the north-east of Scotland, used an ingenious method in which strips of mica were painted with heat-sensitive paints which changed colour at different temperatures. These were then

*Controlled burning/
Nature Photographers,
F. V. Blackburn*

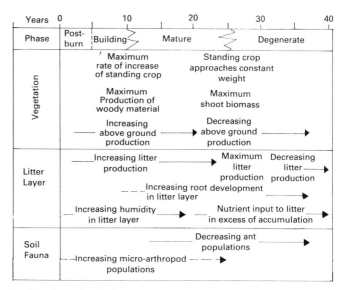

Fig. 24
Summary of Changes within the Heathland Ecosystem in the Years Following a Fire

placed in the path of a fire; Whittaker found that at ground level temperatures were in the range 300–500°C, while in the canopy, at 20 cm (8 in) above the ground, they reached 840°C. Comparable results were obtained by Kenworthy (1963), who recorded maxima in the canopy of 940°C, with an average of 670°C. The duration of the temperature rise was from 0.5–1.0 minutes, the temperatures then returning to ambient. Kyall (1966), who like Kenworthy, used thermocouples rather than strips of heat-sensitive paints, obtained very similar results. There are no comparable studies on lowland heathlands, but my own observations of soil temperatures using thermistors showed that although temperatures at the litter surface were similar to those found by other workers, at 1 cm (0.4 in) depth maximum temperature reached was 65°C, and at 2 cm (0.8 in) maximum was 45°C, and below 4 cm (1.6 in) there was no detectable change (Fig. 25). These results were similar to those of Whittaker (1961), who also found that the upper layers of the litter had extremely good insulation properties, and to those of Hobbs & Gimingham (1984a), who found that temperatures did not exceed 100°C at 1 cm depth beneath the soil surface. On the soil surface, temperatures may exceed those in the canopy (ranging from 140–840°C), depending on the stand (Hobbs & Gimingham, 1984a), but the extent to which the soil is warmed may depend on its moisture content as well as the insulating properties of the surface layers.

The factors affecting the temperature and intensity of fires have been studied in more detail recently. Some of the variability can be attributed to the method of recording temperature. Strips of mica coated with heat-sensitive paints may not be valid for comparing stands differing in age, species composition and structure (Hobbs, Currall & Gimingham, 1984). Detailed studies relating fire to the growth phase of heather and stand structure show that temperatures increase with age of the stand up to the late mature phase (20–25 years), and range from 340°C to 790°C; thereafter there is a decline but temperature variability increases. The duration

THE DYNAMICS OF HEATHLAND VEGETATION

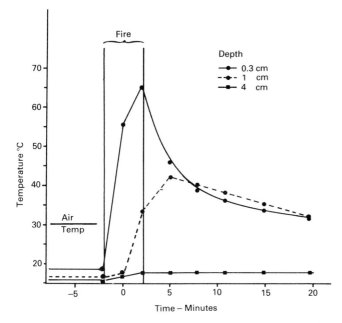

Fig. 25
The Range of Soil
Temperatures during
Burning

of high temperatures (over 400°C) also increases with stand age and only declines in the degenerate phase. These general observations were fitted into a predictive framework using the statistical technique of multiple regressions analysis. Vegetation height (which reflected both the age of the plants and the quantity of fuel available) was the most influential factor, followed by the width of the burning front. Wind speed was shown to have relatively little effect.

Wind and moisture content of the vegetation can affect the intensity of a fire (Whittaker, 1961) to the extent that if the temperature is not high enough, only 30% of the combustible material will be consumed, compared with up to 90% in a hotter fire (Kyall, 1966). Maximum temperatures may also be generated with optimum weather conditions and a large quantity of vegetation; in stands of 10 years, temperatures reach 500°C, but in a 35-year-old stand, in which considerable quantities of plant material have built up, temperatures may be up to almost 900°C (Kenworthy, 1963). A successful fire will remove almost all of the above-ground vegetation but leave rootstocks unharmed, and if temperatures at ground level do not exceed 400°C, this can be expected. But only canopy temperatures over 500°C will ensure successful combustion of all the vegetation.

The fire may modify the regrowth of *Calluna* in two ways: by affecting regeneration of rootstock or, if the roots have been killed, by affecting germination of heather seed buried in the soil. If the stem bases of the *Calluna* plant are exposed to temperatures higher than 500°C for more than one minute, they may be killed (Whittaker, 1961). However, the stems at the plant's base are often protected by litter or bryophyte layer and these temperatures are seldom experienced. Heather plants decline in their ability to regenerate with age; in 12–13-year-old plants, up to 58% of the stems will regenerate, but in 23–25-year-old plants, only about 10% will regenerate successfully because the number of points from which regeneration can take place diminishes as the stems become longer and more lignified (Mohamed & Gimingham, 1970). Miller & Miles (1970) have similarly shown that 6–10-year-old plants regenerate best, and most recently the regrowth of both *Calluna* and Bell Heather has been shown to decrease with increasing age: if the stand is young, regrowth is mainly vegetative, but seedling regeneration becomes increasingly important in the older stands (Hobbs & Gimingham, 1984b).

Post-fire Succession

It takes up to two years after a fire for *Calluna* to re-establish its dominance in the vegetation, and during this time other species are able to establish (Mallik & Gimingham, 1983). Regeneration of heathland plants can be vegetative, by seed dispersing from surrounding areas, or by seed stored in the soil, and each of these processes can vary in their importance,

	Pioneer	Building	Mature	Degenerate
Seeds produced	101,000	92,900	183,000	223,000
Seed dispersal in existing canopy	1,940	304	406	1,800
Seed storage per m²	3,380	3,340	8,750	7,080

Fig. 26
Heather Seed Dynamics in the Various Phases of Growth

depending on the age of the heather when it was burnt. On a species-rich *Calluna*/Bearberry heath in Scotland, Heather up to 15 years old was found to regenerate vegetatively, but this capacity declined with age and when older stands were burnt, seedling regeneration became increasingly important. As Heather grows older, the viability of both the rootstocks and the seed bank decline (Hobbs, Mallik & Gimingham, 1984).

Three regeneration strategies were recognized among the plants on this type of heath. First, woody plants which regenerate from adventitious buds at surviving stem bases. Typical members of this group (nonophanerophytes or chamaeophytes) are *Calluna*, Bell Heather and – in Scotland – Bearberry (*Arctostaphylos uva-ursi*). Second, small herbaceous plants (hemicryptophytes) such as grasses and rosette herbs, in which the main growth apices are protected during the fire by the old leaf bases; growth of some of these species may be stimulated after the fire. Third, the plants which regenerate from underground dormant buds on their rhizomes (geophytes).

In the two years after a fire on the same Scottish heath, the number of vascular species increased; lichens and bryophytes decreased. The first plants to reappear were representatives of the second and third groups – mainly grasses and perennials. Ericaceous species of the first group followed, but numbers remained stable, while the vascular plant species continued to increase until the middle of the second growing season.

Vascular plant numbers were checked when the *Calluna* canopy expanded; hence, the high densities of the first years were not maintained as the more vigorous dominant species grew up. Group three species were very important in the first few seasons, when they grew rapidly, having persisted weakly during the pre-fire dominance of *Calluna*. In these early years, not only was competition reduced, but the litter layer was thinner and there was less competition for nutrients (Mallik & Gimingham, 1983).

On southern lowland heaths, Purple Moor Grass and Tormentil (*Potentilla erecta*), representatives of the second group, soon appear because they can draw on reserves from their rhizomatous roots. For this reason, Purple Moor Grass is often difficult to eradicate where it has become established in place of heather. In such circumstances, Bristle Bent (*Agrostis curtisii*), Wavy Hair Grass (*Deschampsia flexuosa*) or other bents and fescues (*Agrostis capillaris, A. canina* and *Festuca ovina*) are also pioneer grasses, the species depending on the region.

Almost all heathland plants store seed in the soil (the seed bank) and, while being poor competitors, they are opportunists, ready to colonize open ground once the dominance of *Calluna* has been reduced. Few of these species regenerate from seed dispersal from surrounding areas (Mallik, Hobbs & Legg, 1984); Birch (*Betula pendula*) is the only exception. Despite this, Mallik, Hobbs & Legg found that fewer plants regenerated as seedlings than that expected from the size of the seed bank. This may be connected with the type of substrate left after a fire for seedling germination.

Production and dispersal of seeds depends on how abundant each species was before the fire, but the performance of some declines when the *Calluna* canopy has closed, and hence their contribution to the seed bank declines. The performance of Bristle Bent (*Agrostis curtisii*) is typical: it rapidly colonizes freshly-burnt southern heaths with seeds from plants surviving in nearby hedgerows and on firebreaks. Recruitment rises to a peak after four years, when there is maximum flowering. Few plants recruited to populations in their first years die, but subsequent recruits soon die. The population of this grass has an uneven age structure dominated by those individuals recruited in the first two years; these are the largest and most fecund, and the later plants are small and non-flowering. Survival depends on proximity to other species, especially Dwarf Gorse (*Ulex minor*), possibly due to the nitrogen-fixing properties of this species (Gray et al., 1985).

There is little seed dispersal into a closed canopy or onto a recently-burnt area (Mallik, Hobbs & Gimingham, 1984), and experimental studies on a southern type of heath in north Hampshire showed that out of 18 regularly-occurring heathland species, 14 established poorly among existing heathland vegetation (Miles, 1972). The amount of seed stored in the soil declines with the age of the stand for most species, but for *Calluna* it increases with age (Fig. 26). The greatest mortality of *Calluna* seed is in the pioneer phase, but once seed is incorporated into the soil, its survival is good. This is also true for many other plants in this species-rich Scottish heath, with the exception of Wavy Hair Grass (*Deschampsia flexuosa*), whose seeds are absent from the soils of both the building and mature phases. This grass colonizes gaps in the canopy of the mature and degenerate phases, setting seed which disperses to colonize freshly-burnt ground (Mallik, Hobbs & Gimingham, 1984). Concentric rings of plants, each one a year younger than its predecessor, may be found round a single parent tussock of Wavy Hair Grass in pioneer heath.

There is a well-developed sequence of plants colonizing freshly-burnt heath, each with different life cycle strategies. Some species colonize rapidly but soon die out through competitive effects; others establish in two to three years but decline as ericaceous species become dominant. *Calluna* shows differences depending on whether it is regenerating from seed or by vegetative means; in the latter case, it reaches maturity more quickly (Mallik, Hobbs & Legg, 1984). On a southern heath, most heathland species established on cleared plots in the associations in which they normally occurred, regardless of what existing species were present. Differences in the abundance of species were attributed to interspecific interactions, past severity of fires, and grazing (Miles, 1972).

The richest flora regenerates when the youngest stands of heather are burnt, and declines with the pre-burn age of the stand. The most abundant growth of herbaceous species and grasses follows the burning of the youngest stands and decreases with their age. In these circumstances, the regrowth of ericaceous species is greater and they soon assume dominance over the herbaceous species and grasses, but where regrowth of *Calluna* is slow, grasses such as Wavy Hair Grass (*Deschampsia flexuosa*) spread rapidly, both by vegetative regeneration and by seed, and it has been found that the floristic composition of the vegetation before it was burnt (itself dependent on the age of the stand) is one of the most important determinants of post-fire succession. The widely-held view that old stands of heather regenerate very slowly when burnt, and that the ground remains bare with few low species-diversity for several years after a fire, is therefore confirmed (Hobbs & Gimingham, 1984b).

On many of the southern heathlands, regeneration is from rootstocks (Chapman & Webb, 1978), but following severe fires, in which the upper layers of litter and humus may be burnt, seedling regeneration is the most important. However, the dry conditions on these heaths may impede seedling regeneration. The microclimate near the ground, and the conditions in the litter and soil are greatly modified after a fire and influence germination and establishment. Burnt soil shows a 75% decrease in the rate of infiltration of water compared with soil beneath an unburnt stand, and moisture retention is increased. This effect is pronounced in the top 2 cm (0.8 in) and decreases with depth. These changes in soil properties are caused by ash particles blocking the soil pores (Mallik, Gimingham & Rahman, 1984).

In the first few years after a fire, grass species often dominate the appearance of a southern heathland. Dwarf Gorses (*Ulex minor* or *U. gallii*) are also species which regenerate quickly; they flower conspicuously, the bright yellow flowers contrasting with the blackened soil surface. Bracken (*Pteridium aquilinum*) is also conspicuous. There is considerable debate about whether burning encourages the spread of Bracken. On some lowland heathland this is undoubtedly true, since the balance of competition between Bracken and Heather is altered in favour of Bracken. But on other heathland, especially where the soils are very poor and thin, although Bracken may be more conspicuous after the Heather has been burnt, it may not increase in abundance. The rhizome of Bracken, which stores food, makes the species particularly well-adapted to survive burning. Nowadays, many heathlands in lowland Britain are surrounded by agricultural land, and weeds such as Rosebay (*Epilobium angustifolium*), Sheep's Sorrel (*Rumex acetosella*) and Groundsel (*Senecio vulgaris*) may be prominent in the early years after a fire; usually these species die out as the Heather regrows, but in some places Rosebay may persist. The open conditions after a fire favour this species, which is noted in North America for its capacity to colonize burnt ground – hence its name, Fireweed.

The nutrient status of the soil may affect the pattern of regeneration. On Dutch heathland, repeated application of fertilizer following turf-cutting, when regeneration is from seedlings, caused changes in the composition of the vegetation, and in some instances regeneration moved away from *Calluna*-dominated heathland, depending on the fertilizer. Phosphorus encouraged lichens but nitrogen reduced *Calluna* while encouraging bryophytes and generally increasing species diversity. Calcium encouraged a different spectrum of bryophytes but did not reduce the *Calluna*. After a single, light application, the vegetation returned to typical *Calluna* heath as nutrients were soon leached, except that where nitrogen was added, the rate of development was accelerated (Helsper, Glenn-Lewin & Werger, 1983). Soils may be modified through the release of nutrients by the fire, or by the drift of chemicals from adjacent, reclaimed heaths.

Lower plants are also conspicuous in the early post-fire stages. The bare ground is frequently colonized by a reddish-brown mat of the alga *Zygonium ericetorum*, which persists until shaded by the new growth of *Calluna*. This mat may be persistent and maintain open spaces in the heathland vegetation for several years, since it prevents the establishment of seedlings. The succession of lichens and bryophytes on freshly-burnt heathland is complex. Coppins & Shimwell (1971) analysed the succession on a heathland in the Vale of York, where they recognized three groupings of species:

First, those characteristic of the pioneer and early building phases. These can be subdivided into two sub-groups – one colonizing the bare humus after a fire and sporadically reappearing in the open conditions of the degenerate phase, such as liverwort *Cephalozia bicuspidata*, and the lichens *Lecidea uliginosa*, *L. granulosa*, *Cladonia floerkiana* and *C. coccifera*. The second sub-group included species such as *Zygogonium ericetorum*, *Coccomyxa* and *Gloeocystis* spp., which occur only in the pioneer phase, not in the degenerate phase.

The second group of lower plants were mainly bryophytes and characteristic of the building and early mature stages. The development of the *Calluna* canopy led, in the Coppins/Shimwell analysis, to the exclusion of bare-ground forms of lichens and algae, which were replaced by a succession of mosses such as *Pholia nutans*, *Calypogeia fissa* and *Cephalozia connivens*. But this stage in Yorkshire differs from the classic description of succession on Surrey heaths (Fritsch & Salisbury, 1915), and in Scotland by Ward (1970)... on the humus remaining on these heaths, the colonists were the mosses *Hypnum cupressiforme*, *Polytrichum juniperinum* and *Dicranium scoparium*, which are succeeded by *Pleurozium schreberi* and *Hylocomium splendens*.

The third group was a collection of heterogeneous life forms in the mature and degenerate phases, characterized by an increase in squamulose lichens, mainly *Cladonia crispa*, *C. chlorophaea* and *C. fimbriata*. Some of the mosses and liverworts of the earlier phases were replaced by others and there was an increase in fructose lichens, such as *Cladonia impexa* and epiphytic species. Many *Cladonia* spp. were prevalent in both the pioneer and degenerate phases, some of which were difficult to identify.

Where heathlands are maintained by burning or grazing, Heather tends to regenerate, and on Scottish moorland it has been suggested that a lack of seeds from potential invaders and the soil infertility under *Calluna* have led to this stability (Miles, 1973; 1974a), although in some instances vegetation structure may influence seedling establishment (Miles, 1974b). Yet when introduced as seed, many species became established (Miles, 1973; 1974a), and in some instances spread (Miles, 1975). Persistence of heathland vegetation depends on poor soil conditions and an increasing degree of podsolization, although it has been suggested that fungitoxic factors in raw *Calluna* humus have an inhibitory effect on the mycorrhiza, on which establishing tree seedlings depend (Robinson, 1972). The establishment of Birch (both *Betula pendula* and *B. pubescens*) – often thought of as soil improvers – reverses podsolization, and on moorland soils in Scotland and the north of England, *Calluna* is replaced by a grassy field layer, moor soils become mull, and pH, base status, rate of nitrogen mineralization and rate of cellulose decomposition all increase (Miles & Young, 1980). There is evidence from 90-year-old Birch woods in Scotland that when the trees begin to die, they do not regenerate and *Calluna* invades in a cyclical process (Miles, 1981). In many southern heathlands, particularly in East Anglia, the London Basin and on the Greensands, invasion by Birch is a major problem. This has occurred since traditional management and rabbit-grazing have ceased, and after some 30–40 years we now have first generation Birch woods. Clearly, if soil improvement has occurred, reversing podsolization, the future management of these heaths will be difficult (see chapter 12).

In conclusion, it must be stressed that the processes taking place within a heath and its ecosystem have been pieced together from research on Scottish, continental, and southern English heaths. Probably the only common feature to all these heathlands is the presence of *Calluna* as the dominant species. Regional differences, especially in soils and climate, will affect the functioning of these systems, and we must therefore be careful in the conclusions which we draw in relation to southern lowland heathland.

The Heathers   CHAPTER 8

The Ericaceae is one of seven plant families which comprise the order Ericales (Fig. 27), and although the Ericaceae are cosmopolitan, there are concentrations of the genera in the Himalayas, New Guinea and South Africa. The family is absent from Australia and is replaced by the related Epacridaceae. The Ericaceae (or Heath) family is well-known for the large number of species which have been cultivated or grown for ornamental purposes; these cultivars are mostly species of Rhododendron, Azalea, heaths and heathers. Several members of the genus *Vaccinium* are

Family	Name	No. of genera	No. of species	Distribution
Clethraceae	Lily-of-the-Valley trees	1	120	Tropical and sub-tropical America and Madeira
Grubbiaceae		2	5	South Africa
Cyrillaceae	Leatherwood and Buckwheat trees	3	14	South-east North America, Meso-America and South America
Ericaceae	Heaths	100	3000	Cosmopolitan
Epacridaceae		30	400	Australasia, Indo-Malaysia, South America
Empetraceae	Crowberries	3	6	Cool, temperate south-west Europe, east and south-east North America
Pyrolaceae	Wintergreens	4	30	Temperate and Arctic

Fig. 27
The Ericales Familes

cultivated for their edible fruits. The commonest and most widespread genera of the Ericaceae are *Rhododendron* (1200 spp.) and *Erica* (500 spp.). Both genera occur throughout the world but there are concentrations of some 700 *Rhododendron* spp. in the border areas of China and Tibet, where the main rivers of Asia break through the Himalayan range. A further 300 spp. grow in New Guinea, and the remaining 200 are distributed from the Himalayas to Japan, and in Europe. A similar distribution pattern is exhibited by the genus *Erica*: about 450 spp. grow in South Africa, almost all of them growing in the Cape Province, and the remaining

Fig. 28
Distribution of Britain's Native Ericaceae Species

Dorset Heath	*Erica ciliaris*	Dorset, Devon, Cornwall
Cross-leaved Heath	*E. tetralix*	Widespread
Bell Heather	*E. cinerea*	Widespread
Cornish Heath	*E. vagans*	South Cornwall
Heather or Ling	*Calluna vulgaris*	Widespread
Bearberry	*Arctostaphylos uva-ursi*	N. England and Scotland
Alpine Bearberry	*A. alpinus*	N.W. Scotland
Bog Rosemary	*Andromeda polifolia*	Upland Britain
Cranberry	*Vaccinium oxycoccos*	Widespread on moors
Cowberry	*V. vitis-idea*	Upland Britain
Northern Bilberry	*V. uliginosum*	N. England and Scotland
Bilberry	*V. myrtillus*	Widespread on moors

fifty throughout Africa, in the Mediterranean region, and in south and west Europe. The distribution of the genus *Gaultheria* (which, although planted frequently, is not native to Britain) rings the Pacific Ocean (Heywood, 1978). Eighteen genera of the Ericaceae occur in Europe, but only *Erica* (with four species), *Calluna* (one species), *Arctostaphylos* (two species), *Andromeda* (one species) and *Vaccinium* (four species) are native to Britain (Fig. 28).

The growth form of the Ericaceae is predominantly that of either dwarf shrubs or small trees; a few species are climbers. The shrubs are usually evergreen with leaves that are modified to enable the plants to grow in dry conditions (sclerophyllous leaves). These leaves are mostly small and needle-like, with a reduced surface area seldom exceeding 25 sq mm (0.4 sq in). In many species, of which *Calluna* and *Erica* are good examples, the leaf margins may be folded inwards, almost meeting in the mid-line. This is an effective way of regulating water loss by transpiration in hot, dry conditions. Leaves of this type are called ericoid. In addition, the cell walls of the leaves may be thickened with lignin or silica, and the cells may contain appreciable quantities of tannins, resin and essential oils. This makes them unpalatable and indigestible to many herbivorous animals, and highly inflammable in dry conditions. The development of sclerophyllous leaves is thought to be an evolutionary response to low levels of nutrients, especially of phosphorus, in heathland soils (Specht, 1979). All Ericaceae tend to be calcifuge and grow in acidic or peaty soils, and all those investigated have been found to grow in association with root-inhabiting fungi (Mycorrhiza). The flowers are normally radially symmetrical, and may vary from umbel-like racemes to clusters or single flowers; they are bi-sexual. The pollen is characteristic (see chapter 3) and is in tetrads; the ovary is superior and the fruits are either berries, capsules or drupes.

Heather or Ling (*Calluna vulgaris* (L.) Hull)

The ecology of *Calluna* is, to a large extent, the ecology of the European heathlands. This plant is familiar to all, especially during the flowering period from July until September. It is the most common and widespread member of the Ericaceae in Britain, present in almost every 10 km square (3.9 sq miles). Its distribution is not, however, an accurate indicator of heath and moorland areas. The range of *Calluna* covers most of western Europe from Iceland and Norway in the north, southwards through France and Spain to Morocco and the Azores. Eastwards, its range extends to just beyond the Ural Mountains in Russia (Beijerinck, 1940; Gimingham, 1960). Throughout its range, *Calluna* grows in a variety of locations from sea level to an altitude of 1040 m (3400 ft). It is a low-growing, much-branched, rather woody shrub, and in Britain its average height is from 60–80 cm (24–31 in); it rarely exceeds 125 cm (50 in) although in very favourable conditions will grow to 1.5 m (60 in) or even 2 m (79 in). The stems are erect or divergent, and branch from the base; the lowest may be prostrate and sometimes root adventitiously into the upper layers of the litter, although the plants do not spread in this way. In very exposed or wet habitats, the plants may creep by a process of adventitious rooting (see, for instance, Watt, 1947) and often grow in stripes aligned at right angles to the direction of the prevailing wind, with bare patches of ground between. Such stripes are characteristic of the very exposed heathlands on the Isles of Scilly and the Cornish coasts. On mountain tops in the Cairngorm Mountains, movements of 9 mm (0.4 in) per year in the direction of the prevailing wind have been recorded (Bayfield, 1984).

Considering its wide geographical range, *Calluna* is surprisingly constant in its growth form and it is hardly possible to recognize any regional variation in the plant. The variation that does occur is confined to single plants or isolated patches; much of the variation is inherited, although there may be plastic variation depending on local environmental differences, such as the availability of mineral nutrients and temperature differences. A large number of local forms of *Calluna* has been recognized. These include variations in size, shape and number of flowers, or in the size and number of the floral parts; leaf-size; different growth forms – from prostrate, spreading or erect to forms that are hairy or have long flowering shoots. The foliage may vary in colour from yellow or golden-yellow to red, copper, greyish-green and white; some forms may have variegated leaves. The principal variations in flower colour are white and shades of pink or purple, and on occasions double-flowered varieties can be found. However, it is unusual to encounter many of these forms, as anyone who has searched for white heather will testify, and the plant is surprisingly constant. The only variety to be recognized by taxonomists is var. *hirsuta* S. F. Gray. Plants of this variety are pubescent, being covered with dense, short hairs, which give the plants a grey, downy appearance. Locally, large stands of this variety may develop. At least sixty forms of *Calluna* have been taken into cultivation, varying in growth form, colour of flowers and of foliage.

Calluna sheds large numbers of very small seeds, which measure 0.60 × 0.35 mm (0.2 × 0.1 in), in the autumn, and are mainly dispersed by wind. Under good conditions, these germinate rapidly in six to eight weeks. The germination rate is affected by the wetness and composition of the soil, and is generally greater on wet soil and peat than on either dry soil or humus. In the driest conditions, full germination does not take place and remaining seeds only germinate when the soil is re-moistened (Bannister, 1964a). Under field conditions, particularly in southern England, seeds which germinate in the autumn produce well-established seedlings before lower winter temperatures check growth. There is a secondary development of seedlings the following spring, but survival is poorer because the upper layers of the soil frequently dry out in summer. On many southern heathlands, regeneration after fires is frequently from rootstocks (Chapman & Webb, 1978), which contrasts with upland moorlands where, in many instances, regeneration is by seedlings (Miller & Miles, 1970). Field experiments have shown that on lowland heathlands, where there is an abundant supply of seeds in the litter beneath the heather plants, germination was increased by removing or disturbing the litter or by reducing root competition (Chapman & Rose, 1980).

Not all seeds shed by *Calluna* germinate in the first season; they may remain in the soil, forming a seed-bank which may persist for up to forty years (Gimingham, 1972; Hill & Stephens, 1981). In most years, there is copious production of heather seed and a considerable seed-bank may build up. Miles (1979) reports densities of from 600 to 1200 seeds per 600 sq cm (93 sq in) from soils beneath *Calluna* in the Scottish Highlands, and Mallik *et al.* (1984b) report densities of germinable seeds of up to 8750 per sq m (813 per sq ft), depending on the age of the heathland (see chapter 8). For a plant growing in extensive stands, a large seed production and persistent seed-bank seem to be inappropriate, but it must be remembered that before forest clearances, *Calluna* would have been much more a plant of temporary open spaces in woodland and forest; hence, this strategy would ensure that the species was able to take advantage of clearings as they were formed.

Seed germination is affected by both temperature and light. Temperature has two effects: a pre-treatment of 40°C–160°C (104–320°F), but for no longer than one minute, stimulates germination, but higher temperatures are lethal (Whittaker & Gimingham, 1962). A pre-treatment of up to 40°C (104°F) is often used in germination experiments, and seed may receive exactly this type of pre-treatment during a heathland fire, and since duration of the temperature has also been shown to be important, the right temperature for the right period of time may stimulate rapid and abundant germination on the ground cleared by the fire. The burning of surface layers of litter during the fire also helps seedlings to become established (Chapman & Rose, 1980). *Calluna* seeds seem to germinate best when subjected to fluctuating temperatures in the range 17°C–25°C (63–77°F), and above 30°C (86°F) there is a considerable decrease in the numbers germinating. This response to fluctuating temperatures is characteristic of the open sites, both on heathlands after fires and in woodland edges or clearings, where *Calluna* colonizes (Gimingham, 1972).

Light, even in short bursts, stimulates germination, but in complete darkness there is almost no germination (Gimingham, 1972). Thus, seeds buried in the upper layers of the soil will not germinate, even when other conditions are favourable. Removing the vegetation cover or disturbing the upper layers of the litter and soil encourage germination (Chapman & Rose, 1980). There is nearly always an abundant supply of seeds in the soil beneath Heather plants, even in places where Heather may have been absent for several years. This property of the seeds has been exploited in heathland restoration (see chapter 12).

The establishment of seedlings requires similar conditions to those for germination: water supply and the humidity (or saturation deficit) of the atmosphere surrounding the plants are critical. If the atmosphere close to the soil surface is very dry, or the soil dries out beyond its field capacity, establishment and development are checked (Bannister, 1964b).

Calluna performs better over a wide range of soil and moisture regimes than either Bell Heather or Cross-leaved Heath. In *Calluna*, germination rates are higher, the proportion of seedlings establishing is greater, and the plants grow better, showing better root development, greater dry matter production and a greater degree of branching (Bannister, 1964a, b, c, d). Although soil and moisture conditions may be important factors affecting germination and establishment of *Calluna*, the water relations of the mature plants are also important in determining their distribution in the field. Generally, the relative turgidity of the *Calluna* plants is low, but there are seasonal variations and values are highest in the spring and summer.

The relative turgidity at which stomatal closure occurs (65–75%) is lower than that for either Bell Heather or Cross-leaved Heath. The stomata of *Calluna* plants from dry sites closed at lower relative turgidity values than those from wet, suggesting that plants from dry sites maintain assimilation by forgoing stomatal protection and not by greater control of their transpiration rates. *Calluna* also reduces transpiration and relative turgidity when waterlogged, but not as much as Bell Heather. The greater flexibility of *Calluna* may contribute to its ability to grow in a wide range of heathland soil types. Cross-leaved Heath lacks this flexibility and is unable to withstand water stress; hence, it is confined to the wetter parts of the heathland, and Bell Heather is restricted to the deeper mineral soils because it maintains higher turgidity than *Calluna* by greater root development, for which deeper soils are needed (Banninster, 1964a, b, c, d).

Sometimes in winter, reddening and death of *Calluna* foliage occurs. This so-called frosting is in fact not caused by low temperatures but by the low atmospheric humidities which may occur during cold weather. Under these conditions, a water deficit may build up, in much the same way as it does in summer when soil moisture is low. The plants are unable to maintain their turgidity, and damage and death of leaf tissue results. It is not certain what causes the reddening (Bannister, 1964a). Frosting of the vegetation seldom occurs on southern lowland heath but is more frequent on the northern moors in Scotland. In summer, a similar form of reddening and foliage death may result in times of drought, again when a deficit in soil moisture builds up. Damage by defoliating insects, especially at times of Heather Beetle outbreaks, also causes reddening because the damage caused by the insects again prevents the plant from controlling its water balance. It is possible to distinguish between drought and insect attacks since, in the latter case, damage to the leaves by grazing can be detected.

At first, *Calluna* seedlings grow unbranched for ten to sixteen weeks. The small leaves are produced in opposite pairs alternately at right angles to each other (decussate). The first lateral shoots grow from the axils of the sixth to tenth pairs of leaves. Further lateral shoots are produced, so that by the first winter the young plants have a pyramidal shape. Growth in the next season differentiates between long and short shoots. The short shoots have very short internodes and bare, small, closely-overlapping leaves (imbricated). The main shoots, called long shoots, have internodes which are longer than the leaves; the leaves themselves are also longer than those on the short shoots.

Each long shoot grows in a characteristic way, and short shoots are produced on it in two zones and separated by the flowering shoots (Fig. 29).

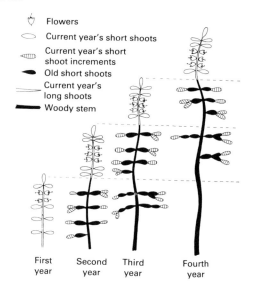

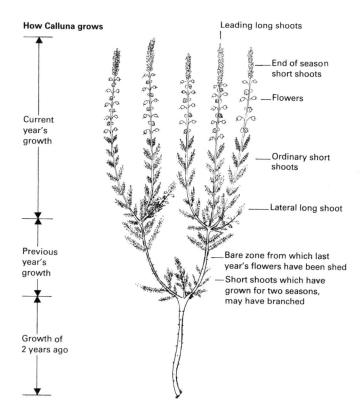

Fig. 29
How Calluna *Grows*
(Mohamed & Gimingham, 1970; Chapman et al 1975a)

The short shoots at the base of the long shoot, which are produced first, often branch, but those at the tip 'the end-of-season short shoots' seldom branch. The flowers, like the short shoots, are borne in alternate pairs at right angles round the stem.

In the next year, the long shoot may continue to grow in the same way from its tip, at first producing a zone of short shoots which later branch, a zone of flowers, and a zone of end-of-season short shoots (Fig. 29). More often, however, growth is resumed from a few end-of-season short shoots just behind the tip (of the long shoot), producing long shoots of the form already described. The short shoots may continue to grow and branch, but they seldom persist for more than three seasons and gradually fall off.

Because of this type of growth, in which each stem is replaced in the following season by two or three new stems from which further growth takes place, the heather plant becomes increasingly branched. The bases of the long shoots begin to become woody (lignified) towards the end of their first year, and gradually a woody section forms at the bases of long shoots. The woody sections of the previous year's long shoots respresent the zone where flowers were formed. Where the plants grow undamaged and without restriction from surrounding vegetation, neat, hemispherical bushes develop, but when crowded or damaged, this symmetrical form is less evident (Mohamed & Gimingham, 1970). In the early years of growth, it is possible to tell the age of a *Calluna* plant by the successive number of long shoots, but later this method is impossible to use, and ring counts must be made from the stems. In the south of England, even this may not produce a reliable estimate of a plant's age, since, in mild seasons, when growth hardly ceases, false rings may be produced and the pattern of rings may not correspond with each season's growth.

The life history of a *Calluna* plant may extend over a period of up to forty years. Besides the detailed growth pattern which can be observed from the structure of the stems, the overall habit of the bush falls into one of four age classes or phases. The identification of these phases is due to the distinguished botanist, Dr A. S. Watt of Cambridge, who, in unique, long-term studies of the plant communities of the Breckland, examined the dynamics and interactions between patches of vegetation (1947). In his studies, Watt recognized pioneer, building, mature and degenerate phases for several types of vegetation; later, these phases were applied to Heather communities (1955), and this nomenclature has persisted for describing the stages in the life cycle of *Calluna*.

The pioneer phase lasts from seedling establishment and development to the early stages of growth over the first five or six years when the plant develops fully into a bush. In this phase, there is a clear distinction between long and short shoots. The building phase lasts until the plant is about fifteen years old; the bush-like form is well-established and there is a clear distinction between the growth of long and short shoots. The mature phase lasts until the plant is about twenty-five years old; growth continues much as in the building phase, although gradually it becomes less vigorous, and, towards the end of the phase, the centre of the bush begins to open and branches grow literally on the soil surface. After thirty years, the plant enters the degenerate phase, which leads to death; the active growth of the leading shoots declines and the plant canopy continues to open and exposes more ground (Fig. 17). Growth productivity and many other

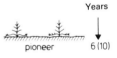

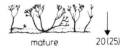

Fig. 30
The Four Growth Phases of Calluna *(A. S. Watt, 1955)*

features of succession (see chapter 7) can be related to these phases.

Watt originally described the succession from Heather which was colonizing bare sand on Lakenheath Warren in the Breckland, in which seedling Heather of the pioneer phase grew through to the degenerate phase, and then new seedlings established in the spaces created by the dead plants. If factors such as fire are absent, a mixed-age community of *Calluna* plants develops, in which each individual plant can be assigned to one of the four phases. But frequently in southern England, as well as on the moors of the north, growth commences from a fire. In these circumstances, the pioneer phase is modified; it may be called a post-fire phase (Chapman & Webb, 1978), and regeneration is not by seedling establishment but from existing rootstocks which survive the fire. Fires produce large, even-aged stands of heather in which all the plants are in the same phase. If this effect is not fully appreciated, the work of various heathland ecologists can be misunderstood.

Bell Heather (*Erica cinerea* L.)

Members of the genus *Erica* are distinguished from *Calluna* by the relative proportions of the calyx and corolla. In *Calluna*, the calyx is longer than the corolla and the same colour, whereas in *Erica* spp., the calyx is shorter. Furthermore, the leaves, which are opposite in *Calluna*, grow in whorls in *Erica*. These and other features form the basis of the lateral key in

	Ling *Calluna vulgaris*	Bell Heather *Erica cinerea*	Cross-leaved Heath *Erica tetralix*	Dorset Heath *Erica ciliaris*	Cornish Heath *Erica vagans*
Flowers:					
Calyx longer than corolla	●	X	X	X	X
Calyx shorter than corolla	X	●	●	●	●
Corolla bell-shaped	●	X	X	X	X
Corolla globular to cylindrical	X	●	●	●	●
Corolla and calyx same colour	●	X	X	X	X
Corolla and calyx different colours	X	●	●	●	●
Stamen within corolla	●	●	●	●	X
Stamen protruding from corolla	X	X	X	X	●
Flowers umbel	X	X	●	X	X
Flowers raceme	●	●	X	●	●
Leaves:					
Opposite pairs	●	X	X	X	X
Whorls	X	●	●	●	●
Glabrous	●	●	X	X	●
Finely hairy	X	X	●	●	X

Fig. 31
Identification Guide to Heathers

(Fig. 31), by which British species of *Erica* and *Calluna* may be identified.

When growing in isolation, Bell Heather forms neat, compact plants up to 60 cm (24 in) in height, with stems that are more slender and less woody than those of *Calluna*, and which arise from the rootstock with few branches. In this condition, Bell Heather grows frequently on sandy banks, along the edges of tracks and in the free-draining soils of disturbed ground. When it grows amongst *Calluna*, the plants are weaker and more straggly, appearing to rely on the more robust *Calluna* for support and it can be frequently overlooked except for early in the flowering season. In the south of England, Bell Heather flowers before *Calluna*, commencing in July and continuing until September; seed is shed in October and November.

Bell Heather is as widely distributed in Britain as *Calluna* but does not form dense uniform stands. A comparison of the two distributions shows Bell Heather to be less common than *Calluna* on calcareous soils, and in the agricultural areas of the Midlands. It has more oceanic affinities and its European range extends eastwards only to the west coast of Norway. It grows in the Netherlands, Belgium and southwards, through central and western France, north-west Spain and Portugal, and occurs in more-or-less the same altitudinal range as *Calluna* (Bannister, 1965). It almost always grows in association with *Calluna*, in Pine or Oak woods and Birch scrub, in all the oceanic heathland communities (including both the *Calluna*; *Ulex minor* and *Calluna*; *U. gallii* heaths, as well as the more continental *Calluna*; *Erica cinerea* heaths (Bannister, 1965)).

Bell Heather sheds its seeds in October and November, and a mature plant may disperse up to half a million seeds per square metre (Bannister, 1965), although recent estimates for a Scottish heath are somewhat less, and indicate range of variation in both germination and seed-production in stands of differing ages (Mallik *et al.*, 1948b (Fig. 32)). Bell Heather seeds lie in the upper layers of the soil; 43% are in the first centimetre, 34%

	Pioneer	Building	Mature	Degenerate
Mean annual seed production No/m^2	48,800	11,500	4,890	35,100
No. germinating per m^2	2,170	646	552	1,210

Fig. 32
Seed Dynamics of Bell Heather
(Mallik, Hobbs & Gimingham, 1984)

between 1–3 cm (0.4–1.2 in), and 23% in the 3–5 cm (1.2–2.0 in) layer. Like *Calluna*, there is considerable mortality of both seeds and seedlings. Nevertheless, a seed-bank builds up and Mallik *et al.* (1984b) report about 16,000 seeds per sq m (1486 per sq ft) in the top 5 cm (2 in) of a 16-year-old Scottish heath. Seedling mortality is greatest in the spring and summer of the first growing season, with lower levels during the winter (Mallik *et al.*, 1984b). Germination of stored seed drops to 20–40% after the first growing season (Bannister, 1964b) and germination can be enhanced by heat treatment, a feature which, in part, may explain why Bell Heather germinates uniformly and rapidly after fires, compared with *Calluna* (Bannister, 1965; Mallik *et al.*, 1984b). (See chapter 7.)

Bell Heather is generally confined to the driest parts of the heathland because germination and establishment of seedlings is poor in waterlogged or peaty soils. The mature plants are able to withstand conditions in dry, mineral soils because they can control water loss more effectively than either *Calluna* or Cross-leaved Heath. These physiological differences may explain why the distribution of Bell Heather is confined to more oceanic regions, compared with *Calluna* which is tolerant of a wide range of mineral and peat soils with considerable variation in water content. Bell Heather and Cross-leaved Heath are closely-related species with similar morphology, yet differ considerably in their distribution within a heathland: Bell Heather is confined to the driest parts and Cross-leaved Heath to the wettest. A variety of factors has been suggested to explain this distributional difference, including response to water deficits (Bannister, 1964b, c, d), or the relative depths to which the plants root (Webster, 1962a, b). Bannister has also suggested that toxic substances in waterlogged soils may determine local distribution patterns. Iron is more toxic to Bell Heather than to Cross-leaved Heath, and plants growing in waterlogged conditions take up more iron than plants growing in drier soils. The transpiration rate of Bell Heather is also higher than that for Cross-leaved Heath, and under waterlogged conditions the uptake and accumulation of iron increases, particularly in the roots. This leads to the death of Bell Heather, whereas Cross-leaved Heath can withstand and survive long periods of waterlogging. Further, valley bog peats tend to have higher concentrations of soluble and exchangeable iron than ombrogenous blanket peat, and therefore Bell Heather tends to survive better in the latter, even if partly waterlogged. Thus, the distribution patterns of these species on a heath is determined by an interaction between waterlogging and toxic substances (Jones, 1971a, b; Jones & Etherington, 1970).

Cross-leaved Heath (*Erica tetralix* L.)

Cross-leaved Heath (Fig. 33) has a British distribution very similar to that of Bell Heather but is less oceanic and more continental. Its European distribution is also similar but it is absent from Iceland and grows in Denmark, Sweden and north Germany, where Bell Heather does not. Cross-leaved Heath tolerates much wetter conditions than either *Calluna* or Bell Heather, and although in Britain is found within a similar altitudinal range, on the Continent it is confined to low-lying places. It is also able to withstand low winter temperatures, and Bannister (1966) suggests that its continental range is due to a water balance intermediate between that of *Calluna* and Bell Heather. In lowland Britain, Cross-leaved Heath grows where there is transition from dry to wet heath, or where the topography causes local water accumulation. In these locations, the plant is unlikely to suffer from shading, although it can withstand moderate shading beneath a woodland canopy (Bannister, 1966).

Cross-leaved Heath occurs in a range of peat communities in the north and in the uplands which contain *Calluna* and Crowberry. It is a member of the short heath community on the Lizard (Coombe & Frost, 1956a), and although it can be a member of dry heath communities in the lowlands, it is more often found amongst wet heath and mire. When it is burnt, it regenerates from rootstocks, and may be locally dominant in a community.

Dorset Heath (E. ciliaris)	Cross-leaved Heath (E. tetralix)
1. Leaves broadly ovate (only twice as long as broad)	Leaves linear-lanceolate (at least three times longer than broad)
2. Abaxial midrib glabrous	Abaxial midrib pubescent
3. Branches short, numerous, tending to be whorled under the current inflorescence	Branches few, long, not tending to be whorled, usually distant from the current inflorescence
4. Inflorescence a unilateral raceme	Inflorescence an umbel
5. Leaves 3 to a whorl	Leaves more than 3 to a whorl
6. Corolla tubular-urceolate, 8–10 mm, ventricose, mouth oblique	Corolla ovoid-urceolate, 6–8 mm, not ventricose, mouth may be slightly oblique
7. Anthers without appendages	Anthers with appendages more than half-length of anther
(Intermediate when appendage present but less than half-length of anther)	
8. Anther surface papillate	Anther surface not papillate
9. Capsule glabrous	Capsule pubescent

Fig. 33
Distinguishing Features of Dorset and Cross-leaved Heath

It is considered to be less palatable to grazing animals than either *Calluna* or Bell Heather and is often resistant to grazing pressure, especially in grass-dominated heaths. The reclamation and drainage of many wet heath areas in southern England may lead to a decline in this species.

Cross-leaved Heath is a small, branched shrub, growing to a height of about 60 cm (24 in). When growing in isolation, it forms a hemispherical bush, but when growing amongst *Calluna*, it tends to become straggly. The flowers, of which there are four to twelve, form a terminal umbel-like cluster (*c.f.* Dorset Heath), and the leaves, which are one of the principal identification characteristics, grow in whorls of four and have a greenish-grey, pubescent appearance. The foliage colour is distinctive, especially where Cross-leaved Heath is growing amongst *Calluna*, and wet heath communities can be recognized at a distance by their colour alone.

Comparative studies on species of the Ericaceae have shown that Cross-leaved Heath has a higher germination rate than Bell Heather, but on dry soils germination and establishment are poor. The seedlings grow better than those of *Calluna* in wet soils, but no more vigorously on peat. The relative turgidity of Cross-leaved Heath is generally higher than that of Bell Heather, and the plants are unaffected by waterlogging and show no consistent reduction in either transpiration or relative turgidity. However, on dry soils, transpiration is reduced and there may be a lethal fall in relative turgidity. There is evidence that Cross-leaved Heath plants growing in soils are physiologically-adapted to these conditions and can tolerate greater water deficits than plants from wetter soils (Bannister, 1965a, b, c, d). Cross-leaved Heath is also more tolerant of iron toxicity under waterlogged conditions than Bell Heather (Jones, 1971a, b; Jones & Etherington, 1970).

The distribution of these three principal members of the Ericaceae on heathland can be largely explained by their water relations, and in the case of the two *Erica* species, to their reaction to iron toxicity; hence, under most conditions, Cross-leaved Heath is confined to the wetter soils, where it competes successfully against *Calluna*.

Dorset Heath (*Erica ciliaris* L.)

The three species of Ericaceae in Britain considered so far are very common and widespread, but Dorset Heath, or Ciliated Heath, is one of two species which have Lusitanian distributions and occur in Britain in only one or two places. The stronghold of this species is in Dorset on the heaths south of Poole Harbour, where there are extensive stands. There are also some isolated localities in Devon and Cornwall. Dorset Heath grows in three 10 km (3.9 sq miles) squares in Dorset and about ten in Devon and Cornwall; but this can be misleading, since there are many acres of the plant in Dorset, yet many of the Devonian and Cornish records are of relatively few plants at each location. The plant was first discovered in

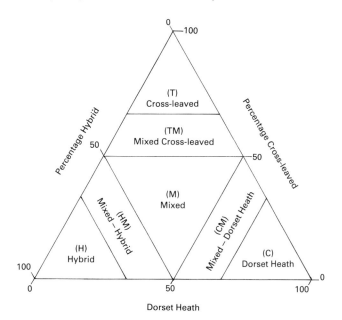

Fig. 34
Chapman's Classification of Dorset Heath Populations

Britain near Truro, Cornwall, in 1828, and was found in Dorset in 1848. The distribution of Dorset Heath extends from north-west Morocco to the western coast of Portugal, Spain and France, and reaches the very northern limits of its range in southern Britain. Superficially, the plant looks like Cross-leaved Heath, and grows in the same habitat. It can be readily distinguished by its longer pyramidal racemes (elongated inflorescences), which are 5–12 mm (0.2–0.5 in) long, whereas the flowers of Cross-leaved Heath are in umbel-like heads of no more than 7 mm (0.3 in) long. Its leaves, which have a marked pubescence due to long, glandular hairs, grow in whorls of three, not four as in Cross-leaved Heath. However, the position is rather more complex since this species hybridises with Cross-leaved Heath, as in Britain, their flowering seasons overlap; elsewhere the flowering seasons are separate and there is no hybridisation. The well-recognized hybrid form has been described as *E.c. watsonii* Benth., although a large number of other hybrid forms exist which are intermediate between the two parent species.

Chapman (1975) examined a sample of flowering plants from every stand in South Dorset, and scored them for nine floral characters. A hybrid index was calculated in which pure *E. ciliaris* scored 0 and pure *E. tetralix* scored 9; intermediate scores represented hybrids (Fig. 34). He classified plants with a score less than 3 as '*ciliaris*', 3–6 as 'hybrid', and greater than 6 as '*tetralix*'. It proved difficult to obtain adequate samples of plants to define the composition and distribution of *E. ciliaris*–*E. tetralix* populations and, as an alternative, populations were classified subjectively as *ciliaris*, hybrid or *tetralix*, from the relative abundance of these forms. Using estimates of halves and thirds, a description (Fig. 34) was constructed into which each population could be fitted. The relative proportion of *ciliaris*, *tetralix* or hybrid are represented by the distances along the triangle. This provided three categories where one type was dominant; one mixed category with all three present in approximately equal proportions; and three categories intermediate between dominant and mixed types. Every 200 m grid square (2150 sq ft) of the area which contained an *E. ciliaris* population was then classified from this scheme, and the type of habitat recorded. In Dorset, the plant's range has changed little since it was mapped in 1937 (Good, 1948). Chapman refuted the suggestion of Moore (1962) that the species was dying out in the periphery of its range, and statistical analysis indicated the association between the *E. ciliaris* populations and the various heath communities. The population of *E. ciliaris* appeared to be expanding, although it remained absent from apparently-suitable habitats.

Chapman (1975) raises the interesting issue of whether this plant is expanding or contracting in range. Many consider, as did Moore (1962), that it was formerly more common and widespread, but if this had been the case, the populations at the edge of the distribution might be expected to contain more hybrid individuals, whereas Chapman found that at the edges of the distribution, as well as in scattered localities, *E. ciliaris* tended to be pure. Sub-fossil remains of this species from the peat deposits of Purbeck suggest that it colonised the area in about 3600 BP, and has been expanding ever since; hence the hypothesis based on the degree of hybridisation in the populations seems to be correct, and it is likely that this species is more common today than it has ever been. It is often assumed that rare species were more common in the past, but often for those living at the edges of their ranges this is untrue. Dorset Heath is a good example: its range is determined by its breeding strategy and the fact that it has no mechanism, in this part of its range, to prevent it hybridising with Cross-leaved Heath.

Cornish Heath (*Erica vagans* L.)

Cornish Heath is confined to the Lizard (Fig. 28), where it was first found by the famous botanist, John Ray, in 1662, and the communities which it forms are unique in Britain (chapter 5). There is a number of horticultural varieties of this species which, together with the wild form, may be found naturalized elsewhere. Cornish Heath is an upright shrub growing up to 80 cm (31 in) long with erect branches. The flowers, which appear in July and August, form an elongated and dense inflorescence or raceme, and are pale pink. Like Dorset Heath, this is, in Britain, another species at the northern limits of its European range. On the continent it grows in west and central France and southwards into northern Spain.

Other Species of *Erica*

Lusitanian Heath (*Erica lusitanica* Rud.) is a native of south-western France, north-west Spain and Portugal; it is naturalized in Dorset and Cornwall. In the British Isles as a whole there are two further species but these are native only to the west of Ireland. They are the Irish Heath (*Erica mediterranea* L.) and Mackay's Heath (*Erica mackaiana* Bab.); both are Lusitanian species occurring in Spain and Portugal, and in the case of Irish Heath, western France. These species are occasionally seen in cultivation and may occur in these circumstances in other parts of Britain, and may occasionally be naturalized.

Uses of Heather

In the earlier chapters we have described how the use of heather and of heathlands for grazing, for animal bedding and for the cutting of turves have been important factors in maintaining open heathland, but the heathers, mainly *Calluna*, have been put to many other uses by the communities which had to live on these poor soils. Besoms and brooms were made by itinerant workers, who cut heather after the sap had risen but before flowering. This was a widespread practice which survived until a late date in Dorset, Surrey, Yorkshire, Derbyshire and parts of Wales (Chapple, 1952). Heather was cut for thatching on small buildings, outhouses and sheds, rather than dwellings, since, although very durable, it forms a looser thatch than either straw or reed; sometimes it was used in combination with these materials. Heather blossom provides a rich and distinctively-flavoured honey and bee hives are frequently placed on heaths in various parts of the country in summer. Formerly, heather was cut for bedding, for making scrubbing and scouring brushes, as fuel for ovens, for woven fences, land drains and packing. Since Roman times, it has been used in road foundations over marshy ground, and is still cut and baled in the New Forest for this purpose today. The astringent properties of the shoots have found a place in beer flavouring (for which Bog Myrtle may also be used), and in the concoction of medicines; and both the shoots and flowers of *Calluna* and Bell Heather have been used in the formulation of dyes.

Other Heathland Plants   CHAPTER 9

Compared with almost all other communities, heathlands have a very poor flora. Dry heath is the poorest, but as we pass along the gradient of increasing soil wetness, through humid and wet heath to valley mire, there is an increasing richness of plants of great interest to the botanist.

Besides *Calluna* and Bell Heather, Bracken and a species of dwarf gorse, the only plants to occur commonly on dry heath are Tormentil (*Potentilla erecta*), Heath Milkwort (*Polygala serpyllifolia*), Heath Bedstraw (*Galium saxatile*), Slender St John's-wort (*Hypericum pulchrum*), Sheep's Sorrel (*Rumex acetosella*), several species of Hawkweed, of which the commonest is Mouse-ear Hawkweed (*Hieracium pilosella*), and on some heaths Harebell (*Campanula rotundifolia*). Many shrubby and woody plants can also be found, especially in their young stages, and oak, birch, rowan and pine seedlings are often common, usually where there are adjacent plantations with seed parents. Creeping Willow (*Salix repens*) is more common northwards and on dune heaths, and other species of willow can sometimes be found, especially in the wetter parts of dune

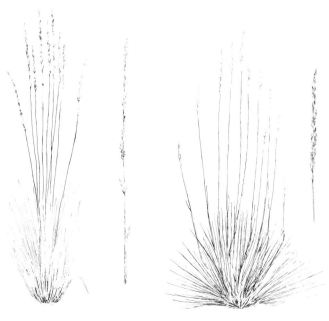

a) Purple Moor Grass   b) Bristle Bent

heaths. The most abundant grasses are Sheep's Fescue (*Festuca ovina*), Wavy Hair Grass (*Deschampsia flexuosa*), both of which are more characteristic of the heathlands of south-east and eastern England; the commonest grass of dry, south-west heathland is Bristle Bent (*Agrostis curtisii*). Occasionally, Purple Moor Grass (*Molinia caerulea*) may be found on dry heathland but is more usual in wetter areas. The Wood Rushes *Luzula campestris* and *L. multiflora* can also be found, and in some heaths, especially on dune heaths and in the Breckland, Sand Sedge (*Carex arenaria*) may be frequent.

Lichens are a common component of the ground flora of dry heathland. In older, more open stands, bare ground may be colonized by the foliose lichens *Cladonia impexa* and *C. arbuscula*. In more well-developed stands of mature heather where there is a well-drained humus layer, crustose species of *Cladonia* predominate, including *C. coccifera* and *C. floerkiana*. In old stands, plant stems are often colonized by *Parmelia physodes*. On mature dry heath, bryophytes such as *Polytrichum juniperinum*, *Hypnum cupressiforme*, *Pleurozium schreberi* and *Dicranum scoparium* occur; *P. juniperinum* and *P. piluliferum* may be present in the younger phases.

Less common plants of dry heathland are the Mossy Stonecrop (*Crassula tillea*), which grows on bare ground and tracks in Dorset, the New Forest and parts of East Anglia. It seems to be decreasing in abundance, possibly because these habitats are no longer maintained by traditional means. Other less common, though widespread, plants are Petty Whin (*Genista anglica*), Shepherd's Cress (*Teesdalia nudicaulis*), Trailing St John's Wort (*Hypericum humifusum*), Dodder (*Cuscuta epithymum*), Heath Cudweed (*Gnaphalium sylvaticum*) and the oceanic species, Sheep's Bit (*Jasione montana*), which grows in the south-west. Another similar oceanic or Lusitanian species is Heath Lobelia (*Lobelia urens*), which grows in a handful of places, mostly dry heath or heathy woodland, from Cornwall through to the New Forest, and in Sussex. On the continent it grows down the west coast of France, in places in Spain, and more abundantly in Portugal. Although perennial, Heath Lobelia often springs up in clearings, only to die after a few years. It may actually require periodic disturbance and persist as buried seed between clearances (Brightmore, 1968). The very rare Yellow Centaury (*Cicendia filiformis*) occurs at a few places on the heaths of Sussex, the New Forest, and Dorset.

On most dry heath, scrub is of gorse, broom or birch, but on many continental heaths, from the Netherlands through North Germany into southern Scandinavia, Juniper (*Juniperus communis*) is often a feature. There is now hardly any Juniper in southern Britain, although it used to be widespread – on Hampstead Heath in the 17th century (Rose, 1974) and on the heaths of Greensands and Wealden deposits in south-east England. The small amount of Juniper which remains is confined to downland (Ward, 1973).

The humid and wet heaths are much richer in plants than dry heath. In these areas, Cross-leaved Heath grows with *Calluna*. In one or two places in Dorset and Cornwall, Dorset Heath (*Erica ciliaris*) grows with the Cross-leaved Heath. Purple Moor Grass (*Molinia caerulea*) is characteristic of the humid and wet heaths, as are Sundews (*Drosera* spp.) and Bog Asphodel (*Narthecium ossifragum*) [it is claimed that if cattle eat the latter, they develop brittle bones, hence its specific epithet *ossifragum*]. These areas have many more species of rushes, sedges and similar species, such as *Juncus acutiflorus*, *J. squarrosus* and *J. bulbosus*, Deer Grass (*Scirpus cespitosum*) and Cotton Grass (*Eriophorum angustifolium*). Less common species include Bog Pimpernel (*Anagallis tenella*), Butterwort (*Pinguicula lusitanica*) and Marsh Gentian (*Gentiana pneumonanthe*). On bare, open areas in some places, the Marsh Clubmoss (*Lycopodiella inundata*) or Stagshorn Clubmoss (*Lycopodium clavatum*) may be found. Both species appear in late summer and both are rare or restricted in distribution. Marsh Clubmoss is predominantly a lowland species, although it is scattered throughout Britain. Its strongholds are the heaths of Dorset, the New Forest, and Surrey, and it also occurs in north Norfolk. Stagshorn Clubmoss is more of an upland species, but occurs on a few heaths in south-west England. It is decreasing in the lowlands and is extinct or very rare at many of its former localities.

A few flowering species which grow on dry heath may also be found on humid and wet heaths, including Milkwort, Tormentil and Lousewort (*Pedicularis sylvatica*). The last species prefers slightly wetter conditions than the other two.

On the Lizard heathlands, the Black Bog-rush (*Schoenus nigricans*) is a component of the tall heath community (chapter 5). It also occurs on other heaths in the south-west peninsula, in Dorset, the New Forest and East Anglia, but is absent from the south-eastern heaths. It is generally locally abundant, especially where there are nutrient-enriched areas. The White Beak-sedge (*Rhyncospora alba*) has a somewhat similar distribution but is much less common in East Anglia. The Brown Beak-sedge (*R. fusca*) occurs only in Dorset, the New Forest and at one locality in Surrey – there are few other stations in Britain for this plant. The most frequently-occurring sedges on heathland are Pill Sedge (*Carex pilulifera*), Carnation Sedge (*C. panacea*) and Green-ribbed Sedge (*C. binervis*). Cotton Grass (*Eriophorum angustifolium*) grows on valley bogs on all southern heaths, but Hare's-tail Cotton Grass (*E. vaginatum*) is very local in southern England, occurring in Surrey, West Sussex and in one or two scattered localities in Hampshire and westwards. However, this plant is very common and widespread on the moors of the north. Another species more abundant in the north is Cranberry (*Vaccinium oxycoccus*), which only occurs in damp communities in Hampshire and Sussex.

The Heath Spotted Orchid (*Dactylorchis maculata*) is common on almost all dry heaths; in the wetter areas, species of Marsh Orchid (*D. praetermissa*) often grow. Undoubtedly, the most interesting orchid is the Bog Orchid (*Malaxis paludosa*). This plant is scattered over a few localities, mainly in Dorset and the New Forest, but seems to have died out on the heaths to the east. It was recorded in Norfolk. It is a dwarf species, not more than 5 cm (2 in) high, with dirty yellowish flowers which make it inconspicuous, and since it grows in the wettest places among the carpet of *Sphagnum*, is frequently overlooked. It flowers in July and August.

The Marsh Gentian (*Gentiana pneumonanthe*), with its striking blue flower heads which appear in late summer, is one of the jewels of the southern heathlands. It is widely distributed from the west coast of Europe to the Caucasus Mountains, and from Scandinavia to northern Spain, occurring in wet heaths, damp grasslands and dune slacks. It tends to be local, but where it occurs it is often common. In Britain it occurs in similar areas, from Yorkshire and Cumberland to Dorset and Hampshire, and in the west its range extends to Anglesey. The occurrence of the Marsh Gentian is determined by availability of suitable habitat and climate, and it is loss of habitat, largely through the drainage of wet areas, that has led to its decline in recent years. The decline has been exacerbated by changes in the quality of the habitats, which has led to increased competition with other plants. However, where the Marsh Gentian occurs, it shows considerable variation in vegetative growth, number of flowers, and seed production. It is a perennial plant, individuals living for a number of

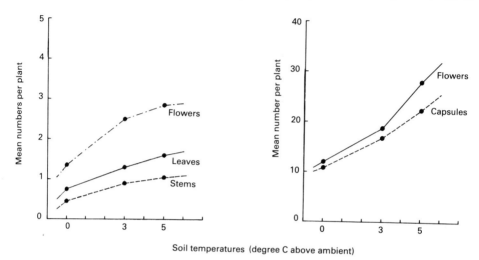

Fig. 35
Effects of Increased Soil Temperature on the Marsh Gentian (Chapman & Rose, 1983)

years, but flowering is variable and often creates the impression that the plant has become extinct at a locality when in fact it persists vegetatively and is difficult to see. Such populations have an annual mortality of about 10%, and population size remains fairly constant.

The Gentian's variability has been investigated experimentally. Soil temperatures influence the numbers of flowers and the production of seed (Fig. 35). The flowering period, which differs in natural populations, can be lengthened by raising soil temperatures. The blackened soil surface left by a heathland fire leads to higher soil temperatures and this leads to a profusion of flowers which often follow a fire on wet heath.

Gentians growing in stands of old Heather also show poor performance, and it has been shown experimentally that there is root competition between the Marsh Gentian and *Calluna* for nutrients. Heathland fires reduce this competition, and with hotter soil temperatures there is greater flowering and seed production, which ensures adequate recruitment to future generations, without which the populations gradually become extinct (Chapman & Rose, 1983).

OTHER HEATHLAND PLANTS

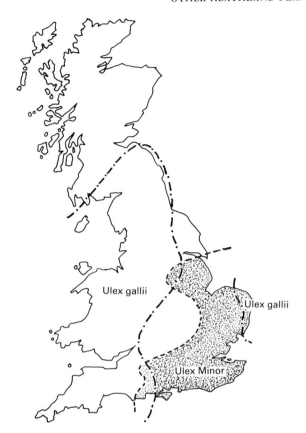

Fig. 36
Distribution of Dwarf
Gorse Species

Gorses, Whins and Broom

These three genera of the Leguminoseae, or Pea, family have species which form a conspicuous component of heathland vegetation throughout Britain. The Common Gorse, or Furze, (*Ulex europaeus*) is the most common and widespread and is a plant of poorer soils, growing on heathland, roadsides, poor grassland and sea cliffs. It is often found on downland where poorer soils develop on deposits of superficial drift. On heathlands, Common Gorse is usually confined to the margins, boundary banks and areas of disturbed soil; it seldom occurs on the open heath, where it is replaced by one of the two dwarf species, *Ulex minor* and *U. gallii*. Common Gorse flowers in the spring from March to May but the two dwarf gorses flower in the autumn from August until October. Unless one is aware of the species of gorse concerned, the flowering seasons of these species give one the impression that gorse is in flower almost all the year round – hence the old country saying that kissing is in season when gorse is in flower provides an almost unlimited opportunity for this activity.

There are seven species of *Ulex* in Europe; four are confined to the Iberian Peninsula and only *U. europaeus*, *U. minor* and *U. gallii* are widely distributed. Common Gorse grows throughout Britain, the Iberian Peninsula, France, Belgium and Holland, and has been introduced to Jutland and southern Sweden (its northern limits depend on its sensitivity to frost); eastwards it extends to Switzerland. Even in Britain this species may be damaged by very cold winters, and Gilbert White made reference in the *Natural History of Selborne* to the death of gorse caused by the excessively cold winter of 1784. In Britain, the two dwarf species have distinct distributions, the Western Gorse (*U. gallii*) grows in Cornwall, Devon, west Dorset, Wales and north-west England. Curiously, there is an outlying colony of the species on the Norfolk and Suffolk coasts. Elsewhere there are scattered plants, especially in north Hampshire (Fig. 36). Dwarf Gorse (*U. minor*) is the eastern species, and Proctor (1965) sketches the dividing line between the two species from Weymouth, Salisbury, Marlborough, Oxford and Sheffield. Dwarf Gorse does not occur any further westwards than the limit of the Tertiary deposits in Dorset. Both species of dwarf gorse occur on the Dorset heaths, where there is a curious distribution. *U. gallii* is only found on the central group of heathlands between the River Stour and an outcrop of London Clay which extends to the shores of Poole Harbour. *U. minor* grows on the remaining heathlands, with the exception of a small area of *U. gallii* in the north-east of the Poole Basin (Fig. 36). There are few places where both species occur, which raises an interesting problem concerning the factors affecting their distribution.

In Europe, both dwarf species have similar distributions, occurring in France and Spain; *U. minor* extends to Portugal and *U. gallii* grows in Ireland. There is a clear geographical separation of these two species in north-western France, where in Brittany *U. gallii* grows west of a line from Dinard to Vannes, and *U. minor* grows eastwards into central France. There are suggestions of a similar pattern of distribution in north-west Spain and in the Basque Country (Proctor, 1965). The causes of this distribution are not really known; they may be caused by soil or climatic conditions or by interspecific competition. Proctor (1965) wonders whether

Dwarf Gorse/N. R. Webb

OTHER HEATHLAND PLANTS

the distribution represents a frozen previous distribution, which the fragmentation of heathland has subsequently maintained. This is a likely hypothesis, since on the Dorset heathlands, which were originally made up of several large tracts – about eight, separated by river valleys – *U. gallii* has colonized one of the original tracts and *U. minor* the others; on none of them do both species occur. It might be that subsequent fragmentation has accentuated this distribution. It seems odd that seed does not disperse from one heathland to another, although we have no real idea of seed production by these species, since all gorses have a rich insect fauna – mostly weevils – which lives in the pods and eats the seeds; therefore, seed production may be highly variable.

Generally, there is little difficulty in distinguishing Common Gorse (*U. europaeus*) from either of the two dwarf species – the difference in flowering

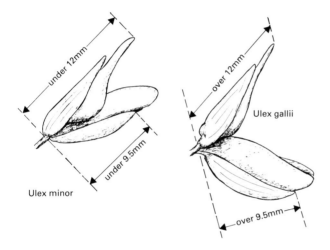

Fig. 37
Identification of Dwarf Gorse Species by Calyx Length

time is usually sufficient. It is also a much more robust plant, growing up to 2 m (6.6 ft) high and often becoming very woody. The dwarf species are more difficult to separate but it is important that this be done accurately so that their distribution can be precisely defined. Both species have a similar growth form; usually *U. minor* is more-or-less prostrate, growing amongst the heather, but on occasions, when shaded by taller vegetation, it may reach 1 m (3.3 ft) in height. *U. gallii* is more vigorous, growing up to 1 m or more in height, but can resemble *U. minor* by adopting prostrate growth form under some conditions. In an examination of floral characteristics, flower colour, bractiole size, fruiting characters and size of vegetative parts, Proctor (1965) found that both species were variable and very plastic; most of these characters were of little use for certain identification. He found that petals and calyx length were the most satisfactory characters: petals, which can only be examined during the autumn flowering period, rarely exceed 12 mm (0.47 in) in *U. minor* and are rarely less than 12 mm in *U. gallii*. Perhaps the best character is calyx length, which it is usually possible to examine all year round since they remain on the plant: mean calyx lengths of less than 9.5 mm (0.37 in) are found in populations of *U.*

minor and mean values greater than 9.5 mm in populations of *U. gallii* (Fig. 37).

Common Gorse, or Furze (*Ulex europaeus*), has been an important constituent of heathland economy, and its cultivation and use has affected the ecological balance (see chapter 4). Gorse was a very useful plant, grown for fodder, used as hedging and cut for fuel. In Ireland, furze was used for many purposes including fuel for ovens and lime kilns, fodder, animal bedding, manure, thatching, wall building, fencing, field drains, harrowing, road foundations, cleaning chimneys, dyeing, and folk remedies (Lucas, 1960). In England we have no such inventory but it seems likely that there were many similar uses. Although the dwarf species, especially *U. gallii*, may have been used, the plants were probably too small to warrant the labour of cutting them, although on the Lizard the poorest cottagers were confined to gathering Western Gorse for fuel while the better off could cut Common Gorse (Hopkins, 1983).

19th-century fuel-gatherers/Dorset County Museum/N. R. Webb

There are about ninety species of whins and greenweeds in Europe; they mostly occur in the Mediterranean region and the Iberian Peninsula, but in Britain there are only three species – Dyer's Greenweed (*Genista tinctoria*), Hairy Greenweed (*G. pilosa*) and Petty Whin, or Needle Furze, (*Genista anglica*). Only the last two species are heathland plants and both have restricted distribution in Britain. These are small spiny shrubs with yellow flowers borne in the axils of the leaves. Except when in flower, they are relatively inconspicuous amongst heathland vegetation. Petty Whin grows in France (Brittany), Belgium, Netherlands and in north-western Germany and southern Jutland. In Britain it occurs scattered through the Hampshire and London Basins including Dorset, Exmoor and central Scotland. It also grows in a number of scattered localities in northern England and Wales. It is nowhere very common and can be easily overlooked. It flowers in May and June, when its yellow flowers make it conspicuous. Hairy Greenweed (*G. pilosa*) is a much rarer plant, growing in coastal parts of Cornwall, the Wealden heathlands, the Breckland and West Wales. On the continent its distribution is similar to *G. anglica* but it is scarcer.

Broom (*Cytisus scoparius*) is a much-branched shrub, rather like Common Gorse, which grows to a height of about 2 m (6.5 ft) and lives for ten to fifteen years. It is sometimes confused with Common Gorse but is not spiny. Broom is widely distributed throughout Britain growing in similar places to Common Gorse – on sandy soils, especially where there has been some disturbance. However, unlike gorse it rarely forms dense stands on the southern heaths and usually occurs in smaller stands or as scattered plants. Its European distribution extends from southern Sweden to Spain and eastwards to Poland and Hungary. The bright yellow flowers, which are very attractive to insects, first appear in March and the plant is in full flower by May. The insect fauna of broom has been studied intensively; there are some twenty-three species associated with the plant and associated with these insects is a complex of some seventy parasites and sixty common predators. The phytophagous insects can be divided into seed- and pod-feeders, sap-sucking species, stem miners and defoliators (Waloff, 1968).

Insectivorous Plants

The bogs, bog pools and surface waters of heathlands and valley mires are acidic and very short of nutrients, especially nitrogen; there are several plant species which can obtain a supplementary source of nitrogen by trapping insects, a habit described in detail by Charles Darwin in his book *Insectivorous Plants*. Some of the most characteristic plants of the wetter areas of heathland are the sundews, of which there are three species in Britain. The commonest is the Common, or Round-leaved, Sundew (*Drosera rotundifolia*), which occurs throughout the British Isles in most boggy, peaty, acid heaths and moors. The Great Sundew (*Drosera anglica*) is rarer, and is found in north-west Scotland, scattered localities in the south-west peninsula, and is most common in a few places in Dorset and the New Forest. It used to occur on the East Anglican heaths but, like many species, has now declined there. The Long-leaved Sundew (*D. intermedia*) is also local, growing on the heaths of East Anglia, Surrey, Hampshire, Dorset and the south-west peninsula. These species can be identified by the shape of their leaves, which form a rosette. On their upper surfaces are longish, red-tipped, fairly stout hairs, which have glandular tips that secrete a viscous fluid; insects attracted to these leaves become entrapped, like a fly on a fly-paper. Then the hairs bend over and hold the insect fast while the glands secrete further fluid which contains proteolytic enzymes and ribonucleases which digest the trapped insect. These products are absorbed into the plant.

The butterworts (*Pinguicula* spp.) catch insects in a similar way to sundews. Their leaves are covered with hairs which secrete attractants and enzymes, the trapped insect is held by the curled margins of the leaf. There are two native species in Britain: the Common Butterwort (*P. vulgaris*) is common on bogs and wet heaths of the moors of Wales, northern England and Scotland, and is not really a lowland plant; the Pale Butterwort (*P. lusitanica*) grows in north-west Scotland and a few places in lowland Britain – Cornwall, Devon, Dorset and Hampshire. The butterworts belong to a small, cosmopolitan family of plants, the Lentibulariaceae, which is also represented in Britain by the bladderworts (*Utricularia* spp.). These small plants grow in bog pools and streams on heathland. They have no roots and consist of a trailing stem in the water bearing numerous small bladders, which catch insects. The flower is produced on a stem which grows out of the water. The bladders are small traps, impermeable to water, the insides of which are covered with small, glandular hairs which extract water from the bladder. The entrance to the bladder is closed by a flap surrounded by sensitive hairs. The plant catches small insects, crustaceans, rotifers and infusoria, which become entangled in the hairs around the flap; in struggling, they activate a mechanism whereby the flap springs open and water rushes into the bladder, carrying the prey on its current. The flap then closes and the prey is trapped. There are three species in Britain: Greater Bladderwort (*Utricularia vulgaris*) occurs in scattered localities throughout Britain; Intermediate Bladderwort (*U. intermedia*) grows in north-west Scotland, Dorset and East Anglia; Lesser Bladderwort (*U. minor*), which is slightly more common than *U. intermedia*, grows in scattered localities in Dorset, Cornwall, East Anglia, Wales and north-west Scotland.

Besides the insectivorous plants which supplement their nutrition on the poor heathlands, there is a number of species – all members of the Scrophulariaceae, or Figwort, family – which are semi-parasitic on the roots of other species. Most of these plants are not true heathland species but are frequently found on many parts of heathlands, especially the more grassy areas. These species include Lousewort (*Pedicularis sylvatica*), Eyebrights (*Euphrasia* spp.), Yellow Bartsia (*Parentucellia viscosa*) (a more oceanic species absent from the eastern heaths), Yellow Rattle (*Rhinanthus minor*) and species of Cow-wheat (*Melampyrum* spp.). All these plants have a more-or-less normal appearance with green leaves, but below ground their root systems are poorly-developed and become attached to grasses and other plants, from which they obtain their nutrition. Among this group of plants, dependence on the host varies. The Cow-wheats cannot develop in the absence of their host, whereas Yellow Rattle and the Eyebrights can grow and reproduce without the host if necessary.

The Common Dodder (*Cuscuta epithymum*) is locally common on many of the southern heathlands and, unlike the previous groups of species, is totally parasitic, with Heather and gorse its principal hosts. Dodder is related to the bindweeds, or Convulvulaceae. The seedlings develop in late spring, sending up a small shoot which twists round to locate a suitable host; when it finds one, it begins to twine upwards, forming an untidy mass of coils, some of which twine tightly round the host stems while others are looser. This stem produces outgrowths which penetrate the host's tissue, and possibly modified roots (called haustoria) eventually link with the xylem and phloem of the host (Fig. 38). The Dodder then becomes

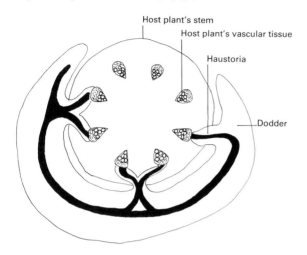

Fig. 38
Cross-section of Dodder on Host Plant

completely dependent on the host for all its nutrition, since it has no roots and the tissues contain no chlorophyll. The thread-like stems of the plant are red and have numerous pinkish-white flowers.

CHAPTER 10 **Heathland Invertebrates**

Many heathlands have long been popular haunts for entomologists, particularly those south of London, like Chobham Common and the New Forest, which were readily accessible to Victorian naturalists by rail. Generally, these heathlands have a rich invertebrate fauna partly because southern England has a richer fauna than the rest of Britain and partly because the microclimate of heathlands provides hot, open conditions not available elsewhere. About forty insect species depend on *Calluna* for food (phytophagous species), and this number, which relates to the plant's architecture and geographical distribution, is about what's expected, although it may appear rather low compared with other woody plants (Lawton & Schroder, 1977).

Thorough investigation of the relationships between plants and the insects which eat them (herbivores) is relatively recent. Plants which are stress-tolerant and from habitats with low nitrogen levels, grow slowly and do not respond rapidly to changes in the nutrient status of the soil. Such plants are sensitive to herbivore damage, especially to their leaves, and it has been suggested that they develop high levels of defensive chemicals to resist herbivore attacks. Plants growing in nutrient-rich habitats containing high levels of nitrogen have high growth rates, and respond rapidly to changes in soil nutrient status; they are thought to be less sensitive to herbivore damage and are less well protected by defensive chemicals (Chapin, 1980; McNiel & Prestige, 1982). Heathland plants such as gorse (*Ulex* spp.), *Erica* spp. and *Calluna* are typical representatives of the former class; their nitrogen content is low and falls through the growing season from a spring peak. Their herbivore fauna is small: 100 sweeps in an ericaceous community will yield 150–270 insects representing up to six species, whereas on a nitrogen-rich plant, such as Creeping Soft Grass (*Holcus mollis*), 1500–2000 insects representing up to twenty species can be caught (McNeil & Prestige, 1982). The stress experienced by heathland plants is reflected in the composition of their insect fauna which contains species that can do without high levels of nutrients. These species tend to be sedentary, preferring to remain on the same plant, and are likely to have only a single generation each year. Some even have life cycles that take more than a year to complete. The diversity of the herbivore fauna of an ericaceous plant community is correlated with changes in the structural diversity of the plants, including the effects of age. The population density of the herbivores has been found by experiment to depend on the plants' nutrient content.

In common with vertebrates, there are relatively few species which can be considered unique and solely dependent on heathland; many species occur in other habitats, and often select heathland because it provides a certain range of physical conditions. These features suggest that we must consider the invertebrate fauna of heathlands from two standpoints. First, there are phytophagous (plant-eating) species that feed on *Calluna, Erica* spp., gorse, broom, Bracken and other characteristic heathland plants; the distribution of these is determined by the distribution of their food plants. Secondly, there are species whose distribution is determined by their requirement for particular physical conditions which are only available on heathland, such as sandy soil for burrowing, hot open spaces, or the structural diversity of the much-branched canopy of dwarf shrubs. Compared with plants and vegetation, there have been relatively few investigations into animals and their ecology on heathlands. The earliest study was on Oxshott Heath and Esher Common, two heathlands in Surrey, on soils derived from the Bagshot Beds of the London Basin (Summerhayes *et al.*, 1924). Here, pine woodland had regenerated on the open heathland, only to be felled for pitprops during the First World War, but presenting an ideal opportunity to study succession in both the plant and animal communities (Summerhayes & Williams, 1926). The fauna of the felling- and burnt-successions on these two heathlands was studied by Richards (1926), who recognized that it was not possible to accumulate the same amount of information about animals as for plants, since animals are much more mobile, seasonal, and difficult to catch and identify. For these reasons, animal succession was not studied in detail. To some extent, these same difficulties apply to all subsequent animal studies, and should be considered when planning new investigations.

Richards highlighted the differences between animal and plant succession. In the latter, dispersal mechanisms were good enough to allow all species to reach bare areas quickly, and develop progressively through a series of dominant species as conditions changed to favour them. But for animals, the concept of dominance did not apply; animals tended to form communities attached to particular plants by food relationships and then radiated outwards through carnivorous species and parasites. Animal succession involved adapting from the food chain associated with one dominant plant, to that attached to its successor. Richards recognized that the animal community might change slowly, without apparent comparable changes in the plant community. The subtle relationships within an animal community have been found to alter frequently, indicating otherwise-unobserved changes in the physical and biotic environments. Richards then described the individual animal communities of bare areas, of heather, Rosebay (*Chamaenerion angustifolium*), and the regenerating deciduous woodland of oak and birch, of aquatic, bog moss and bare wet areas, of Purple Moor Grass, dead wood, stumps, and fungi. Comprehensive species lists were presented for the animal communities of each on the two heathlands.

There was a characteristic fauna of bare sandy areas, such as paths and sandpits, consisting mostly of nest-burrowing bees and wasps, tiger beetles (*Cicendela* spp.), dung beetles (*Geotrupes* and *Typhoeus*), ants and spiders. Few of these live entirely on bare areas, and most obtain their food from within the plant communities. However, most of them require bare sand in which to nest, and do not occur where there is a well-developed humus layer.

Richards concluded that the fauna associated with *Calluna* was very definite, and probably more-or-less the same for Bell Heather (*Erica cinerea*) and Cross-leaved Heath (*Erica tetralix*). He thought that detailed study was likely to reveal differences, and that the fauna of *Calluna* seemed to be controlled by the plant rather than by any special edaphic (soil) or physiological conditions. One of the most important factors affecting the distribution of the animals associated with *Calluna* was the power of dispersal: some species, especially some of the carabid beetles, were flightless, and consequently absent from earlier stages of the succession. Richards was not able to detail the changes in the fauna throughout the succession, but recognized that there was room for further study, especially since many species – in the older stands of *Calluna* – live beneath the plant and depend on a well-developed dense and moist layer of litter and moss. This was probably important in determining the presence of some species while restricting others.

Richards' species lists provide us with a comprehensive view of heathland fauna, but thirty years passed before Delany (1956) published his work on animal communities of pioneer heathland in south-west England which complemented his previous study on the Bristle Tail (Thysanura), *Dilta littoralis* (1954). He studied three heathlands: the Pebble Bed Commons near Exeter, which were pioneer heath recovering from fires and heavily grazed by rabbits; an area in the New Forest; and pioneer coastal heath on Lundy Island in the Bristol Channel. Larger organisms were collected by hand and the smaller ones extracted from litter samples with a Tullgren funnel. The fauna was divided into a mesofauna composed of animals over 0.5 mm (0.2 in) in length and a smaller microfauna. He concluded that the mesofauna comprised species that occurred widely in habitats other than heathland, and that only a few species were associated with heather. The Hemiptera (bugs) had the greatest number of Heather-associated species, while the Coleoptera (beetles) and Araneae (spiders) had few such species. Much the same picture was revealed by the microfauna, which also consisted mostly of species (especially the mites) with a wide distribution. These findings were very similar to those of Richards for the Surrey heathlands.

The mesofauna of pioneer heathland consisted mainly of species adapted to a wide range of habitats, a feature of the fauna of the early stages of colonisation noticed by Richards. This is to be expected, and it is only as the habitat matures that the number of characteristic heathland species rises. Delany (1956) noticed, as did Richards, that the ratio of predatory to non-predatory species on heathlands is rather high, and very much higher for the mesofauna than the microfauna. Spiders, which undoubtedly contribute most to this phenomenon, together with bees and wasps and some predatory species of beetles, are noticeably common on heathlands. The distribution of many of these species is probably determined more by the structure of the vegetation canopy than by the species-composition of the vegetation. For example, ideal conditions exist for spiders to build webs, whereas phytophagous species may be expected to be less since heathland vegetation contains rather few host plants.

Moore (1962) made use of four invertebrate indicator species when reviewing conservation problems of Dorset heathlands. He used pairs of species, one of which was restricted to heathland and the other more widespread over other habitats. The indicator species selected were: the dragonflies (Odonata) – the Small Red Damselfly (*Ceriagrion tenellum*) –

restricted to heathland and bog pools, and the Large Red Damselfly (*Pyrrhosoma nymphula*) – which occurs widely; the butterflies (Lepidoptera) Silver-studded Blue (*Plebejus argus*) – restricted to heathland, and the Grayling (*Hipparchia semele*) – which is widespread. The ability of these species to withstand changes in land-use, which caused increasing isolation of the remaining Dorset heathlands, was assessed. Moore showed that there was a tendency for the heathland species of each pair to be absent from smaller or more isolated heathlands.

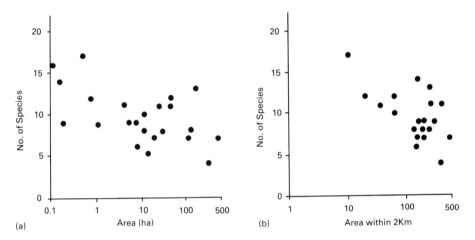

Fig. 39
a) and b) Effect of Heathland Fragmentation on Richness of Plant-feeding Beetle Species

The problem of fragmentation and isolation, which he identified on Dorset heathlands, has affected all heathlands in southern England. What were formerly large, unbroken areas have now become split up into many small, sometimes very isolated, fragments, and if these are burnt or managed rotationally to restore earlier successional stages of heathland, it is difficult for recolonisation to occur. This problem affects both plants and animals (see chapter 12); but whereas living roots or seeds frequently remain from which plants can regenerate, in many cases animals have to migrate from other heathlands. The ease with which they can do this is impaired by isolation of heathland patches. In addition, animals characteristic of later successional stages may not find regenerating heathland suitable until after some years have elapsed.

The invertebrate fauna of Dorset heathlands has recently been investigated from this point of view (Webb, 1983; Webb & Hopkins, 1984; Hopkins & Webb, 1984). Twenty-two heathlands were surveyed, ranging in area from 0.1 ha–500 ha (0.25–1235 acres), which were at different distances from each other; thus, the effects of both the area and of its degree of isolation were examined. Generally, it is considered that a greater number of species are found on a large area of the same habitat, than on a smaller one – more species occur on large islands than on small. The more isolated an island is from its source of colonisation, the fewer species will occur on it. These two observations, forming some of the basic concepts of biogeographical theory [which attempts to explain the distribution of species

(MacArthur & Wilson, 1967)] have been extended by analogy to patches of habitat. But sampling of the Dorset heathlands revealed a surprising departure from this theory: the smallest and most isolated pieces of heathland had the largest number of species (Fig. 39). When this phenomenon was examined closely, it was found that many of the species did not originate from the heathland, but from surrounding habitats. Analysis showed that the vegetation surrounding small heathlands was the most important determinant of the invertebrate fauna on the site (Webb *et al.*, 1984); mixed deciduous woodland contributed most species and grasslands the least (Fig. 50).

In these studies, the problem arose of how to differentiate between species which were members of the heathland community and those which were not; in practice, it proved very difficult to identify true heathland species since, as we have already seen, relatively few use heather as a foodplant, and many occur on heathland simply because it provides the right physical conditions. A good example is provided by the Grayling (*Hipparchia semele*), which was used as an indicator by Moore (1962). The foodplants of the Grayling are grasses, but it likes the hot, dry, open spaces found on heathland. However, it finds similar conditions on chalk downland.

The studies which we have described have all illustrated the difficulty of recognising a heathland invertebrate fauna, and all of them, particularly Richards (1926), allude to the succession of animals on heathland. For general information on the process of invertebrate succession on heathland, we must turn to the studies on the heather moors of Scotland by Barclay-Estrup (1974) and Miller (1974). The Barclay-Estrup study was essentially preliminary; pitfall samples, collected for about a year, showed that the greatest abundances of invertebrates occurred during pioneer and degenerate phases. In the former case, ants were the most prolific, drawn to the high levels of insolation (sunshine) on the bare ground which characterizes the pioneer phase. Spiders, he found, declined as the pioneer phase closed, but then built up to a maximum in the degenerate phase. Millipedes and centipedes (Myriopoda) were most abundant in the building and mature stages. Barclay-Estrup concluded that of the microclimatic influences, which he had studied simultaneously (1971), the humidity change which occurred when the vegetation canopy in the building phase closed was the most important.

Miller's similar, more detailed investigations were undertaken in a mixed-age community representing all the stages of the *Calluna* cycle, and in even-aged stands produced by a regime of burning. Invertebrates were sampled from the soil surface, the litter, the vegetation canopy, and the air above the canopy - by heat extraction of soil and litter cores, pitfall trapping, sweep-netting and by sticky traps. In the mixed-age heather stands there was little change in either size or diversity of the invertebrate populations in the different growth phases. By contrast, in the heather managed by burning, population densities were highest and diversity second highest, in the pioneer phase. Burning resulted in a less diverse fauna in the litter and in the air above the plants; an increase in that on the litter surface, and almost no change in the canopy. In mixed-age heather communities, there is little difference between the faunas of the patches of plants representing the different phases, but in managed, even-age stands, although the faunal composition may be similar from phase to phase,

densities are highest in the oldest phases.
Similar conclusions have originated from studies of individual invertebrate groups on heathlands in southern England. The four commonest heathland ants, *Lasius alienus*, *L. niger*, *Tetramorium caespitum* and *Formica fusca*, occur in different parts: *L. niger* and the red ants, *Myrmica scabrinodis* and *M. ruginodis* inhabit the cool, wet areas where the 83% plant cover is made up of Purple Moor Grass and Bristle Bent, with Cross-leaved Heath and some *Calluna*. The larger, active species, *Formica fusca* prefers similar, but drier, areas where there is a well-developed litter layer, almost complete plant cover, and a greater proportion of *Calluna*. *T. caespitum* prefers dry heath, which is higher and warmer, and where plant cover is less (62%). Finally, *L. alienus* inhabits the driest heath of all, where plant cover is less (Brian, 1964). The interactions of the ants with the vegetation is summarized in Fig. 40. This pattern of ant distribution

has been tested experimentally (Elmes, 1971) by transplanting whole colonies of *L. niger* into the habitats of *T. caespitum* and *L. alienus*. Colonies transplanted to other areas of wet heathland survived well but *L. niger* was unable to survive in the areas occupied by *L. alienus*. These two sympatric species were isolated by ecological as well as behavioural differences, the mechanism being reinforced by territorial selection by the fertilised, colony-founding queens.

Fig. 40
Ant Succession following Fire

After ten years, the vegetation on this ant study site developed from the early post-burn phase to the late building phase; bare ground had decreased from 36% to 6% and *Calluna* had increased its cover from 10% to 54%, reducing insolation. The proportions of *T. caespitum* increased from 17% to 24%, *F. fusca* from 6% to 15%, but *L. niger* and *L. alienus* decreased from 28% to 19%, and 42% to 24%, respectively (Brian *et al.*, 1976). The regeneration of the vegetation had altered the competitive balance in favour of *T. caespitum*, since this species stores the seeds of heather for food and can build nest mounds to avoid shading by the plants. Species such as *L. alienus*, which require high levels of insolation, decline as vegetation regenerates, and the original balance of species is only restored when fire occurs again, creating the sparse vegetation suitable for *L. alienus*. The two species co-exist because they occupy opposite ends of the burning cycle.

The succession of ants was studied on Hartland Moor National Nature Reserve in Dorset; on this same heathland the distribution and phenology of 195 species of spiders were investigated by Merrett (1967, 1968, 1969). The succession of spiders over ten years on burnt heathland was also investigated in stands of different ages, while the vegetation composition and cover were recorded simultaneously (Merrett, 1976). The activity of ground-living species was not markedly affected until after ten years, when the vegetation canopy closed and there was a well-developed litter layer. Merrett recognised six categories of species:

1. Pioneer species, which colonised heathlands soon after fire but declined quickly, and were absent when plant cover reached 90%.
2. Pioneer species which persisted throughout the ten years and declined slowly in numbers.
3. Species whose peak numbers were reached five to ten years after the fire. Studies from adjacent older areas suggested that numbers would then decline ten to fifteen years after the fire.
4. Species which reached peak numbers after ten years.
5. Species typical of mature heathland (over fifteen years old). These fell into two classes: web-spinners, living mainly in the canopies of *Calluna* and gorse, and ground-living species.
6. A group which occurred in most phases without any well-marked peak.

These results demonstrated a clearly-defined succession of spider species on heathland regenerating after burning, which, like ants, depended on changes in the vegetation structure, and probably microclimate (Fig. 41).

A very similar pattern of succession is shown by the soil and litter fauna of mites, springtails and other small arthropods. Most species survive the heat of a heathland fire but, without the cover of vegetation, the microclimate becomes much harsher and species which require very moist conditions for survival die out. The soil and litter fauna does not begin to build up until the canopy has closed in the building phase. At this time, the litter layer begins to form; prior to this stage, when the canopy is open, most of the litter blows away. The developing litter layer retains moisture as the microclimate beneath the plants stabilizes, and the fauna develops quickly. In the late mature and degenerate phases, when the canopy begins to open again, conditions beneath the plants become less humid, although

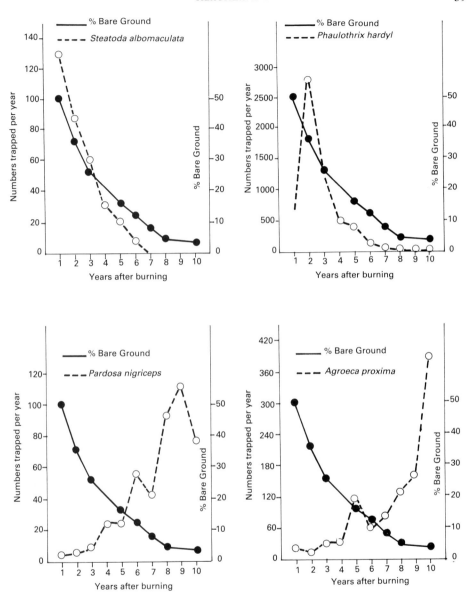

Fig. 41
Spider Recolonization of Burnt Heathland

the litter remains moist since it is both deep and covered with moss, enabling the fauna to retain its diversity (Webb, 1972; Chapman & Webb, 1978).

Two points emerge from these general surveys of heathland arthropods. First, although there are species which can be considered as heathland-dwelling, many can also be found elsewhere or are associated with plants not necessarily confined to heathland. Because of this, it is difficult to recognize a heathland fauna as such, although groups of species which depend on particular species of plants can be identified: we shall consider these later. Secondly, the succession in the plant communities influences the distribution and abundance of many of the species of invertebrates, largely through changes in the vegetation structure, which in turn affects the microclimate near the ground and in the vegetation canopy.

Many of the heathlands of southern England are considered to have a rich insect fauna, despite the low diversity of plants, and the low diversity of insects associated with the Ericaceae. On the heathlands south of London, up to 60% of the species of heteropteran bugs, 47% of British spiders, 32% of craneflies and 66% of dragonflies have been recorded (Stubbs, 1983). These figures are for heathland in its widest sense, consisting of a mosaic of many habitat types and including such plants as birch and gorse, which have large numbers of associated species. But if we only consider the dwarf shrub communities, the species count is much lower.

The heathland soils are, as we have already seen, highly acidic, and this limits the range of animals which live in them. In many richer soils, earthworms and millipedes are responsible for the first stages in the breakdown and decomposition of plant remains, but there is only one species of earthworm (*Bimastos eiseni*) which is common in heathland soils. Mites and springtails (micro-arthropods) also assist in this process, but in heathland soils their numbers are low compared with woodland soils (Webb, 1972). In wetter heathland soils, and on moorlands, pot-worms (Enchytraeidae) can be very abundant and are important in the decomposition processes. Pot-worms are closely-related to earthworms; they look superficially like nematodes, but when examined closely they can be seen to be very small, white, and segmented. Because many of the animals which play important roles in the decomposition processes are absent from heathland, decomposition is often slow and relies on the activities of micro-organisms. A variety of other small arthropods lives in the litter layers. Often, the millipede *Polxyneus largurus* is found in samples; this is a rather attractive creature and unlike other millipedes in appearance. The Bristle-tail (*Dilta littoralis*), a primitive insect, is often found in the litter beneath heather plants, but also ascends into the canopy where it grazes on algae growing on the stems of heather plants.

The litter surface beneath the plants is the haunt of many spiders. One of the largest and most distinctive species is the Purse-web Spider (*Atapus affinis*) which lives at the end of a silken tube extending 15–50 cm (6–20 in) below ground level; an above-ground portion of the tube is used to catch prey, which the spider drags into the tube. This species prefers hot, dry soils and also occurs on downland.

The very rare Ladybird Spider (*Eresus niger*) lives in a similar way; both sexes live in burrows, and when mature, the males leave their burrows to mate but the female never does so. The Ladybird Spider lives in a tube ending in a small sheet of web spun above ground to trap other spiders and beetles (especially the large, active Tiger Beetles) on its upper surface; the spider then attacks its prey from beneath. The male of this species is exceptionally attractive, having a scarlet abdomen with large, black spots. The species was once thought to be extinct in Britain, but it was found in 1979 on Dorset heathland. Previously it had been known from the outskirts of Poole, but had not been recorded for almost seventy years since its only known site had been built upon.

One of Britain's largest spiders may be found on the bog pools of many of the southern heathlands. This is the handsome Raft Spider (*Dolomedes fimbriatus*), which is brown with a creamish-white edging to its body. It sits on the surface of the water waiting for prey, which may sometimes be quite large insects.

In 'July and August, the nursery webs of the very common species *Pisaura mirabilis* are a common sight amongst heather branches. One of the most typical heathland spiders is the Crab Spider (*Thomisus onustus*) which is coloured to match the heather flowerheads on which it sits, ready to pounce on bees and other insects. Once located and removed from the plant, this spider is quite conspicuous, but is surprisingly difficult to find when hidden in the heather flowers.

In summer, gorse bushes are often covered with a dense and spectacular mass of webbing which is formed not by a spider but by a small mite called *Tetranychus lintearicus*. This is a plant-feeding mite closely related to the red spider mites which are pests of fruit trees and vegetable plants. The mass of webbing protects the colonies of the young and adult mites. It may also serve as a dispersal mechanism, the mites 'ballooning', like some spiders, to new host plants. The web is secreted by glands which open through the mouth parts.

Thrips (Thysanoptera) are an important and numerous group of insects. They are herbivorous, living in flowers where they eat pollen. Three species are associated with *Calluna* and other members of the Ericaceae: *Ceratothrips ericae* (formerly called *Taeniothrips ericae*), *Aeolothrips ericae* and *Frankiniella intonsa*, all of which are common and widespread.

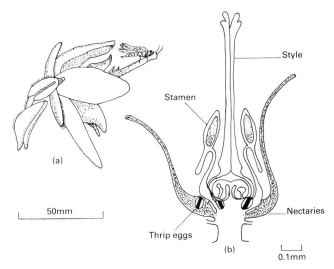

(a) Heather thrip *(Taeniothrips ericae)* pollinating a *Calluna* flower.
(b) Longitudinal section of a *Calluna* flower with thrip eggs in base. To reach and leave the oviposition site the thrips squeeze between stamens and style, collecting pollen

Fig. 42
Life Cycle of Heather Thrip (C. Hagerup, 1950)

C. ericae often flies in large numbers over heathlands but it seldom appears to migrate (Lewis, 1973). Because they spend almost all their lives within flowers, they are important pollination agents, bringing about self-pollination under conditions where cross-pollination may be difficult. This process has been studied in detail in *Calluna*; normally this plant is wind-pollinated, but in wet conditions this may not be effective. *C. ericae* lives within the flower, up to six thrips to each (Fig. 42), when they are mature, they squeeze their way out and, in so doing, pollen adheres to their bodies. These young females fly to other plants, where they mate and enter the flowers to lay their eggs. While doing this, they transfer pollen from one plant to another. The thrip's eggs are laid on the nectaries at the base of the flowers and the new generation of thrips lives on the pollen in the plants (Hagerup, 1950).

Three grasshopper species occur fairly commonly on heathland; none eats heather and all feed on grasses. The most typical species on heathland is the Mottled Grasshopper, *Myrmeleotettix maculatus*, which is a small, dark grasshopper with distinctly clubbed antennae. It can probably be considered as a heathland species since that is undoubtedly its favourite habitat. The Meadow Grasshopper (*Chorthippus parallelus*) and the Common Field Grasshopper (*C. brunneus*) are both often common, especially at the margins, although neither is really a heathland species. The same is true of the Common Green Grasshopper (*Omocestus viridulus*).

Two of Britain's rarest grasshoppers occur on heathland in southern England: the Heath Grasshopper (*Chorthippus vagans*) was first reliably identified on Studland in Dorset in 1933; since then it has been discovered at a number of places on the heaths of Dorset and the New Forest. The *Sphagnum*-filled valley bogs of the same areas are also the best habitat for the largest British species, the Large Marsh Grasshopper (*Stethophyma grossum*). It is difficult to locate since it inhabits the wettest parts of the bog and flies readily on hot days; it is most easily recognized by the sound it produces during stridulation. Besides Dorset and the New Forest, it has been recorded from East Anglia and several other southern counties.

Several species of bush cricket are found, the commonest being the Bog Bush Cricket (*Metrioptera brachyptera*) which, despite its name, occurs on both wet and dry *Calluna* heath. In the wetter areas, the Short-winged Cone-head (*Conocephalus dorsalis*) may also be found; it is quite common in suitable habitats in southern and eastern England. The much rarer Long-winged Cone-head (*Conocephalus discolor*) occurs on some Dorset heathlands and in the New Forest, and in the last few years has been recorded from a number of new localities in these areas (Haes, 1984). Both species are best recognized by their songs.

All three native British cockroaches (*Ectobius* spp.) occur on the southern heathlands. They are ground-living, very active, especially in warm weather, and have similar distributions in most of the southern counties. The litter surface is the ideal habitat for the Common Ground-hopper (*Tetrix undulata*) which is common on almost all heathlands; it feeds on algae and mosses. The New Forest and the heaths of south-east Dorset are also well known for the richness of their orthopteran fauna, and this is described in detail by Ragge (1965).

A glance at the distribution maps of British dragonflies reveals that a significant proportion have southerly distributions, and the heathlands of southern England, particularly those in Surrey, the New Forest and Dorset, have long been recognized for the variety of species they support. The habitat preferences of dragonflies vary: some prefer running water and others still; some prefer small pools while others frequent larger ponds and lakes; some species tolerate a wide range of pH, others are confined to either acid or alkaline waters. Climate, too, is important, since many of the southerly species are at the northern limits of their ranges in southern England. This is true for two Mediterranean species, the delicate Small Red Damselfly (*Ceriagrion tenellum*) and the Scarce Ischnura (*Ischnura pumilio*); both are confined to pools in valley bogs in the New Forest and south-east Dorset. Another species almost entirely restricted to these same heathlands is the delicate blue Southern Damselfly (*Coenagrion mercuriale*) which seems to be associated with the presence of Bog Myrtle (*Myrica gale*). The Scarce Libellula (*Libellula fulva*) prefers more alkaline water than those usually found on heathland so its stronghold is the Norfolk Broads, but it can sometimes be found in the New Forest and Dorset. The Keeled Orthetrum (*Orthetrum coerulescens*) is more widespread, and besides occurring in Dorset and the New Forest is also found in Surrey and the south-west peninsula. By contrast, the metallic green species, the Downy Emerald (*Cordulea aenea*) although occurring in Dorset and the New Forest, is most common in Surrey. The Black Sympetrum (*Sympetrum scoticum*) and the Green Lestes (*Lestes sponsa*) are more widespread, with strongholds on the southern heathlands. The Brilliant Emerald (*Somatochlora metallica*) has similar habitat preferences to the Downy Emerald and, although known from Ashdown Forest, Sussex, has also been reported from Surrey and Hampshire. The White-faced Dragonfly (*Leucorrhinia dubia*) is known mainly from one heathland in Surrey, but also occurs in Cumbria.

Several species of the large hawker dragonflies can be seen on many of the southern heaths, including the Southern Aeshna (*Aeshna cyanea*), the Scarce Aeshna (*A. mixta*), and the Emperor Dragonfly (*Anax imperator*), but the Common Aeshna (*Aeshna juncea*) and the Gold-ringed Dragonfly (*Cordulegaster boltoni*) prefer open water. All these species can be seen hawking over adjacent heathland and are important prey for the Hobby.

Moore (1964) recorded fifteen species from a heathland study area at Arne in Dorset, and, latterly, Pickess (1980) has reported twenty-two species from the same area. More widely, in the Isle of Purbeck, Moore reported twenty-six species; the British fauna contains a total of forty-four species. In southern England, landscape changes have adversely affected dragonfly populations; practices used in the intensification of agriculture, with the drainage of ponds and other wet areas, and the loss of heathland to 'cultivation', have all been detrimental.

A few moments' hand-collecting from heather plants and leaf litter surface – or, better still, a few strokes with a sweep net – will result in the capture of a number of species of bug – Hemiptera. This order is divided into the Heteroptera and the Homoptera on the form of the wings and the structure of the mouth parts. These sub-orders almost have the status of orders themselves.

There are about thirty-two species of Heteroptera on heathland (Fig. 43); eight feed only on heather, a further fourteen on various plants and ten are predators. About half are common but the remainder have restricted distributions. The largest and most easily recognized are shield bugs

Rhacognathus punctatus	C	III	UL	XXX
Alydus calcaratus	P	III	L	XXX
Rhopalus parumpunctatus	P	II	L	X
Rhopalus rufus	P	III	L	XXX
Nysius helveticus	M	IV	L	XXX
Ortholomus punipennis	P	V	L	XXX
Kleidocerys resedae	P	II	L	X
Kleidocerys truncatulus	M	II	L	XXX
Magalonotus dilitatus	P	III	L	X
Rhyparochromus pini	M	III	L	XXX
Trapezonotus arenarius	P	I	L	X
Macrodema micropterum	M	II	L	XXX
Stygnocoris pedestris	P	I	UL	XX
Ischnocoris angustulus	M	II	UL	XXX
Drymus sylvaticus	P	I	UL	X
Scolopostethus decoratus	M	I	UL	XXX
Eremocoris plebejus	P	V	UL	XX
Berytinus crassipes	P	II	L	X
Coranus subapterus	C	I	L	XX
Nabus ferus	C	II	L	X
Nabus ericetorum	C	II	UL	XXX
Stalia boops	C	III	L	X
Orius niger	C	II	L	XX
Deraeocoris scutellaris	C	V	L	XX
Systellonotus triguttatulus	P	II	L	XX
Globiceps crucuatus	C	III	L	XXX
Orthotylus ericetorum	M	II	UL	XXX
Mymecoris gracilis	C	III	L	XXX
Lygus pratensis	M	II	UL	X
Phytochoris varipes	P	II	L	X
Phytochoris insignis	P	V	L	XXX
Micracanthia marginalis	C	V	L	XXX

M   Monophagous, eating only *Calluna* and possibly other species of *Erica*
P   Polyphagous, eating other heathland plants besides *Calluna*
I–V   Scale of abundance, I=Common, V=Very rare
U   Upland species and frequently northern in distribution
L   Lowland species and mainly southern in distribution
XXX   Stenotopic, occuring on heathland and not in other biotopes
XX   Generally a heathland species, but occuring in other biotopes
X   On heathlands, but occuring regularly in other biotopes

Fig. 43
The Occurrence and Features of Heathland Bugs

(Pentatomidae): the Gorse Shieldbug (*Piezodorus lituratus*) feeds on gorse and related species and is frequently found; the Green Shieldbug (*Palomena prasina*), the Birch Shieldbug (*Elasmostethus interstinctus*) and the Forest Bug (*Pentatoma rufipes*) may also be found, but these are widespread and not particularly associated with heathland. Another important shield bug is the carnivorous *Rhacognathus punctatus*, which occurs widely, but not commonly, on both upland moors and heathlands. Its prey is the Heather Beetle (*Lochmaea suturalis*) larvae and it is thought to be useful in the biological control of Heather Beetles (Cameron et al., 1944). Two other species which prey upon the Lepidoptera and Coleoptera larvae are *Trolius luridus* and *Picromerus bidens*, although neither can really be considered to be heathland species. The lygaeid bug *Scolopostethus decoratus* is exceedingly abundant on all heathlands and is to be found running actively over the ground surface or on the plants, especially in warm sunshine. Although common, little is known about its habits and food. It has been suggested that it feeds on springtails (Collembola) or on another very common heathland species, the green mirid *Orthotylus ericetorum*, which attacks heather flowers and leaves (Southwood & Leston, 1959).

Two common predatory bugs frequently found are the Heath Assassin Bug (*Coranus subapterus*), a member of the Reduviidae family, and the Heath Damsel Bug (*Nabis ericetorum*) from the Nabidae. Both species prey on a variety of insects or their larvae, and spiders.

Froghoppers (Cicadellidae) are probably the most frequently-seen species of Homoptera on heathland, and a few strokes with a sweep-net will capture a number of specimens of *Ulopa reticulata*, and probably a few of the other five species which occur on heather. Psyllids, or Jumping Plant Lice (Psyllidae), are important herbivores on many plant species. Generally they are host-specific, and members of the genus *Strophingia* are specific to the Ericaceae. Two species have been recorded in Britain: *S. ericae*, which is common on *Calluna* everywhere, and *S. cinerea*, which occurs mainly in south-west Britain and restricted to Bell Heather, although on the continent it also occurs on other species of *Erica*. The adult psyllids sit in the axils of the leaves where they feed. They can be sampled by heat extraction of the heather shoots and the larvae may be recovered from litter samples, by heat extraction in Tullgren funnels. In this genus, the psyllids overwinter as nymphs, and *S. ericae* has two races with differing lifecycles. The one which inhabits southern Britain below about 304 m (1000 ft) completes its lifecycle in one year, but the race which lives above 304 m in northern Britain requires two years (Parkinson & Whittaker, 1975) – a parallel with some of the heather-feeding Lepidoptera. In upland Britain, *S. ericae* has been shown to be the most important herbivore of *Calluna* (Hodkinson, 1973). A single species, *Livilla ulicis*, is associated with gorse.

Other Homoptera associated with *Calluna* are *Tetralicia ericae* (Aleyrodidae), which is related to the whiteflies, and the aphid (*Ericaphis ericae*), which feeds on young *Calluna* shoots, fastening itself between the leaves. There are about five Coccidae species (scale insects and mealy bugs) associated with *Calluna*; these live on the roots where they are often tended by ants, especially *Lasius niger* (Brian, 1977).

Of the butterflies, the Grayling (*Hipparchia semele*), the Green Hairstreak (*Callophrys rubi*), and the Silver-studded Blue (*Plebejus argus*), are the only ones which can be considered as part of heathlands fauna in southern England. A number of common species, such as the Meadow Brown (*Maniola jurtina*), Gatekeeper (*Pyronia tithonus*), Common Blue (*Polyommatus icarus*), and the Large and Small Skippers (*Ochlodes venatus* and *Thymelicus flavus*), together with the whites and other actively-flying common species, can often be seen, especially at boundaries between heathlands and other habitats. The Small Heath (*Coenonympha pamphilus*), is widespread on heathlands, flying close to the ground, especially where grass is growing with the heather. Despite its name, it also occurs widely in most types of rough, dry grasslands.

The Grayling is most often seen as it flies up in front of you as you walk across bare heaths which provide the hot, open conditions it likes. Once disturbed, it flies a short distance, then suddenly settles on bare ground. It first flashes the eyespots on the forewing; it then closes this wing, hiding the eyespot behind the hind wing, which has a camouflaged pattern closely resembling the ground, thus making the butterfly very difficult to see against its background. In addition, the Grayling will settle parallel to the direction of the sun and then tilt slightly in order to cast the least possible shadow. It has recently been suggested that this is not a defensive action but one designed to regulate the insect's body temperature (Findlay et al., 1983). Besides heathland, the Grayling occurs in a wide range of well-drained locations where vegetation is sparse, such as dunes and unimproved chalk and limestone grasslands. Grasses are the larval foodplant, principally fescues and bents, on which eggs are laid. The larvae hatch in early autumn, feeding until they hibernate, and then again before they pupate in the spring. The adult butterfly, flying strongly, is on the wing from July to September. The Grayling is common throughout the southern counties from Cornwall to Sussex, frequenting both heathlands and downlands, in the Breckland and East Anglian coasts, south and west Wales, north-west England and western Scotland, and with scattered colonies on the east Scottish coasts.

The Green Hairstreak is fairly common and widespread throughout most of England and in the west of Scotland, and although it is on the wing from May to June, it is frequently overlooked. It is unique among British butterflies for its green colour, which is caused by structure of the scales on the underwing and not by green pigments. The larval foodplants are gorse (*Ulex* spp.), broom (*Sarothamnus scoparius*), Dyer's Greenweed (*Genista tinctoria*) and other closely-related members of the Leguminosae. The Hairstreak is common wherever these plants grow, and consequently is not restricted to heathlands. The larvae feed on the tender young shoots throughout the summer. They also have a tendency to be cannibals in all their larval stages. The winter is passed as a pupa among the leaf litter at the bases of foodplants.

The larvae of the family Lycaenidae, to which the hairstreaks and blues belong, frequently have an association with ants. The caterpillars have glands in the seventh abdominal segment which secrete a sugary, honeydew-like substance which the ants 'milk'. The larvae of the Green Hairstreak are attractive to ants in this way and have been found in the nests of *Myrmica sabuleti* (Heath et al., 1984), but this relationship is most highly developed in the Large Blue (*Maculinea arion*) (Thomas, J. A., 1980), and to a lesser extent in the Silver-studded Blue (Thomas, C. D., 1985 a & b).

The Silver-studded Blue is very much a butterfly of heathlands, occurring in the coastal heaths of Cornwall, the south Devon heathlands, abundantly in Dorset and the New Forest, in northern Hampshire and Surrey and in Sussex, and in one or two localities in East Anglia. The southern heathlands are the strongholds and the distribution map is very much that of lowland heath (Fig. 44). The species was formerly more widespread, although local. A form (*P. argus cretaceus*) formerly occurred on the limestone downs of southern England, and other forms occur in North Wales.

The adult butterfly is on the wing in July; the eggs are laid on the foodplants, and after about eight months' diapause, hatch the following spring. The larvae feed on the soft, growing tips of *Calluna*, Bell Heather, Crossleaved Heath, gorse spp., and *Genista*. On sites in North Wales, Bird's-foot Trefoil (*Lotus corniculatus*), and Rockrose (*Helianthemum* spp.) were also eaten (Thomas, 1985a). The larvae are attended by either *Lasius alienus* or *L. niger*, and from the third larval stage are taken into their nests (Thomas, 1985b). The newly-emerged butterfly is also attractive to ants, possibly

Fig. 44
Distribution of Silver-Studded Blue

as a device to escape from the nest. The Silver-studded Blue forms discreet colonies on the heathlands; it is usually associated with the humid heath type of *Calluna* and Cross-leaved Heath. The colonies seem to be sedentary, but may move slightly as succession makes the vegetation structure unsuitable. These butterflies require a certain vegetation height and the correct proportion of open space and bare ground in their habitat. Their heathland distribution may, in part, be determined by the distribution of the ants, for we have seen earlier how *Lasius* species differ in their habitat preferences, and the differential effects of heathland succession (Brian, 1964; Brian *et al.*, 1976). This beautiful butterfly is decreasing, partly through loss of its habitat but also because of changes in habitat quality, a factor which can be corrected with appropriate conservation management.

Although there are only three butterfly species which can be considered as heathland species, there are many more moths – about thirty – almost all of which eat *Calluna*, and seven or eight are monophagous on this plant. The most spectacular is the Emperor, (*Saturnia pavonia*); it is the only representative of the silk-moth family in the British fauna and, with its characteristic eyespots on the wings, resembles a smaller version of the large silk moths found in warmer countries. The females fly only at night, but the males fly strongly and actively over the heather in the daytime in April and May. The eggs are laid in batches on the foodplant, principally

Larger Moths (Macro-lepidoptera) from Heathland

Pale Eggar	Trichiura crataegi	P	II	UL	X
Northern Eggar	Lasiocampa quercus callunae	M	II	UL	XX
Fox Moth	Macrothylacia rubi	P	II	UL	XX
Emperor	Saturnia pavonia	P	I	UL	XX
Ling Pug	Eupithecia goossensiata	M	I	UL	XXX
Narrow-winged Pug	Eupithecia nanata	M	II	UL	XXX
Double-striped Pug	Gymnoscelis rififasciata	P	I	UL	X
Horse Chestnut	Pachycnemia hippocastanaria	M	III	L	XXX
Bordered Grey	Selidosema brunnearia	P	III	UL	XXX
Ringed Carpet	Cleora cinctaria	P	III	L	XXX
Common Heath	Ematurga atomaria	P	I	UL	XXX
Dark Tussock	Dicallomera fascelina	P	II	UL	XX
Four-dotted Footman	Cybosia mesomella	P	II	UL	XXX
Scarce Footman	Eilema complana	P	II	L	XX
Speckled Footman	Coscinia cribraria	P	V	L	XXX
Wood Tiger	Parasemia plantaginis	P	II	UL	X
Clouded Buff	Diacrisia sannio	P	III	UL	XX
Lesser Yellow Underwing	Noctua comes	P	I	UL	X
Autumnal Rustic	Paradiarsia glareosa	P	II	UL	XXX
True Lover's Knot	Lycophotia prophyrea	M	I	UL	XXX
Ingrailed Clay	Diarsia mendica	P	I	UL	X
Small Square-spot	Diarsia rubi	P	I	UL	X
Neglected Rustic	Xestia castanea	M	II	UL	XXX
Heath Rustic	Xestia agathina	M	II	UL	XXX
Beautiful Yellow Underwing	Anarta myrtilli	M	II	UL	XXX
Black Rustic	Aporophyla nigra	P	II	UL	X
Dark Brocade	Blepharita adusta	P	II	UL	X
Yellow-line Quaker	Agrochola macilenta	P	I	L	X
Flounced Chestnut	Agrochola helvola	P	I	UL	X

M   Monophagous, eating only *Calluna* and possibly species of *Erica*
P   Polyphagous, eating a range of heathland plants including *Calluna*
I–V   Scale of abundance, I=Common, V=Very rare
U   Generally an upland species and frequently northern in distribution
L   Generally a lowland species and southern in distribution
XXX   Stenotopic, occuring only on heathland and not in other biotopes
XX   Heathland species, but occuring in other habitats
X   On heathlands, but occuring regularly in other biotopes

Fig. 45
Occurrence and Features of Larger Heathland Moths

heather, although bramble and sallow may be used. At first, the caterpillars are dark-coloured with an orange line along the side and feed communally in a small web at the tips of the heather plant; it is during this stage that they are most easily found; but after the third stage they assume the striking green colouring with black rings, and become solitary. For their large size, they are surprisingly difficult to find; they feed until August, at which time they spin a silken cocoon among the twigs of heather plants, emerging the following spring.

The Fox Moth (*Macrothylacia rubi*) is another large species widespread on heathlands and moorlands. It is on the wing both by day and night, at the same time as the Emperor (May to June), but has a slightly different lifecycle. The eggs hatch into hairy caterpillars which feed until the autumn, when they bask in warm sunshine on the tops of the heather plants before hibernating. Many of the caterpillars are parasitised by braconid wasps

(*Apanteles* sp.), and one can watch the gruesome sight of the wasp larva emerging through the side of the Fox Moth caterpillar and spinning a small, white, cigar-shaped cocoon; some caterpillars may be covered in these cocoons. The Fox Moth hibernates in the larval stage, feeding again in the following spring before pupating.

The Fox Moth belongs to the Lasiocampidae family, or 'eggars', and two other members of this family have an interesting association with heather and heathland. The Oak Eggar (*Lasiocampa quercus quercus*), may occasionally occur on southern heathlands but it is more a woodland-edge and hedgerow species. However, on the moors of northern England, on Dartmoor, Exmoor and a few other places in the south, another, darker, form – the so-called Northern Eggar (*L. callunae quercus*) occurs which feeds on heather. Not only does this form differ in its choice of food-plant but its lifecycle takes two years to complete, compared with the annual lifecycle of the form *quercus*. An extended lifecycle is also found in the Pale Oak Eggar (*Trichiura crataegi*), considered by some authorities to have a subspecific form (*ariae*), which inhabits the northern moors and also has a two-year lifecycle.

Differences of this type, particularly in choice of foodplants, are said to occur in a number of other closely-related pairs of species (not always recognized as distinct by some authorities), forms, or races of moths. For instance, the Wormwood Pug (*Eupithecia absinthiata*), which feeds on *Artemisia*, *Senecio* and *Achillea*, and the closely-related Ling Pug (*E. goossensiata*), which feeds on heather, form such a pair; so do the Autumnal Moth (*Oporinia autumnata*) and the Small Autumnal Moth (*O. filigrammaria*), which feed on birch and alder, or on heather and bilberry respectively. In the case of the Ringed Carpet (*Cleora cinctaria*) and the Bordered Grey (*Selidosema brunnearia*), the British races of these species are heather-feeders, but on mainland Europe they feed on other plants. It has been suggested that they colonised Britain in the third inter-glacial period and survived the last glaciation by adapting to tundra conditions by feeding on heather and closely-related species. When the ice retreated, these species spread northwards but retained their heather-feeding habit, while new colonists from the continent continued to feed on the normal foodplants for the species. In this way, separate races or species, with either different food preferences or (as in the case of the eggars) lifecycle differences, evolved (Beirne, 1952).

Besides the Emperor and the Fox Moth, there are four or five other common moths on heathland (Fig. 45): True-lover's Knot (*Lychophotia porphyrea*), Beautiful Yellow Underwing (*Anarta myrtilli*), Narrow-winged Pug (*Eupithecia nanata*), Ling Pug (*E. goossensiata*) and Common Heath (*Ematurga atomaria*). Adults of the Common Heath fly actively in the sunshine in May and June, but the other species are best seen in light trap catches. The True-lover's Knot is exceedingly abundant and the catch from a single night's trapping may exceed over a thousand individuals. However, the caterpillars are surprisingly difficult to find unless one searches at night when they ascend the heather plants to feed, having rested by day in the litter. The caterpillars of Narrow-winged Pug, Ling Pug, Common Heath and Beautiful Yellow Underwing can be obtained easily from sweep-net samples; the caterpillars of the last-named closely resemble a shoot of ling. Two commonly-seen, day-flying species are the Grass

True-lovers' Knot/N. R. Webb

Emerald (*Pseudoterpna pruinata*), and the July Belle (*Ortholitha plumbaria*); their larvae feed on gorse and broom and both species are out in July and August. The Silver-Y (*Autographa gamma*), is very common, feeding on a wide range of plants; it is very often seen on heaths throughout the summer, flying in sunshine.

Less common, but widely distributed, are three other heather-feeding species: Neglected Rustic (*Xestia castanea*), Heath Rustic (*X. agathina*) – both of which fly in August and September – and Dark Tussock (*Dasychira fascelina*), which flies in June and July. The larva of the last is most often seen sunning itself on heather in April or May, before pupating. It has tufts of yellow and dark hairs towards the head and tail but brushes of black hairs in the middle of the body. The Clouded Buff (*Diacrisia sannio*), an arctiid moth frequently seen by day on the southern heathlands, is not really a heather-feeding species; neither are the Scarce Footman (*Lithosia complana*), or the Four-dotted Footman (*Cybosia mesomella*), the larvae of which graze algae from the stems of heather plants. The Horse-chestnut (*Pachycnemia hippocastanaria*), which, despite its name, has no connection with the tree, feeds on *Calluna*. It is a small, grey moth with longish, oval wings; it can sometimes be seen by day or be swept from the heather, but most easily captured by light trap. This species is locally distributed over most of the heathlands of southern England, and in East Anglia. Generally, the moths are seen early in the year, and again in August and September, but, in the south, they may be continuously brooded and encountered throughout the year.

Parley Heath near Bournemouth became famous among entomologists in the latter years of the 19th century; it was from here that a colony of Mazarine Blue (*Cyaniris semiargus*), was known, although today the species is extinct in Britain. In the same locality, the distinguished 19th-century entomologist, J. C. Dale, first recorded the Large Bagworm (*Pachythelia villosella*), and the Ringed Carpet (*Cleora cinctaria*). It was partly in the quest for these rarities that Parley Heath became well-known and led to other discoveries, including the first record of the smooth snake. But the discovery which perhaps, above all, made Parley famous was that of the Speckled Footman, (*Coscinia cribraria*). It was found in about 1820 by both J. C. Dale and a Mr Bentley. The species is confined to the New Forest and south-east Dorset and flies in June and July; it is active by day and night. The Speckled Footman occurs in discreet colonies and is seldom encountered away from them. Of late, rather more colonies have been located than previously known. The species does not feed on heather but on grasses; Tufted Hair-grass (*Deschampsia cespitosa*) is said to be the larval food, but since it is hardly characteristic of the habitats in which the moth occurs, other species are probably eaten. An immigrant form of the Speckled Footman occurs from time to time in southern England, but can be distinguished from resident individuals by their much lighter-coloured wings.

About forty species of the so-called Microlepidoptera can be found on heathland: some twenty feed on *Calluna* of which one of the commonest is *Aristotelia ericinella* and a further eighteen on *Erica* spp.; others feed on gorse, broom and other common heathland plants, and a single species, *Stenoptilia pneumonanthes*, has larvae which inhabit the flowers and stems of the Marsh Gentian. Many of these small moths live in silken cases attached to the plant. There are two species of Case-Moth (*Coleophora juncicolella* and *C. pyrrhulipennella*), which form cases on *Calluna*, but perhaps the most remarkable is the Bag Worm (*Pachythelia villosella*), which makes large cases up to 5 cm (2 in) long hanging from heather plants and resembling the caddis fly cases. The case is made from longitudinally-placed fragments of heather litter. The females of the Psychidae family are apterous, with considerably reduced wings and legs, making them quite unable to leave the case. Mating takes place within the case and the eggs subsequently develop within the abdomen of the female during June and July. The larvae feed on *Calluna* and Bell Heather from September until May, when they make a new pupal case; in some instances, development may take two years. The males fly in June in search of the females within their cases (Heath, 1946).

Most of the ground beetles common to heathland are predatory. One of the most characteristic is the Green Tiger Beetle (*Cicendela campestris*), which is widespread on hot, dry, sandy heathlands throughout Britain and most often seen in spring and early summer, when it flies readily. The Wood Tiger Beetle (*C. sylvatica*), occurs in much the same habitat but its distribution is restricted to Surrey, Hampshire and Dorset heaths. Both species have highly carnivorous larvae which live in burrows, resting at the entrance with powerful mandibles poised to seize passing ants or similar prey. These burrows are often concentrated on exposed, sandy patches, or along the sides of tracks, forming what is, for many ground-living insects, a minefield. Violet Ground Beetles (*Carabus violaceus* and *C. problematicus*), are both widespread, and frequently the most commonly-seen carabid in the latter part of the year. The distributions of these species suggest that there might be a closer association between *C. problematicus* and heathland than for *C. violaceus*.

HEATHLANDS

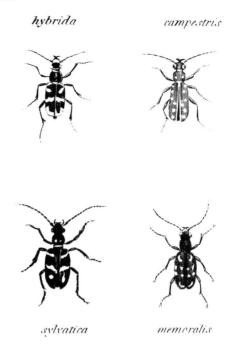

Tiger Beetle from Shaw's Zoology, 1806

On a few wet heath areas in Hampshire and Dorset, the beautiful, iridescent-green beetle, *Carabus nitens* may be found; it is only found elsewhere scattered over some northern moors.

Altogether, some twenty-five carabids can be considered as heathland species, but only about ten are really common. The dependence of many species on dry sand heaths varies; many of them also occur in dry, sandy grasslands, dunes, etc., as well as on agricultural land. Some species such as *Harpalus* spp. prefer high temperatures, but several others are attracted to dry conditions. The preferences of *Harpalus* for each condition has been investigated experimentally and shows a range from species to species. Several sand-loving species form the genera *Amara*, *Harpalus* and *Dyschirius*, and, as diggers, their distribution is determined by sands of differing particle size (Thiele, 1977).

Not all carabids are predatory: *Amara* and *Harpalus* species are phytophagous, and *Amara infirma*, which occurs on heathland, may feed on ripe seeds. Although most carabids are active, walking beetles, some species fly; others have well-developed wings but cannot fly, while a third group does not possess functional wings. In some there is an alternation between winged (macropterous) forms and non-winged (brachypterous) forms. The ability to fly considerably affects dispersal, a feature which has been intensively investigated for both heathland and non-heathland species in the Netherlands (Den Boer, 1977). These, and similar studies in Britain, have shown that the flying and the macropterous species, both with and without wings, are characteristic of pioneer heathlands. Hence, there are interesting problems, yet to be studied in detail, on carabid dispersal and succession on heathland.

Other large, ground-living beetles likely to be seen all depend on hot, dry conditions. The Oil Beetle (*Meloë proscarabaeus*) – so called because of the defensive oily secretion it produces when provoked – is a sluggish beetle with a complex lifecycle, and now somewhat restricted in its distribution. The female lays large numbers of eggs which hatch into larvae that then attach themselves to bees. In this way they are transported to the bees' nests, where development is completed, the larvae feeding on the brood of the bees (see Linssen, 1959, for full details of the lifecycle). The remaining large beetles are likely to be Dung Beetles or Dor Beetles (Geotrupes spp.) and the Minotaur (*Ceratophyes typhaeus*). The last makes distinct, circular burrows in firm, sandy patches, into which it rolls balls of rabbit dung, laying an egg on each of them. The larvae feed on the dung supply in the burrow until they emerge the following year. Related to this family is the leaf-feeding species, *Euchlora dubia*, which is said to feed on *Calluna* and birch.

Weevils (Curculionidae) are a distinctive group of plant-feeding beetles, with a characteristic anterior elongation of the head, called the rostrum. Most species are small but are often distinctively marked. Three species are commonly associated with *Calluna* and *Erica* and widespread over all heathlands: *Acalles ptinoides*; *Micrellus ericae*, a distinctive species with red legs and antennae, and a black body; and *Strophosomus sus* – a small, shiny black species. Rarer species include *S. nebulosus*, which is associated with *Erica* and *Ulex minor*, *S. curvipes* and *S. capitatus*; *Coniocleonus nebulosus*, which is restricted to the southern and eastern heathlands and found among the roots of *Erica* plants, and *Caenopsis fissirostris* which inhabits sandy places where there is damp moss. Many weevils are associated with gorse and broom. These are mostly from the genus *Apion*, of which there are some ten species. *Apion ulicis* and *A. difficile* are the most typical, and found easily on gorse plants. Larvae of many of these species live in seed pods and, as a result, little of the seed is viable in some years. *Sitona griseus*, which lives in sandy places, and *S. striatellus*, are associated with gorse shoots and roots.

All the beetles considered so far have relied on heathlands to furnish them with particular physical conditions, but members of the family Chrysomelidae (leaf beetles) rely on heaths for food. The most important of these is the Heather Beetle (*Lochmaea suturalis*), which during all stages of its lifecycle feeds on *Calluna*. The defoliation of heather by this beetle, often over wide areas, causing the death of the plants, has been reported regularly throughout the whole of north-west Europe since the middle of the last century. The Heather Beetle was first recognized in 1876; until then it was considered to be a closely-related species, *L. repens*, which feeds on willow (*Salix* spp.). Defoliation by Heather Beetle varies in intensity from year to year. In the north of England, outbreaks are regular and may occur annually in different localities, to the extent that it is considered a pest on grouse moors. In the south, although present on all heaths in very small numbers all the time, major outbreaks are much less frequent,

154   HEATHLANDS

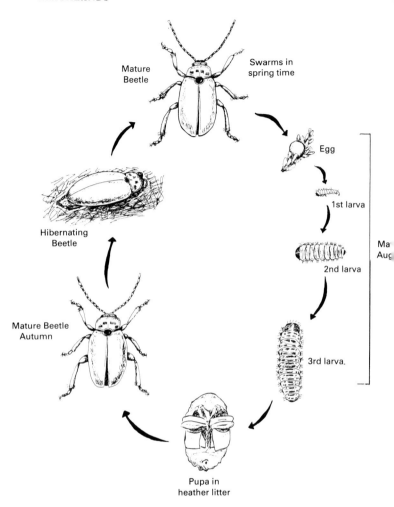

Fig. 46
Life Cycle of the Heather Beetle

perhaps only attaining major proportions every ten years or so.

Concern about the damaging effects of this beetle on the northern grouse moors led to a major study of Heather Beetle ecology by Cameron *et al.* (1944), and their monograph remains to this day the standard text on the subject. The adult beetles fly in March and April, when they mate (Fig. 46); in years of abundance, swarms are encountered which may fly some distance from the nearest heathlands. The eggs are laid in damp heather litter or *Sphagnum*; they hatch after three to four weeks and the three larval stages feed on *Calluna* shoots from June until early August, when they pupate in the heather litter. In September, beetles emerge which begin to feed on the heather plants until the onset of winter, when they hibernate in the litter, emerging again in the spring to mature. The dynamics of Heather Beetle populations are poorly understood, and there is no satisfactory ex-

HEATHLAND INVERTEBRATES

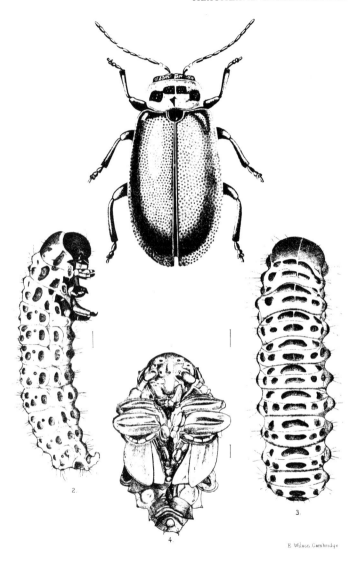

Heather Beetle from The Grouse in Health and Disease, *1912*

planation of why they attain such high densities from time to time. Cameron et al. (1944) thought that the balance between two important predators – the Pentatomid Bug (*Rhacognathus punctatus*), which preys upon the larvae, and the coccinellid beetle (*Coccinella hieroglyphica*), might be important factors, but were unable to demonstrate any effects. Likewise, during the large outbreaks which occurred on the heathlands in southern England in 1979, I was unable, from an analysis of population counts, to detect any relationship between the Heather Beetle and its predators.

Heather Beetle eggs/
M. M. Brooks

In many years, most of the large larvae which can be swept from the heather on the southern heaths are parasitised. The small eulophid wasp (*Aescodes mento*), has been described from the north of England by Golightly (1962), and may be an agent of biological control. Samples of larvae from southern heaths during the 1979 outbreaks did not appear to be parasitised, although subsequent samples have been. It is therefore possible that parasitism may hold Heather Beetle populations in check, with outbreaks only occurring when the parasite is absent. The size and topography of many southern heathlands, which are now small and fragmented compared with the extensive and uniform northern moors, may affect the dynamics of Heather Beetle populations. In the Netherlands, a shortage of food is considered to encourage swarming in the spring (Brunsting, 1982), and survival of hibernating beetles may be lessened by attacks from a fungus, *Beauveria bassiana*, but neither effect has been demonstrated in British populations.

On the continent, particularly in the Netherlands, the Heather Beetle is considered to be an important initiator of changes in the composition of heathland vegetation (Diemont & Heil, 1984; De Smidt, 1977; Brunsting, 1982). Increased nitrogen levels in the vegetation, which may be caused by contamination from farmland or atmospheric pollution, lead to increased population densities of herbivorous insects, particularly the Heather Beetle. This leads to defoliation and death of *Calluna* plants. Grasses, mainly Wavy hair Grass (*Deschampsia flexuosa*), replace *Calluna*, because of pollution and the enrichment of soil from nutrients released by the beetles feeding on *Calluna*. Besides the Heather Beetle, species of *Altica*, and other genera of the Chrysomelidae, may feed on *Calluna* and *Erica*; among these are *Altica ericeti*, *A. britteni* and *A. oleracea*.

Representatives of the various Hymenoptera families are conspicuous and important members of the heathland community. In particular, the fauna of aculeate Hymenoptera is rich and varied on the hot, sandy heaths of the Tertiary areas of Dorset, Hampshire, Surrey and the London Basin. For instance, 236 species of bees and wasps – 50% of the British fauna – have been recorded from Chobham Common in Surrey (Stubbs, 1983). Many of these prefer more continental conditions and reach the northern limits of their ranges in southern England, and western limits in Hampshire and Dorset. They like hot, dry, sandy soils, into which they can burrow easily, and are thus confined to sparse heather with bare, sandy patches, tracks or cuttings; one should look carefully in such places in the hottest summer months to see these species.

Females of the spider-hunting wasps (Pompilidae) search mainly for wolf spiders (Lycosidae), which they paralyse before excavating the burrow in which the spider is stored. An egg is laid in each cell and the larva feeds on the stored spiders before hibernating; it emerges the following summer. There are about forty British species in this family; many are smallish, black and red wasps, of which species of *Pompilus*, *Cryptocheilus* and *Priocnemis* are the most common on heathlands. The male wasps are not predatory and can be seen visiting flowers, especially the Umbelliferae, in adjacent areas.

Very similar to the Pompilidae in habit are the Spheciidae, or True Digger wasps; this is a larger family, not all members of which make burrows, but all capture prey, which is paralysed and stored as larval food. *Astata boops* stores paralysed pentatomid bugs; *Tachysphex pompiliformis* stores grasshopper nymphs in sandy heathland soils; and *Ammophila subulosa*, *A. pubescens* and *Podalonia viatica* are all species which capture and paralyse caterpillars. These are some of the most characteristic, widespread species in open, sandy parts of the southern heathlands. The female wasps can often be seen straddling large caterpillars, which they drag to their burrows. In addition, *Ammophila*, which is a handsome black and orange-coloured species, reprovisions its burrows as its larvae eat the caterpillars.

A number of species from the hymenopteran superfamily Apioidea also burrow; the so-called mining bees from the genera *Andrena* and *Halictus* (also called leaf-cutting bees) make their nests in the ground, preferring dry, sandy soil. These are also important pollinators and are most frequently seen visiting the flowers of *Calluna* and *Erica*. *Colletes succincta* and *C. fodiens* are similar, visiting flowers frequently and nesting in the sand. Probably the most conspicuous visitors to heather flowers are bumble bees; the Heath Bumble Bee, *Bombus jonellus*, is common and widespread in the south-west, Dorset, the New Forest, north Hampshire and Surrey, Ashdown Forest and East Anglia. Other heathland species include the widespread *B. leucorum* and the local *B. muscorum*. Generally widespread species, such as *B. terrestris* and *B. lapidarius*, are also often seen visiting heather flowers. Bumble bees visit flowers to collect both pollen and nectar, and in so doing are important pollinating agents. Their ability to pollinate flowers has been shown to depend on the ratio of the length of their tongues to that of the corolla of the flower (Brian, 1957). Both *B. leucorum* and *B. terrestris* have relatively short tongues and resort to biting the base of the corolla to obtain nectar. The holes they leave are then used by other

head magnified

Europæa

Velvet Ant from Shaw's
Zoology, *1806*

species which cannot bite through the corolla, to obtain nectar, thereby pollinating the flowers. If Cross-leaved Heath and Dorset Heather flowers are examined, bites can frequently be seen at the bases of the flowers, and by careful observation bumble bees can be watched as they bite holes in the corolla.

Females of the so-called Velvet Ant (*Mutilla europaea*), which is really a wasp, can be found wandering in open spaces on heathland during late summer. It is handsome with a red thorax and black abdomen with cream markings, and unlikely to be confused with any other insect. The females search for bumble bees nests, where they lay their eggs on the bee grubs; the larva develops, feeding on the grubs and on the honey stored in the nest.

On the heathlands of Dorset, the New Forest, north Hampshire and Surrey, as well as the coastal heathlands of Devon and Cornwall, the Turf Ant (*Tetramorium caespitum*), is a dominant species. It is a continental species at the northern limits of its range in Britain, and, unlike most other ants, which collect insects and scavenge, *T. caespitum* collects and stores seeds in underground galleries. It may defend foraging territories of up to 80 sq m (96 sq yds), and lives in deep nests which enable it to survive dessication and probably heathland fires (Brian, 1964; 1977). Two very interesting parasitic ants have been recorded from nests of *T. caespitum* on these southern heathlands: *Strongylognatheus testaceus* has a queen and a few workers which live in a *T. caespitum* nest, relying on the other workers to maintain them. They produce winged sexual forms, which fly and mate; then the fertilized females seek new nests of *T. caespitum* to parasitize. Similar, but with a more reduced polymorphism, is *Anergetes atratulus*,

crabroniformis m.&f.

Robber Fly from Shaw's Zoology, *1806*

which has no workers; the queen lives in a *T. caespitum* nest, killing the host queen and making use of the workers to raise her own sexuals. These do not fly but mate in the nest, after which the fertilized queens fly to another nest. Since the *T. caespitum* queen has been killed, there is no recruitment to the worker population and after about two years the colony dies.

Tetramorium caespitum lives in the best dry heath areas; the remaining space is occupied by *Lasius alienus* and, as conditions become wetter in the areas dominated by Cross-leaved Heath and Purple Moor Grass, it is replaced by *Lasius niger*. Elsewhere on the heathland, *Formica fusca* nests may be found; this species defends no more than the area of its nest. In the boggy areas dominated by *Sphagnum* and Purple Moor Grass tussocks, the rare species *F. transkaucasica* sometimes occurs. Three red ants – *Myrmica ruginodis*, *M. scabrinodis* and *M. sabuleti* – occur on heathland. Brian (1964; 1977) has described the ant communities of southern heathlands.

In summer, the blooms of both *Calluna* and *Erica* attract large numbers of hoverflies (Syrphidae). Many of the species which are found visiting these plants are common and widespread and not restricted to heathland. Among the more distinctive are *Episyrphus balteatus* (which has a yellow abdomen with distinct double black bands), *Metasyrphus corollae*, *Scaeva pyrastri*, *Rhingia campestris* and *Syritta pipiens*. Some, such as *E. balteatus* and *M. corollae* spp., have their resident populations augmented in some years by immigrants, when they are very abundant. Species which occur regularly on southern heathlands are *Paragus haemorrhous*, which may visit Tormentil (*Sphaerophoria philanthus*) (more common on southeastern heaths), and *S. rueppellii*, both of which are species of dry habitats. Among the rare species are *Chrysotoxum octomaculatum*, from the Surrey, New Forest and Dorset heathlands, *Pelecocera tricincta*, a small, wet-heath species reported from Dorset, the New Forest and Surrey, and *Parargus tibialis*, which can be confused with the other heathland species *P. haemorrhous* and *Microdon eggeri* (Stubbs & Falk, 1983). *M. eggeri* occurs on the heathlands of the London Basin, Ashdown Forest, the New Forest and in Dorset, and has an unusual lifecycle. The slug-like larva is parasitic in the nests of ants, principally *Lasius niger*, feeding on tiny pellets of food regurgitated by the worker ants. These larvae, like those of Lycaenid butterflies, are tolerated by the ant, and pupate in the nest, emerging in summer.

A wide variety of other flies lives amongst the heather; some, such as the crane flies, have larval stages which are abundant in the wet heath areas. Blood-sucking flies of the family Tabanidae are also frequent on many of the southern heaths, although these are associated with Man and cattle. Horseflies (*Tabanus* spp.) are the largest species, and the New Forest is a noted haunt for *Tabanus sudeticus*, the largest of them. *Chrysops relictus*, a small species with iridescent green eyes and delta-shaped wings, is also troublesome on the dry heathlands. Robberflies (Asilidae) may be seen on many tracks, where they wait, motionless, ready to pounce on insects such as grasshoppers; *Asilus crabroniformis* is the largest species.

Heathland Vertebrates   CHAPTER 11

The Sand Lizard, the Smooth Snake, the Natterjack Toad and the Dartford Warbler are amongst the rarest vertebrate animals in Britain. All four species are more or less dependent on heathland, and at the forefront of conservation issues concerning this community in southern England. The publicity that surrounds them tends to eclipse the fact that vertebrates in general are not particularly common, and few are dependent upon heathland. In this chapter, we shall look at the biology and ecology of these species, but the problems which they present to conservationists will be considered in chapter 12.

Amphibians

There are three species of newt, two toads and one frog native to Britain. The commonest newt found on heathland is the Palmate Newt (*Triturus helveticus*); it was formerly thought to be mainly a montane species (Smith, 1951), but occurs widely in lowland Britain in pools and beneath turves. Cooke and Ferguson (1975) found that it tends to avoid calcium-rich areas, and may be the most abundant species in heathland pools in Dorset, Hampshire, Surrey, and the London Basin (Beebee, 1973). The Smooth Newt (*T. vulgaris*) may also be found on heathland, but is much less common. The Warty (or Great Crested) Newt (*T. cristatus*) has similar distribution in Britain to that of the Smooth Newt, but is seldom, if ever, found on heathland. In the New Forest, all three species of newt occur and the factors which limit their distribution were examined by Cook and Frazer (1976). Smooth Newts were rarely found in waters where the pH was less than 6.0, but the Palmate Newt tolerated pools with a pH as low as 3.9. They found throughout Britain that the Smooth and Warty Newts were less common in acid water and that the Palmate Newt avoided calcium-rich waters, preferring those deficient in metal ions, especially potassium. Thus, the three species were separated ecologically by differences in water chemistry. These general conclusions have been supported by Beebee (1983a), who showed that ponds at the interface between farmland and heath were well used by all species, but those on open heathland were frequented by only the Palmate Newt. He found also that newts living in heathland pools were significantly smaller than those on farmland. The reason for this is not clear, but may be due to poorer nutrition or to reduced longevity.

The Common Frog (*Rana temporaria*) and the Common Toad (*Bufo bufo*) may both be encountered on heathland, but occur in a wide range of wet habitats, not necessarily associated with heathland; the toad is more frequently seen.

In contrast, the Natterjack Toad (*Bufo calamita*) requires sandy soils into which it can burrow easily. In Britain, therefore, its distribution is confined to sandy heathlands and coastal sand dunes. In the past, it was common on the heathlands of the London Basin, Surrey and northern Hampshire. In the south it occurred in Dorset, the New Forest and southwest Hampshire, and in eastern England at several inland locations near Cambridge, in the Breckland and in Norfolk. On the coasts its most important areas were in the north-west between Southport and Alcar, and on the Norfolk and Suffolk sand dunes (Prestt et al., 1974). In almost all these areas the Natterjack has declined dramatically, particularly at the inland locations, so that it is now confined to the coasts of Lancashire, Cumbria, Norfolk and Suffolk, and to one or two places on the Hampshire and Surrey heathlands (Beebee, 1977; Frazer, 1983). Its range extends from Spain eastwards through France and Germany to Russia, and northwards to southern Scandinavia; in Britain, the Natterjack Toad is at the north-west limits of its European range.

The Natterjack prefers mixed-age dry heath with a well-developed bryophyte flora, where there are enough sandy, open patches suitable for burrowing. The Natterjack's limbs are not modified for burrowing; normally it uses its hind limbs, but where the soil is firmer, it also uses its forelimbs (Smith, 1951). The Natterjack tends to be gregarious and often forms colonies. It prefers to breed in pools which are not too acidic, with pH in the range 6–7, and heathland pools which are more acidic are unsuitable (Beebee, 1977, 1983b). Many heathland pools become more acidic through the ion exchange activities of Sphagnum species growing in them. These mosses exchange cations (their nutrients) for hydrogen ions and thereby increase the acidity of the water (Moore & Bellamy, 1974). This natural process tends to make the pools unsuitable as breeding sites for the Natterjack. Sometimes colonies change pools, possibly in response to adverse conditions, but most colonies breed in temporary pools, where they are less likely to encounter increasing acidity. Recent research has shown that there is also less predation, since many aquatic predators of the tadpoles cannot survive the periodic drying out of the pools which generally takes place outside the Natterjack's breeding season. The toads spawn between April and June; the tadpoles leave the water by mid-August, and hibernation is from November until February. They eat insects mainly, such as beetles, moths, and the larvae of Diptera and Lepidoptera (Smith, 1951; Frazer, 1983).

Beebee (1977) investigated the causes for the decline of this species, and the spread of the Common Toad into some of its habitats. He found it difficult to attribute this to either habitat loss, climatic change, or increased public pressure. In the London Basin, he noted that the decline was accompanied by changes in the composition and structure of heathland vegetation, such as increases in pine, gorse and birch scrub, and bracken. As a result, the open, sandy places preferred by the Natterjack became shaded, causing changes in the microclimate and inducing cooler soil temperatures. The Natterjack burrows to maintain an equitable body temperature, and therefore prefers warm conditions. The Common Toad, however, is unable to burrow; it prefers cooler surroundings, and maintains equitable body temperatures by moving in and out of the shade of vegetation. The less open conditions which have developed on heathlands, possibly through the cessation of rabbit-grazing, have thus favoured the spread of the Common Toad and brought about cooler conditions less suitable for the Natterjack.

HEATHLAND VERTEBRATES

Where the Common Toad has spread into the habitat of the Natterjack, it competes successfully – which may be a further cause of its decline; in the coastal dunes which remain open, the Natterjack's decline and competition with the Common Toad has been much less.

Reptiles

All six native species of British reptile occur on many of the heathlands of southern England; the Sand Lizard (*Lacerta agilis*) and Smooth Snake (*Coronella austriaca*) are more or less confined to them. The Grass (or

The Smooth Snake, from Dorset Natural History & Antiquarian Field Club, Vol VII

Ringed) Snake (*Natrix natrix*) has a predominantly southern distribution, but is not associated closely with heathland. The remaining species – Common Lizard (*Lacerta vivipara*), Slow Worm (*Anguis fragilis*) and Viper (or Adder) (*Vipera berus*) – are widespread, but none is particularly associated with heathland (although the Viper tends to be considered a heathland and moorland species because it is common there).

The British reptile fauna is characteristic of a continental, cool temperate, and recent island. Most species are slow to disperse and colonized Britain before the land bridge with the continent was lost. The continuing improvement in the climate encouraged them to spread northwards, but subsequent cooling (about 5000 years ago) caused a retreat. Isolated remnants were left, especially in north-west Britain, as is suggested by the localized colonies of both the Natterjack Toad and the Sand Lizard on the Lancashire coast. Later, the establishment of more open conditions, following forest clearances by Neolithic Man, produced local, warmer places suitable for reptiles. The creation of heathland on the sandy soils of southern England was particularly important, since egg-laying (oviparous) species could find suitable breeding sites. The most successful and widespread reptiles in Britain are those which are viviparous (giving birth to live young). There is some evidence, derived from measurement of critical minimum temperatures, that some species in the British fauna are distinct physiological races, and differ from those on the continent (Spellerberg, 1975). The species with exacting physical requirements for the incubation of eggs have tended to decline in Britain, through the loss of hot, open habitats. The Sand Lizard and Smooth Snake have both suffered in this way because the extent of the southern heathlands has decreased. In addition, changes in the vegetation structure may have contributed to their decline. Both species are heliothermic and move between open, sunny conditions and shade to maintain an equitable body temperature. Although the Sand Lizard may be adjusted to the British climate, vegetation structure is important so that it can thermoregulate effectively (Spellerberg, 1975).

Neither the Slow Worm nor the Common Lizard are particularly associated with heathland, although both may be found there regularly. The Slow Worm is widely distributed in England, living in dry ground and burrowing in softer soils and leaf litter, or among grass tussocks. Its food consists mainly of slugs and snails (Fraser, 1983), both of which are scarce on heathland through a shortage of calcium. This species is ovo-viviparous (the eggs maturing in the mother) so it is not dependent on the hot microclimates of the exposed, sandy areas of the southern heaths. The Common Lizard, is also ovo-viviparous, widespread, and frequently seen on heathlands. It prefers dry, hot places such as embankments; the open, sunny patches on many heathlands and on surrounding boundary banks are ideal. Its food is a variety of invertebrates, all of which may be commonly found on heathland, such as adult and larval insects, spiders, myriapods and harvestmen (Avery, 1966; 1971).

Up to this century, the Sand Lizard occurred in a number of localities, but the main concentrations were in what remain its strongholds today, namely the coastal sand dunes of south-west Lancashire, the heathlands of Surrey, north-east and south-west Hampshire and the New Forest, south-east Berkshire, north-west Sussex, and the coastal sand dunes and heathlands of south Dorset. Besides these main areas, it used to occur at a number of other scattered localities, including the coasts of Cheshire, Flintshire, Sussex and Kent, and inland Wiltshire and Berkshire. At all of these the Sand Lizard is now extinct (Prestt et al., 1974). In Lancashire today, only a few hundred lizards survive, whereas the population was previously estimated to be 8000–10,000. This decline can be attributed to habitat loss and increased public pressure. Since 1801, some 60% of the dunes have been destroyed or rendered unsuitable (Jackson, 1979), but the decline may have been exacerbated by climatic deterioration. The May 6.5 hours isohel corresponds closely with the distribution boundaries of the Sand Lizard in Britain, but during the 1960s the May sunshine in north-west Britain (but not in the south) was significantly lower than in the previous two decades (Jackson 1978). This decline of the remnant population in the north-west stresses the importance of the remaining heathland in southern England for the survival of the Sand Lizard as a British species.

Even on the southern heathlands there has been considerable decline in the status of the Sand Lizard: the number of colonies in optimum habitats, carrying up to 360 lizards per ha (145 per acre), has been reduced by some 90%; many of the New Forest colonies have disappeared, and, at localities in Dorset, there has been an estimated 80% decline in recent years (Prestt et al., 1974; Corbett & Tamarind, 1979). In almost all instances, these losses have been caused by destruction or modification of habitat. In Surrey, 67% of the decline has been attributed to habitat loss and a further 28% to habitat change; in Dorset, similar figures are 44% and 57% (Corbett & Tamarind, 1979). In addition, dispersal between remaining fragments of heathland is difficult, if not impossible, and recolonization following local extinctions, such as those caused by heathland fires, may now be impossible. The biological consequences of habitat fragmentation are discussed in chapter 12.

The Sand Lizard is widely distributed throughout Europe, extending to central Asia, and is found in a wider range of habitats than in Britain, including steppes, agricultural grasslands, hedgerows and woodland (House & Spellerberg, 1983a). This suggests that being at the north-western limits of its European range in southern England, it survives only in the locations that meet its thermal needs and, because of this, is unable to colonize few habitats other than heathland. In Britain, its optimum habitat is dry heathland and related communities where the structure of the vegetation is similar, such as mixed grasses with scattered shrubs and bare patches. The choice of habitat does not depend on the richness of the plant species present, but upon the structural diversity of the vegetation. The optimum habitat is often quoted as mature dry heathland with bare, hot, sandy areas which are not shaded, but lizards can in fact be found in a variety of other habitats on sandy soils. Although the Sand Lizard may have home ranges of up to 1000 sq m (10,763 sq ft), its distribution may be limited by the availability of sandy areas for the incubation of eggs since, unlike the Common Lizard, it is oviparous, laying its eggs in loose, sandy soil in early summer. The young Lizards hatch in mid-August and feed actively until September when they retreat into their burrows for hibernation. The adults normally make regular use of a burrow, which is often modified from that of a small mammal.

The population density on heathland – that is, the number of lizards per unit area – is difficult to estimate. Where the species is locally abundant, densities may be 345 adults per ha (140 per acre) (Prestt et al., 1974), but other estimates vary from 0.3 individuals per ha (0.1 per acre) in an area of wet and dry heath with acid bog, to 19.3 individuals per ha (7.8 per acre) in mature *Calluna* heath on dune ridges (House & Spellerberg, 1983b). Densities may be very difficult to estimate because of high rates of im- migration and emigration on study areas. Mark and recapture methods for population estimates are often not valid, since marked individuals do not mix randomly within populations, but maintain home ranges which may vary from 1924 sq m (2301 sq yds) for females to 2130 sq m (2547 sq yds) for males (Frazer, 1983).

In an intensive study of the autecology of the Sand Lizard on Dorset heathland, House and Spellerberg found that the lizards occurred at much lower densities in open, exposed heathland than where the vegetation was structurally more diverse, the topography more varied, and there was a maximum amount of edge with other biotopes. In these more complex environments, where lizard density may be higher, home ranges were smaller. The range of variation in the Sand Lizard's habitat was analysed statistically, using principal components analysis and caononical dis- criminant analysis. By these means, the contributions of various features of the habitat, such as vegetation structure and composition, soil type and structure, topography, and microclimate were assessed to determine which, or which combination, best described the optimum habitat. Structural complexity of the vegetation proved to be more important than the species composition or the presence of particular species, such as *Calluna*. Topography was also important, and good Sand Lizard locations generally had a south-east – south-west aspect, small-scale variation in the soil surface in the form of ruts and depressions, and with moss, lichen, or dark-covered surfaces. This reflected the lizards' need for basking sites and was associated with their thermoregulatory and foraging behaviour. Suitable hibernating sites were also important, and a bank or knoll up to 2 m (6.5 ft) high with a south-facing slope with 20°–60° incline was a common feature of thriving colonies.

The study showed that on open, exposed, or dune heath, where the lizards occurred in low densities, the habitat could be manipulated by the traditional methods of heathland management, but where the lizards occurred in high densities, such as in small, isolated patches of heathland which often showed succession to grassland or scrub, the habitat was difficult to maintain. This confirms the synoptic view of the Sand Lizard's habitat requirements which has frequently been expressed (Prestt *et al.*, 1974; Corbett & Tamarind, 1979; Frazer, 1983), and maintains that deep, mature *Calluna* with a well-developed litter stratum is essential. Such conditions provide the Lizard with the greatest abundance of prey in the form of beetles and spiders, with a smaller proportion of flies, winged Hymenoptera and harvestmen – for all of these reach their maximum abundance in mature *Calluna* heathland (Nicholson, 1980; Frazer, 1983). House and Spellerberg (1983b) consider that the Lizard's habitat must meet its requirements for both its thermoregulatory and foraging behaviour, while others place greater emphasis on the need for mature heathland to supply food. Strangely, there has been no detailed study of either the Lizard's feeding ecology, or the carrying capacity of various types of heathland; until there is it will not be possible to provide prescriptions for the conservation of this species. It is, perhaps, interesting that some of the highest densities have been recorded from small heathlands surrounded by other biotopes; House and Spellerberg drew attention to this point in their analysis. Such heathlands may have an abundance of prey derived from the surrounding habitats (Webb *et al.*, 1984), and the Lizard may depend on this food source in addition to that of the heathland.

The Viper, or Adder, is widely distributed throughout Britain but much less abundant in central Wales, and in the central Midlands from mid-Lancashire to Cambridge. The snake occupies a wide variety of habitats which, besides heathlands and moorlands, include coastal areas, chalk downland, open woodland and marshy areas. Outside Britain, the Viper is one of the most widely distributed reptiles in the world (Prestt *et al.*, 1974). It is less often encountered on open heathland being normally found in marginal areas, disturbed ground, embankments and similar places. Boundary banks on the edges of heaths are favourite sites, especially those which are thickly vegetated and dry during winter. After hibernation, the Viper disperses only a short distance from the hibernating area to bask, feed, and ultimately to mate. Later, it moves to its summer areas, which, at a study site in Dorset heathland (Prestt, 1971), was a valley with a stream some 500 m (550 yds) from the hibernation site. The vegetation

Adder/J. R. Cox

included Purple Moor Grass, sedges, willows and Bell Heather and merged with dry *Calluna* heath on the higher ground (Prestt, 1971). It is during the migration to and from the hibernation areas that the Viper is most likely to be encountered on open heathland. Most feeding is during the summer phase, when Vipers catch small mammals including the Field Vole (*Microtus agrestis*), shrews (*Sorex* spp.) and Wood Mouse (*Apodemus sylvaticus*); the young snakes may also eat lizards (Prestt, 1971). Many of these small mammals are less common on heathland than on the marginal areas, which may account for the Viper's preference for heathland surroundings.

Whereas the Viper and Grass Snake occur in a wide variety of habitats besides heathland, the Smooth Snake (*Coronella austriaca*) is (at least in Britain) uniquely a heathland animal: it has only been recorded on the heaths of Dorset, Hampshire, Berkshire and Surrey. The Smooth Snake is dependent on mature, dry *Calluna* heathland and has declined within its range in recent years. It is now absent from Berkshire and, ten years ago, the populations in the remaining counties were thought to number between 1000 and 3000 adults (Prestt *et al.*, 1974); numbers are likely to have declined even further since then. Estimates vary because the snakes are difficult to locate, and in the years before the extensive fires on Hartland Moor National Nature Reserve (a single heathland of some 300 ha (750 acres) in Dorset) in 1976, the population was estimated to be between 700 and 1050 individuals (Spellerberg, 1977). Recently, New Forest populations have been estimated to have densities of one and two snakes per ha, and assuming that in southern Britain there are some 26,656 hectares (65,840 acres) of suitable habitat, the total number could be as high as 53,312 individuals, an estimate considerably higher than any other made previously (Goddard, 1984).

The range of the Smooth Snake extends from Greece and Italy northwards to southern Scandinavia and from northern Spain eastwards to Russia. In Britain it is yet another species living at the very edge of its European range. Although in Britain it is found exclusively on heathland, on the continent it is found in a variety of habitats, including hedgerows, open woodland, field edges and embankments.

The Smooth Snake was first recorded in Britain on Parley Heath near Bournemouth by Mr Frederick Bond in 1853. The occasion has been described by the great Victorian naturalist and famous arachnologist, the Reverend Octavius Pickard Cambridge, FRS, of Bloxworth, who 'was present on that occasion, entomologising with Mr Bond'. But although they recognized the snake as an unfamiliar specimen, it was forgotten 'amid the distractions of the height of the entomological season' and the record was not published until another record appeared in the *Zoologist* in 1859 (Pickard Cambridge, 1886). The publication of these records led to the discovery of many further specimens, not only from Dorset but from the New Forest, north Hampshire and Surrey – roughly the area in which it is known today. The engraving is reproduced from Pickard Cambridge's original paper.

The Smooth Snake is difficult to locate, even in prime habitat – but is the snake most likely to be seen on open heathlands within its range. Its preferred habitat is dry, sandy slopes covered with mature *Calluna* heath with Dwarf Gorse, sometimes with woodland nearby and often adjacent to wet heath or a stream. The soil must have a texture suitable for the snakes to burrow (Spellerberg & Phelps, 1977). Goddard (1983) considers that the essential features of the habitat described by Spellerberg & Phelps can be provided by a mosaic of vegetation types from mature, dry heathland to lowland bog communities. Although there has been some research, relatively little is known about the snake's ecology and behaviour. Traditionally, it was thought to prey on the Sand Lizard, hence its distribution and abundance was determined by that of the rare Lizard. However, it is evidently less specialized in its choice of prey than previously thought. An examination of the gut contents of snakes in the New Forest showed that 84% had eaten small mammals and that almost half had eaten the nestlings of shrews and rodents; lizards made up the remainder. Faecal samples showed a similar composition, with a preponderance of small mammal remains together with those of the Common Lizard (Goddard, 1984). Young snakes also eat young small mammals as well as invertebrates (Spellerberg, 1977). The Smooth Snake does not poison its prey but is a constrictor, wrapping itself around captured animals.

The females, which are ovo-viviparous, normally breed biennially, between August and October, producing litters with a mean size of 3.9 young. This litter size is much smaller than those reported from the continent and may be caused through the failure of the females to reach sufficient condition before mating. Abnormalities in reproduction include non-fertilisation of ova, incomplete absorption of the yolk sac, abortion of embryos and still-births. The females can only breed every two years under English conditions because of the time they require to build up their reserves. Females which breed late in a season, or which breed in a poor season, may not be able to reproduce until the third year. Poor breeding performance is one of the factors limiting the Smooth Snake's range in Britain, and even without the loss and deterioration of habitat, it finds survival difficult in the English climate (Goddard & Spellerberg, 1980). The heathlands of southern England are the only biotopes which provide suitable habitats for all native British reptiles – all of which seem to be declining and those depending solely on heathland have declined the most. This can be attributed to three factors. Firstly, there have been losses of heathland to afforestation, agriculture and urban development, causing a decrease in the absolute numbers of reptiles. Secondly, much of the remaining heathland has deteriorated as reptile habitat, reducing the densities attained. This change was initiated when rabbits were killed by myxomatosis in the 1950s. In the thirty years since, many prime heathlands, especially in north Hampshire and Surrey, have turned into scrub and birch woodland. Thirdly, the incidence of uncontrolled fires has increased, and reptiles suffer considerably during them.

Management of heathland by burning must now be considered inappropriate for these rare reptiles. If the fire is cool and sweeps across the heath quickly, few animals may be killed, and others may survive by sheltering in burrows, but frequently such survivors fall prey to predators such as the Kestrel. When the fires are hotter, burning the upper litter layers, even reptiles sheltering in burrows are killed. Unlike plants, which may bank seed in the soil, these reptiles have no ready means of recolonizing burnt heathland. The Common Lizard may not recolonize from the heathland periphery for two years, and take a further year before building up its population to the former level (Simms, 1969). The Sand Lizard recolonizes more slowly, and only when there are strong colonies nearby. Pre-fire densities may not be attained for several years and the population build-up may depend on a simultaneous increase in prey populations. Often this only occurs when the mature phase of heathland vegetation has been reached, some fifteen years after a fire. Snakes also colonize slowly, and may even lag behind the growth of their prey populations. On a Yorkshire heathland, the Viper did not colonise until the vegetation had reached the mature phase (Simms, 1972). For the Smooth Snake, the problem is even more difficult, since not only must it recolonize but its poor breeding performance in Britain limits population growth (Goddard & Spellerberg, 1980).

Birds

In common with other vertebrates, birds are scarce on heathland. Not only are relatively few species regularly seen but their abundance is much lower than elsewhere. This paucity is due to an inadequate supply of food and, since the British avifauna is largely woodland in origin, an insufficiently diverse structure to the habitat. In the New Forest there are no large winter flocks of finches, starlings and other passerines to be seen on open heathlands because there is a shortage of food, both of insects, and especially of seeds (Tubbs, 1968). The general picture for the lowland heathlands emerges from the study of Bibby (1978b) on a heathland nature reserve in Dorset, the fauna of which he describes as sparse in both species diversity and overall density. He walked a 7 km (4.3 miles) annular transect weekly for almost two years on 150 ha (370 acres) census plot on Hartland Moor NNR. There the vegetation comprised 95 ha (235 acres) – 63% of the total area – of dry heath and 3.2 ha (8 acres) (2.1%) gorse scrub. Five

	Numbers of birds per 1 hectare square				
Vegetation	Number of squares	Goldcrest	Stonechat	Wren	Dartford Warbler
0 gorse (over 80% dry heath)	26	0.1	3.5	1.5	0.2
0 gorse (less than 80% dry heath)	39	0.1	1.9	3.7	0.5
1% gorse	19	1.5	10.9	16.1	3.0
2% gorse	18	2.4	13.9	21.6	5.6
3% gorse	15	6.0	21.5	37.6	13.3
4–5% gorse	17	5.6	11.4	31.7	8.8
5+% gorse	15	8.7	16.3	44.7	12.3

Fig. 47
Distribution of Birds in Relation to Vegetation (Bibby, 1978b)

species were commonly recorded. There was a breeding population of 10–14 pairs of Wrens, the numbers of which were increased by immigration in October. The Goldcrest did not breed on Hartland Moor but there was an autumnal influx of 36–47 birds during both years. The Meadow Pipit was the most numerous breeding species and the population was estimated to be 50 pairs; however, numbers increased at the times of the spring and autumn passages, and even throughout the winter there were flocks of 5–20 birds on the heath. Besides the Meadow Pipit, the Stonechat was also a conspicuous and regular breeding species, with 10–12 pairs. Peak numbers were recorded in the post-breeding period, falling gradually through emigration to leave a few birds present throughout the winter. A particular feature of the Dorset heathland was its breeding population of the Dartford Warbler, of which there were 4–7 breeding pairs. Like the Stonechat, peak numbers occurred in the post-breeding period in late summer and early autumn, after which numbers fell to a much lower level; there were a few adults present throughout the winter, which subsequently bred on the heathland in the following season.

Only a few other passerines were commonly recorded, and these included the Linnet and Yellowhammer, which were summer visitors with estimated populations of 10 and 5 pairs respectively. A few pairs of Willow Warblers, Whitethroats, Robins, Dunnocks and Blackbirds, together with the Green Woodpecker and the Nightjar, were also recorded. In the past, vegetation structure has been found to be an important factor affecting the distribution and abundance of heathland birds (Lack, 1935). Bibby (1978b) also found that the distribution of breeding birds was strongly correlated with the distribution and cover of Common Gorse (*Ulex europaeus*), and all these species were rarely recorded in open heather (Fig. 47). The Meadow Pipit and Stonechat were the main dry heath species but even they sought food away from the heath in winter. So although Gorse was relatively scarce and comprised no more than 2.1% of the total vegetation cover, it was vitally important for the food supply it provided throughout the year, and the most important factor determining the distribution of heathland birds. Bibby found that the greatest exploitation of the Gorse was by the immigrant winter populations of Wren and Goldcrest, and by the resident Dartford Warbler. In Gorse, the density of birds was greatest in October and least in June. Gorse was particularly important for its supply of insects as food, and Bibby found that the potential food supply in the Gorse was some 40 times that of the birds' needs in autumn, but by January was only 15 times greater. The importance of Gorse for heathland birds has also been demonstrated for the Linnet by Eybert (1980) from the heathlands in Brittany. Here, the structure of the Gorse is particularly important for nest sites, but for the seed-eating Linnet, the availability of food in surrounding habitats may also be important.

Green Woodpeckers may also commonly be seen collecting food from the many ants' nests on heathland. The Wren, a very adaptable species, often frequents tall, rank Heather in search of insects.

The Red Grouse, now considered to be a subspecies of the Willow Grouse, is one of the most common inhabitants of Britain's upland moorlands, grazing on heather shoots, but it is absent from the lowland heaths. Its distribution is another way in which heathland is distinct from moorland, since the Red Grouse generally occurs at altitudes over 250 m (800 ft) in zones where the vegetation contains species of *Vaccinium*. Many of the upland grouse moors are on better soils where the quality of the heather food source is better. So although productivity of *Calluna* throughout the range of climatic and soil conditions of Britain varies little (Chapman & Clarke, 1980), the poor nutrient content of lowland *Calluna* may be a factor restricting Red Grouse to the uplands. Shooting bags of Red Grouse were very small during the last two decades of the 19th century because of outbreaks of Grouse Disease (Leslie & Shipley, 1912), and several attempts were made to introduce Red Grouse to the lowlands; almost all failed, but Red Grouse did become established on Dartmoor and Exmoor, both of which have upland characteristics, in 1915–1916 (Sharrock, 1976).

The Black Grouse (*Lyrurus tetrix*) was formerly widespread and, in many

Black Grouse, from Shaw's Zoology, *1806*

places, common on the southern heathlands, but it disappeared from most locations by, or soon after, the turn of the century. Today in southern Britain, the Black Grouse only occurs on Dartmoor and Exmoor. The species has fluctuated in numbers – probably affected by over-shooting – and from time to time in many places, such as the New Forest and Woolmer Forest, introductions were made (Tubbs, 1968). The species probably became finally extinct through the combined effects of excessive hunting and deterioration in habitat. Curiously, much suitable new habitat has been created in forestry plantations, but an introduction of the birds would be needed since there are no adjacent populations to act as a source of colonists. Black Grouse eat the shoots of Heather and other plants and are often destructive to young plantations, but, like the Red Grouse, the young are dependent, during their first weeks, on invertebrate food. In occupying the ecotone (the transition zone) between heathland and woodland, the Black Grouse occurs where there is the greatest supply of invertebrate food (Webb *et al.*, 1984).

The valley bogs on many of the southern heathlands support a few species of birds such as the Lapwing, Redshank, Curlew and Snipe. On some of the open pools duck may occur, such as Mallard and Teal, with numbers often increasing during winter. On many of the heathlands, duck decoys were constructed in former times; all are now derelict, leaving remnant pools often overgrown with *Sphagnum*.

Areas of birch and gorse scrub, both on the edges of heathland and in patches of open heath, together with naturally-regenerating woodland, have a richer bird fauna. This fauna includes many species which are generally common in open, scrubby habitats, such as the Linnet, Yellowhammer, Stonechat, Whinchat, Wheatear, Willow Warbler, Whitethroat, Long-tailed Tit and Redpoll. The Redpoll has increased in recent years since suitable new habitat has been created in young plantations. The Wheatear may often be seen on lowland heaths during the migration periods, but it breeds mostly on the moors of northern and western Britain, although the Breckland is also used. There, in prime habitat consisting of short grassland, the density of breeding pairs is 0.4–0.5 per ha (0.2 per acre), and in less suitable habitat of mixed *Calluna*-grass heath, with tall Heather, Sand Sedge, grass and Bracken, the density is 0.1–0.2 pairs per ha (0.08 per acre). The birds breed mostly in old rabbit burrows and are preyed upon by Stoats (Tye, 1980).

Heathland specialities in edge habitats are Dartford Warbler, Tree Pipit, Woodlark, Nightjar and Red-backed Shrike. The Tree Pipit is widespread throughout Britain, but the Woodlark is a southern species, and now increasingly confined to heathland. Both species depend on scrubby areas in otherwise open habitats for feeding and nesting, but with scattered, taller young trees or bushes which are used as song posts. Woodlarks have declined in recent years over much of the northern part of their European range, probably because of climatic changes, but habitat loss has hastened the decline (Sharrock, 1976). The Red-backed Shrike has been affected similarly: it has been declining for the last century, not only in Britain but also in Western Europe, due mainly to climatic deterioration (Bibby, 1971; Sharrock, 1976), and may be extinct as a breeding species in Britain. The Red-backed Shrike used to occupy a range of habitats, consisting of scrubby, open ground including heathlands, but today it is almost confined to heathland, principally that of the New Forest, Breckland and the coasts of East Anglia. The decline in suitable heathland has accelerated the effect of climatic factors, and possibly pollution has contributed too, and there are now probably fewer than 50 pairs in Britain (Sharrock, 1976).

The Nightjar has suffered a similar fate, and there has been a widespread decline in numbers since the beginning of the century, which can be attributed to climatic change and habitat loss. The Nightjar is very much a species of dry, sandy heaths, especially where there is early successional woodland or plantations encroaching onto the heathland. Like the Black Grouse, it is a species characteristic of the ecotone between open heath and woodland, using the woodland edge for feeding and the heathland for nesting. The distribution of the Nightjar in Britain corresponds closely with the distribution of lowland heathland (Sharrock, 1976), although the definition of lowland heathland used was somewhat broader than that adopted in this text. The Nightjar nests on the ground in open patches in the Heather, in clearings, or at woodland margins especially those containing birch (Berry, 1979).

The only bird more-or-less confined to heathland is the Dartford Warbler. This is a species of the south-western Palaearctic, breeding in Western France, the Iberian Peninsula and Morocco. In the Mediterranean its range extends to Italy, Sicily and Tunisia, where it is characteristic of the dwarf shrub community called *maquis* or *garrigue*. In southern Britain, the Dartford Warbler is another species at the very northern limit of its range, and was first recorded in Britain in 1787 from Bexley Heath in Kent. In Britain today, the species breeds regularly on the heathlands of Dorset and the New Forest only, but in years of high abundance, colonies establish in Devon, Hampshire, Surrey, the Isle of Wight and Sussex (Bibby & Tubbs, 1975). In the past, its distribution seems to have been wider and, besides the localities mentioned, was said to be regular in Berkshire and Wiltshire, with scattered records for Oxfordshire, Hertfordshire, Shropshire, Staffordshire (Cannock Chase), Kent and Middlesex (Witherby *et al.*, 1940). In the late 19th century, the Dartford Warbler also bred in the Suffolk Sandlings, but was last recorded breeding there in 1927 (Chadwick, 1982). We must be cautious of this assessment of a wider and more abundant distribution, since many casual, rather than breeding, records may have been included.

A noticeable feature of this species is a large fluctuation in numbers, especially following severe winters. The Dartford Warbler, unlike other British warblers, remains in Britain throughout the winter and, as a result, suffers considerable mortality if winters are unduly severe. Following a series of mild winters, the population builds up, mainly through breeding by survivors but also supplemented by immigrants from the continent. There is also a post-breeding dispersal of immature birds, which are frequently caught at bird observatories in south and west Britain. It is probably these birds which colonise the peripheral areas of the range in Britain, surviving until there is another severe winter.

Records of past population fluctuations are no more than anecdotal, but from 1960, reliable counts have been made in the main breeding areas. Fig. 48 shows clearly the crash in the population after the cold winters of 1961–1963, and the subsequent build-up in numbers in the mild winter which followed; in Dorset, the population doubled every two years. In-

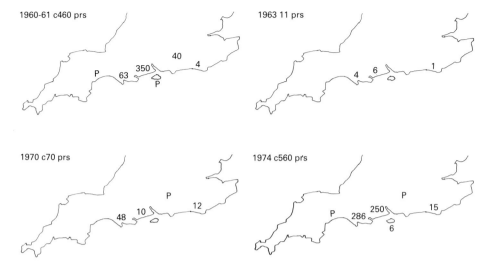

Fig. 48
Distribution and Breeding
Patterns of the Dartford
Warbler (Bibby &
Tubbs, 1975)

terestingly, there was no recolonisation in north Hampshire and Surrey, and this has been attributed to a deterioration in the quality of the habitat because of scrub and birch invasion, and extensive damage from uncontrolled fires (Bibby & Tubbs, 1975). Locally within Dorset, there is a tendency for the Dartford Warbler to be absent from the smaller or more isolated heaths, unlike the Stonechat; this is attributed to the fragmentation and isolation of these heathlands, which may be detrimental to the dispersal of the species (Moore, 1962).

The local name for the Dartford Warbler – the Furze Wren – indicates how this species has always been regarded as being dependent on gorse. Generally, its habitat is considered to be rank heather with gorse or young pine trees, but every birdwatcher has his own prescription of the ideal habitat, and habitat management for this species has often been based on eccentric views. An analysis of 202 territories in Dorset and 180 in the New Forest showed gorse to be a component in 83% and 75% of them, with ericaceous ground vegetation in 79% and 73% of the territories; these findings confirm the traditional view of the bird's habitat. A small number of territories differed, but none was without ericaceous ground vegetation, and some were in young pine plantations, resembling the habitats of France and Spain (Bibby & Tubbs, 1975). It is difficult to estimate the density of the Dartford Warbler population since there is relatively little uniform habitat: the mixture, composition and topography of the heathlands, and the fact that the Common Gorse grows on boundary banks and disturbed areas, all contribute to the difficulty. Bibby & Tubbs (1975) estimated densities of 2.38 ha (0.9 acre) per pair, and in optimum habitat, densities were 10–20 pairs per sq km (2.6–5.2 per sq mile). They found that populations on small heathlands were less dense than those on large ones, but found no evidence of the effects of fragmentation and isolation, which has been suggested by Moore (1962).

Gorse has a richer and more abundant invertebrate fauna than *Calluna*, and good stands are important feeding areas. They are used for seeking food more frequently than their abundance in the birds' territories would suggest. On study sites where gorse occupied 2.1% of the territory, it was used for 68% of the feeding time; deep *Calluna*, with a ground cover of 65%, was used for only 19% of the time, and birch, pine and other plants for the remaining 13%. Other heathland plants, such as Bracken and Bog Myrtle, were hardly used at all. In the spring, when invertebrate food may be in short supply on most heathland plants, the warblers spend nearly all (87%) of their time in the gorse. Their food is mainly beetles, spiders, lepidopterous larvae and bugs; some species such as ants and sawfly larvae are avoided, as are woodlice and harvestmen perhaps because they are nocturnal (Bibby, 1979a). Nestlings are fed large spiders and caterpillars with the birds being prepared to fly some distance, often over deep *Calluna*, to reach the important gorse hunting grounds. The Dartford Warbler differs from many other warblers since it is confined to invertebrate food throughout the year, whereas the other species may supplement their diet with fruits and berries (Bibby, 1979a).

Pure *Calluna*, or mixed *Calluna* and gorse, was used in 43% of cases for nesting, and 14% of nests were built in gorse only. Since territories with *Calluna* also contained gorse, it was concluded that the Heather was chosen in preference to gorse. Clutch size varies from three to five; four is the most common and there is a tendency for average size to increase as the season progresses (Bibby, 1979a). The maintenance of optimum habitat, particularly gorse, is crucial to the survival of the Dartford Warbler in Britain as a breeding species (Bibby, 1978a); the detailed prescriptions for habitat management will be discussed in chapter 12.

The Stone Curlew is not generally regarded as a heathland species, as its habitat requirements are for dry, open ground often on calcareous soils; but these habitats have diminished to such an extent that the species may now be found in heathland in East Anglia, both in the Breckland and in coastal areas. The dry, open conditions there with short vegetation suit this species, and it has benefited from firebreaks around forestry plantations in the Breckland.

A variety of raptors can be seen from time to time on heathland. However, only two, the Hobby and Montagu's Harriers, are dependent on lowland heath for breeding. Kestrels may be frequent too, preying on small mammals, beetles or small lizards. Where there are woodlands adjacent, or where there has been afforestation, other species such as Buzzard, Sparrowhawk and some owls may be seen. The Hen Harrier and Merlin both winter on lowland heaths, although they are characteristic breeding species of upland moorland. From time to time, immigrant Red-footed Falcons are reported from the New Forest (Tubbs, 1968).

Montagu's Harrier, unlike the other two British species, is a summer visitor, and has been reported breeding from a variety of heathlands and young plantations throughout England and Wales. Like the Hen Harrier, it nests on the ground amongst Heather or other low, shrubby vegetation, and is probably most common in south and south-west England and East Anglia. Numbers have tended to decline, but there is some evidence that the breeding population is mobile, breeding in one area, then colonising elsewhere (Sharrock, 1976). The species is now very rare indeed, and may become extinct in Britain, despite a recent slight increase in breeding.

The Hobby is a small falcon which inhabits both heathland and farm-

Hobby with chicks/ Nature Photographers, F. V. Blackburn

land, although on the latter it tends to be overlooked. Like many other raptors, its numbers have declined and most of the British population is confined to the southern counties which contain heathland; although it is largely absent from East Anglia, the New Forest and Dorset are its strongholds. Sharrock (1976) estimated the British population to be about 100 pairs, but recent estimates have been as high as 500 since many of the birds in farmland may be overlooked. The Hobby is a summer visitor, arriving rather later than many species; it prefers open land, especially heathland, and often uses old crows' nests in scattered pines, since it does not build its own nest. Pairs have been known to return to the same nest site year after year. The birds prey on dragonflies and large insects which are a conspicuous feature of heathland fauna, and on swallows and martins. The decline of the Hobby is in part due to climatic variation but also to loss of open habitats in its breeding areas. It has suffered less from the effects of chemical pesticides than many raptors, since it generally hunts over uncontaminated land.

Mammals

In common with birds, the mammal fauna of Britain is dominated by woodland species, and none can be considered characteristic of heathland. The Hedgehog (*Erinaceus europaeus*), although a common and widespread animal, is seldom, if ever, encountered on heathland. The Mole (*Talpa europaea*) is also common throughout Britain, and although it is often found in marginal, acid grasslands, it seldom occurs on heathland, because fine, sandy soils are often unsuitable for establishing systems of runs and burrows. Food is also scarce, for there are hardly any earthworms in heathland soils and there are few larger invertebrates such as ground beetles or molluscs. The absence of such species also restricts the hedgehog.

Of the nine most common small mammals, the majority are woodland or scrub species; only those found in more open habitats, such as fields, grassy banks and low scrub, are also to be found on heathland. These include the Pygmy Shrew (*Sorex minutus*) and, less commonly, the Common Shrew (*Sorex araneus*), both of which feed on a variety of small invertebrates, such as woodlice, springtails and insect larvae. The only other common species are the Wood Mouse (*Apodemus sylvaticus*) and Short-tailed Vole (*Microtus agrestis*); the Bank Vole (*Clethrionomys glareolus*) is much less common. The Short-tailed Vole is almost exclusively vegetarian and eats the basal parts of grasses; the Bank Vole eats mainly plants but may eat a proportion of small invertebrates; and the Wood Mouse eats a wider variety of food, such as plant material, seeds and a range of small invertebrates. The lack of palatable plants and an abundance of the large invertebrates restricts the distribution of these mammals on heathland. There are no population studies available, and we have little idea of the density and distribution of these mammals in heathland communities, but it is likely they are low compared with other habitats, and individuals may be concentrated in marginal areas, on boundary banks, and similar places where there is likelihood of food and shelter. However, these are often the places where their predators, such as the Viper, are also concentrated.

Both the Stoat (*Mustela erminea*) and the Weasel (*M. nivalis*) may occur on heathland, but abundance is also limited by lack of mammalian prey. The Stoat, which may also eat insects and berries, is the more common, but there is very little information.

The Rabbit (*Oryctolagus cuniculus*) used to be considered a major pest of agriculture and forestry, but it was not until populations were greatly reduced by the introduction of myxomatosis that its effects on a wide range of plant communities were realized. Even now, we are inclined to underestimate the extent to which vegetation was modified by grazing Rabbits. Rabbits were introduced on the light soils of southern England at a very early date, and may have been important agents in checking woodland regeneration and encouraging the formation of open heaths and grasslands (Sheail, 1971). Latterly, on many of the southern heaths, particularly in Surrey and northern Hampshire, there has been encroachment of scrub since Rabbit grazing ceased, which now poses severe conservation management problems.

The Rabbit had an important influence on the East Anglian heathlands (both in the Breckland and the Suffolk Sandlings), where extensive warrens were maintained, in addition to sheep walks. The ground was riddled with their burrows, which collapsed to create bare, sandy areas. The vegetation became denuded, thus leading to soil erosion – the blowing sands that are characteristic of the Breckland, were partly caused by overgrazing by Rabbits and sheep. When grazing was in short supply, the Rabbits were fed turnips, hay, and even gorse. They were displaced from their warrens and spread to open countryside by the end of the 19th century when the Brecklands were reclaimed for agriculture. In Sussex, in the forests of Ashdown and St Leonards, warrens were established and maintained by burning the open heath; Bracken may have been cut to provide supplementary winter food, and, hence, open heathland was encouraged (Sheail, 1971).

The effects of Rabbit-grazing (right) *on Foxhole Heath, Breckland/A. S. Watt, c. 1930*

The Rabbit's influence on the Breckland heathlands led Farrow (1925) to examine its role more closely. The main *Calluna* associations were degraded into grass heath, the Rabbit first eating *Calluna* growing round the heathland margins and gradually penetrating along trackways until, eventually, almost all the Heather was eaten. The Rabbit determined the relative distribution of the plant associations through differential grazing effects. By erecting Rabbit-proof enclosures, Farrow demonstrated that grass heath could be restored to *Calluna* heathland as long as live *Calluna* roots existed.

Rabbits were also responsible for the establishment of large areas of Sand Sedge (*Carex arenaria*) by causing the degeneration of *Calluna* heath. Subsequent investigations on these heathlands have shown that the competitive power of *Calluna* against Bracken varies from phase to phase of the Heather, being greatest in the mature phase. The balance between these species may be modified by spring rainfall and frost, and particularly by the presence of Rabbits; this creates a Fescue-dominated acid grassland (Watt, 1971a).

The rabbit eats a wide range of plants but generally avoids Bracken, except the emerging frounds, although they will nibble the stalks of fully-developed fronds, causing them to collapse, and there is a tendency for only the fronds on the edges of patches to be attacked. Cross-leaved Heather (*Erica tetralix*) is also avoided and only eaten when other plants are in short supply. On heathland, Rabbits generally establish burrows where the soils are slightly deeper, sometimes where the depth has been increased by luxuriant Bracken growth, and also in disturbed areas or boundary banks. The vegetation around the burrows is often considerably modified, generally grassy, and nearby Heather and gorse plants are grazed to a short turf. Rabbits living on heathland graze on dry and humid heaths throughout the year, but prefer the humid to wet heath during the summer (Chapuis, 1980). Feeding preferences can be determined by examining epidermal fragments remaining in the faeces. On dry heath, Rabbits eat *Calluna* mostly in the winter, Bell Heather in the autumn, gorse species throughout the year but in the greatest proportions during winter, and during summer a range of grasses, mostly Purple Moor Grass. The choice of plant species may vary, depending on availability, nutrient content, growth phase, and on physical factors such as aspect, moisture and canopy height (Chapuis & Lefeuvre, 1980).

A similar study on Fitzhall Heath, part of Iping Common in Sussex, compared the proportions of leaf epidermis from twenty-two different species of plants in Rabbit droppings with the proportions of the plants growing on the heath. The Rabbit's order of preference was *Calluna*, Sand Sedge, Bell Heather, Bulbous Rush, Heath Rush, Purple Moor Grass, Dwarf Gorse and mosses of the genus *Polytrichum*. They avoided eating Cross-leaved Heath, Bracken and mosses of the genus *Campylopus*. Eight species of plant growing on the heath were not found in the droppings. The radius of the feeding range was at least 120 m (393 ft) (Bhadresa, 1981 & 1984).

The Red Deer (*Cervus elaphus*) is one of the two species of deer considered to be native to Britain. The native stock is now thought to be confined to the moorlands of Scotland, the Lake District, Exmoor and adjacent areas, and perhaps the New Forest. Herds occur elsewhere in southern Britain – in Surrey, Sussex (Ashdown Forest), the Breckland – and a number of localities in the north of England, but mostly these herds are the descendants of introductions. The Red Deer is primarily an animal of woodland and its margins, but in the summer, especially in the uplands, may graze on open moorland. The Roe Deer (*Capreolus capreolus*) is the only other British native species; it was formerly thought to have been widespread, but declined considerably in numbers when it occurred only in Scotland. Its subsequent spread stems largely from introductions in the south of England (Whitehead, 1964). Today, Roe Deer are widely distributed over the north of England and Scotland; in the south they are confined to the southernmost counties and occur in the heathland areas of Devon, Dorset, Hampshire (including the New Forest) and Surrey. It is a species of open woodland and plantations with dense undergrowth; it can also be found on heathland where there is scrub encroachment or adjacent young plantations.

The Fallow Deer (*Dama dama*) is thought to have been introduced to Britain, perhaps by the Romans, but possibly earlier (Whitehead, 1964). It occurs in a number of southern areas, including the New Forest, the Breckland and Cannock Chase, but it is the least likely of the British deer to be encountered on heathland, being a woodland animal. Sika Deer (*Cervus nippon*) were first introduced to Britain from Japan in 1860 (Whitehead, 1964). They were subsequently introduced in a number of places, including heathland areas such as Dorset, the New Forest, Woolmer Forest and other parts of northern Hampshire. However, feral populations seem now to be established only in south-east Dorset, the New Forest and in Somerset. This species is much less confined to woodland, and can be seen on heathland where feral populations have become established. It prefers mixed woodland with well-developed scrub and often inhabits patches of scrub on heathlands. The Sika can be confused with Roe Deer.

The Muntjac (*Muntiacus reevesi*), introduced from China, has established feral populations in, amongst other places, the New Forest and East Anglia, but is an elusive species. In general, deer are not heathland animals, but where there is adjacent woodland cover they often graze on heathland, eating young Heather, saplings, grasses and herbs. The Red Deer, in particular, will graze Heather on open moorlands (Miller, 1971).

`# What the Future Holds   CHAPTER 12

During the last thirty years, wildlife conservation in Britain has developed into a highly organized movement, supported both locally and nationally by a range of official and voluntary bodies. The roots of this movement stretch back further – but throughout its history, its practices at all levels have been firmly based in ecological science. Indeed, many of the founders were themselves eminent and pioneering ecologists.

The word 'ecology' was coined by the distinguished 19th-century German biologist Ernst Haeckel, for the science which investigated the relationships or interactions between living organisms and their surroundings. The surroundings are made up of both the physical environment of the organism and the society created by the presence of other organisms.

Thirty years ago, ecology provided scientific criteria for the selection of conservation areas and a basis for conservation management. In 1963, MacFadyen saw conservation as 'perhaps the most important field in which applied biology has made headway', and felt that nature reserves could be managed so that the organisms and communities present in them were maintained in perpetuity. He stated:–

'The most satisfactory feature of a positive approach to conservation is that one is working towards a state in which stability of numbers, productivity and aesthetic satisfaction, which comes from taxonomic variety, are all combined.'

Today, we can see that the contribution of ecology to all aspects of wildlife conservation was over-emphasized. Its insistence upon rigid scientific criteria to select conservation areas was inappropriate because a much wider variety of valuations must be taken into account ... One chooses a painting to hang in an art gallery on the basis of a variety of valuations, not upon the chemical composition of the paints and the mechanical actions involved in applying them! However, in the management and maintenance of populations and communities, ecology still has a central and increasing role. To continue my analogy, we need the science of materials and paints to keep the painting we have chosen in good condition.

There has been a considerable expansion in ecological research, much of it directed towards wildlife conservation. The research is approached from two standpoints: the first seeks to understand the patterns and processes which affect populations and communities and the functioning of ecosystems. From this one can predict the effects that change may bring. For example, if we understand *how* heathland ecosystems function, we can then predict the effects of rotational management, such as burning. The second approach is empirical: on the basis of existing knowledge and some intuition (which naturalists often possess), a scheme of management is put into action and its effects monitored. This type of research has much less predictive value but, at least, some management is done. Often in conservation there is too little management because we are afraid, or uncertain, of the consequences: but, if nothing is done, because we are waiting for more knowledge, valuable communities or species populations may be lost.

We shall examine how an understanding of the ecology of the plants and animals which form the heathland community can be used to develop a conservation strategy. How can that knowledge be applied to the selection of reserves, and to the development and carrying out of management? And what observations should we make during our conservation practice to add further to ecological knowledge?

The Need for Heathland Conservation

Lowland heathland everywhere has been considerably reduced in area. In Dorset, one of the best documented examples, only 15–20% of the heathland which existed in the early 19th century remains (Webb & Haskins, 1980) (Fig. 13). In southern Sweden, heathland occupied about 75% of the area of uncultivated land, but today it accounts for only about 5% (Damman, 1957). In Denmark there have been similar changes: in the mid-18th century 26% of Jutland (658,200 ha/1.6 million acres) was heathland, by 1961 this had decreased to about 2% (or 12,000 ha/29,640 acres) (Nørrevang & Meyer, 1975). Most of the losses of the Danish heaths were brought about by the Danish Heath Society, when they promoted farming and forestry on the poor lands of Jutland. In the Netherlands, heathland areas fell from about 800,000 ha (2 million acres) in 1835 to 40,000 ha (98,000 acres) today, 50% of which consists of fragments of 50 ha (120 acres) or less; that remaining is mostly nature reserve, and 5000 ha (12,350 acres) of this is managed by sheep grazing (Diemont et al., 1982).

Recently, the Nature Conservancy Council has calculated that on the six main heathland areas in southern Britain the total extent has decreased from 143,250 ha (353,828 acres) in 1830 to 39,450 ha (97,442 acres) in 1980 (Fig. 49), a decrease of 72%. The losses recorded for Dorset (Webb & Haskins, 1980) are typical of most of southern England. The Lizard in Cornwall is an exception; here there has been a gain of 14%, but in Surrey and on the Suffolk Sandlings, losses have been as much as 90%.

Most heathland has been lost through conversion to pasture or arable land, afforestation or used for building. Even where heathland remains its management has changed; it is seldom grazed and there is no turf, gorse or bracken cutting. Under these conditions, there is succession to woodland – a problem common to many areas (e.g., Moore, 1962; Froment, 1981). Many of the Surrey heathlands became birch woodlands when Rabbits disappeared after the outbreaks of myxomatosis in the 1950s. It is thought that losses of heathland through lack of grazing, or similar neglect, are small. What is much more important is the continuing fragmentation and isolation of the remaining heathland. This has important consequences for many of the rare species which rely on the southern heathlands for their habitat. We do not know the biological effects of this isolation fully and there is clearly a need to conserve as much heathland as possible.

Location	Date	ha	acres	
Breckland, Suffolk, Norfolk	1824	16469	(40678)	
	1950	9268	(22892)	
	1963	5973	(14753)	
	1980	4529	(11187)	An overall loss of 73%
Suffolk Sandlings	1783	16403	(40515)	
	1960	1823	(4503)	
	1983	1580	(3903)	An overall loss of 90%
Surrey	1804	55400	(136838)	
	1983	5901	(14575)	An overall loss of 89%
Hampshire	1819	37000	(91390)	
	1982	18000	(44460)	An overall loss of 51%
Dorset	1750	39960	(98701)	
	1811	30400	(75088)	
	1896	22672	(56000)	
	1934	18200	(44954)	
	1960	10000	(24700)	
	1973	6100	(15067)	
	1978	5832	(14405)	
	1983	5670	(14005)	An overall loss of 86%
Lizard, Cornwall	1813	2270	(5607)	
	1880	3610	(8917)*	
	1908	3660	(9040)*	
	1963	3280	(8102)*	
	1980	2580	(6373)	An overall gain of 11%
All areas	1830	143250	(353828)	
	1880	112750	(278493)	
	1930	82000	(202540)	
	1950	64500	(159315)	
	1980	39450	(97442)	An overall loss of 72%

* Gains occured on the Lizard when, through economic depression, reclaimed heathland was allowed to revert.

Since 1950, 17% of the heathland existing at the beginning of the 19th-century has been lost.

Fig. 49
Changes in the Extent of the Main Areas of Lowland Heaths (NCC, 1984)

Choice of Reserves

The reasons for choosing a particular area as a nature reserve are manifold. Often land is acquired opportunistically because it is threatened. What features contribute to the quality of a piece of heathland? What are the criteria we should use for selection? Ratcliffe (1977) suggests ten criteria: size (or extent), diversity, naturalness, rarity, fragility, typicalness, recorded history, position on an ecological or geographical unit, potential value and intrinsic appeal. It is not clear whether these are in order of importance.

Size (or extent) is clearly important: a large heathland contains a greater variety of habitats – dry heath, wet heath, bog, gorse scrub and acidic grassland. It has greater potential for rotational management and this is important for a community in which successional change needs to be controlled.

Ideally, we should look for a complete unit which can be easily managed, such as a bog or valley mire, together with its surrounding dry heath catchment, so that there is less risk of run-off of nutrients from surrounding land, which would lead to eutrophication. However, the acquisition of large areas may be difficult in the fragmented landscape of southern Britain.

Diversity is a term which has several meanings in ecology. It might refer to the number of species present in an area (a value which increases as the area increases), or to the variety of habits present in an area.

It is evident that size and diversity are closely related, and for many areas they are the most important criteria. The diversity of species on heathland is low compared with, say, woodland. On dry heath there are no more than four or five common plants, but in humid, wet heath and bog communities, there are many more, diversity increasing with moisture. The early successional stages of heathland are frequently more diverse than the mature, since a dense canopy of *Calluna* prevents the establishment and growth of other species. In the later successional stages, when *Calluna* cover decreases, diversity increases. However, by this stage, succession may be moving towards scrub and woodland. On heathland, diversity appears to decrease with age but this is really only a part of the succession from bare sandy ground to woodland, in which overall diversity increases.

Heathland is a species-poor community, and it has been shown that the number of species of invertebrate animals at a point on small heathlands is frequently greater than at a comparable point on a large heathland (Webb & Hopkins, 1984). This is no more than a reflection of the fact that edge effects are greater on small heathlands. The magnitude of the edge effect depends on the surrounding community; woodlands, particularly mixed deciduous, contribute far more species than agricultural grasslands (the effects of different plant communities are summarized in Fig. 50 (Webb et al., 1984)). When selecting an area for a reserve, it is important to con-

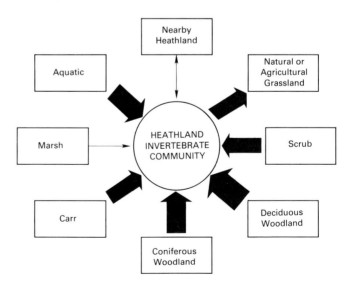

Fig. 50
Influence of Surrounding Vegetation on the Invertebrate Community

sider the surroundings, to avoid unwanted species invading the heathland community. Undoubtedly, the edge effect factor exists in other habitats, but is less apparent because they are generally richer than their surroundings.

Diversity has often been considered to be one of the most important criteria for choosing nature reserves. After all, given two similar areas, one will intuitively choose that which contains most species or greatest variety of habitat. However, on heathland, diversity alone should not be taken as the most important criterion, since diversity may arise through the presence of species which are not characteristic of heathland.

Naturalness in Ratcliffe's criteria referred to the extent to which a habitat was unmodified by human activity. Again this is a difficult criterion to apply to heathland, which is an anthropogenic community. Indeed, it is only in the last century, as Man's activities have declined, that it has become difficult to maintain. Less apparent may be the effects of drift by fertilizers and sprays from adjoining land. For heathlands, we may adapt naturalness to mean those areas maintained by traditional land uses. The grazing, cutting and burning of the open heathland of the New Forest, Ashdown Forest and Exmoor are examples of traditional practices which continue, although they have ceased elsewhere.

Rarity is a criterion which can be applied at both the community level and at the population level. The losses of heathland, which we have already detailed, lead to the conclusion that heathland, throughout its range in Western Europe, is a rare and threatened community, and that good examples, especially those representing its geographical variation, should be protected as nature reserves. The protection of rare species is popularly seen as the most important part of wildlife conservation, but the protection of rare communities is less appreciated.

On the southern heathlands of Britain, a number of rare species occurs, and the places where they are found need to be protected, not because they are heathland but because they are the habitats of these species. The list of rare species in this category is impressive; the most widely mentioned are the Dartford Warbler, the Smooth Snake and the Sand Lizard. But, as we have seen, there are many others, such as the Hobby, Nightjar and Red-backed Shrike, and invertebrates, including the Large Marsh Grasshopper, the Heath Grasshopper, the Ladybird Spider, the Raft Spider and the Scarce Ischnura Dragonfly. All of these are frequently cited in support of heathland protection, but we still need to protect heathland as a community in its own right. Neither must we forget that species may be rare for a variety of other reasons. In southern Britain, for example, many are living under less than optimum conditions at the northern limits of their ranges. The decline of some heathland birds is only partly attributable to loss of habitat; some ornithologists believe that small changes in the climate may have an effect. Crashes in the Dartford Warbler population whenever there is a severe winter are unavoidable, no matter how much suitable habitat we are able to protect. However, by providing as much optimum habitat as possible, we can ensure recovery of the populations. Implicit in many of the arguments of conservationists is the fact that many rare species have declined because of human activity. Often this is far from true; for instance, Dorset Heath (*Erica ciliaris*) has been cited in such arguments, but without supporting evidence (see chapter 8). Nevertheless, rarity is one of the most useful criteria for use in assessing the quality of an area for a nature reserve.

Ratcliffe considered fragility to be a criterion which reflected the sensitivity of species and communities to environmental change. Heathland, with its various phases of development, may be particularly sensitive. Heathland communities may be damaged by changes in their physical surroundings, such as alterations in the pattern of ground water movements, eutrophication of acid bog systems, and drift of sprays and fertilizers, all of which affect the growth and composition of heathland vegetation. Where heathland has been converted to agricultural land or forest, it becomes a source of seed from certain species which tend to dominate the remaining heathland. For instance, the regeneration of pine trees is now a problem on many lowland heaths which have pine plantations adjacent to them. Moreover, heathland vegetation is very sensitive to physical damage from trampling or from vehicles. Vehicle tracks, in particular, remain for many years after no more than a single traverse. Trampling also damages the vegetation, and may lead to changes in its composition. On the Surrey heathlands it has been shown that grass-dominated vegetation develops where there is excessive trampling (Harrison, 1980).

In earlier chapters, the range of variation in lowland heathland was described, and it is desirable that this range of variation should be represented on reserves. Thus, the entire heathland community, or at least an acceptable proportion of it, must form the criterion.

The remaining criteria are perhaps of less importance than those so far discussed. Recorded history is a criterion which relates to the knowledge of a particular site which may make it of value to ecological research, such as sites of long-term research – the Breckland used by Dr A. S. Watt, or Studland Heath in Dorset used by Captain Cyril Diver are good examples. Some bogs are important for the pollen records which they contain, and should be protected for this reason alone. The position of a piece of heath in an ecological or geographical range has been partly considered under the criteria of rarity and typicalness.

Potential value poses something of an interesting question. It considers the value of a site for nature conservation if it is subjected to a programme of suitable management or rehabilitation. The prospects for this activity with a habitat so obviously man-made as heathland is very great: if any of the old practices such as grazing, turf-cutting or furze-gathering were to be restored on heathland, many areas now of poor quality could be restored. Likewise, there is the opportunity for disused mineral workings to be restored as heathland. This, however, is a topic which poses some difficulties since conservation activity is primarily directed at the protection of existing sites.

Finally, intrinsic appeal considers the more aesthetic reasons for selecting a reserve. This aspect of conservation is much less well developed in Britain than in some continental countries, where wildlife conservation takes place within the context of country- or landscape-management. In Britain we have tended to regard wildlife conservation as an end in itself. Some of the heathland areas of Britain are an important feature of our heritage: the way of life on the heaths of Wessex, so skilfully described by Hardy; the New Forest and Woolmer Forest, as described by Gilbert White; the great heaths and sheep-walks of the Breckland; all reflect a similar history. But today it is no longer possible to see the heathland our forefathers described; it is difficult to recapture their spirit, but where this perspective persists, it should be retained.

These criteria form a checklist which can be used to assess a particular piece of heathland as a nature reserve. However, the importance given to the major criteria – size, diversity, rarity and representativeness – may vary from one assessor to another. Sites of top quality are usually recognized by all assessors, as are the poorest, but for sites of intermediate quality, assessment may vary (Margules & Usher, 1984). Quite obviously, the approach must be flexible and sites chosen for the combination of qualities they possess. Thus, a reasonably large site, with an appropriate diversity of range of heathland types (such as dry, humid and wet heath, with perhaps some peatland and gorse scrub), should certainly be a reserve; the presence of rare species is a bonus. In contrast, the sites of colonies of rare species associated with heathland, such as the Sand Lizard, the Dartford Warbler or Scarce Ischnura, or the Ladybird Spider (*Eresus niger*), will probably qualify for protection irrespective of the quality of heathland. However, this may cause management problems at a later date. It is important to appreciate that there are no objective, scientific criteria by which to choose nature reserves; inevitably the choice must represent a valuation of a site involving many factors. The role ecological science can play in this valuation may be small, and we should not be afraid to recognise this point.

Aims of Management

Once a site is chosen, the management aims must be clearly defined. All too often in the past management has been haphazard. Since heathland is seral, it is essential to identify the periods of succession and ensure that each is represented in the right proportion. Management principles and techniques are generally available for climax communities, but the management of stages in a succession is less advanced; in other instances, management is directed towards rare species and less towards succession considerations. However, the balance between these aims is difficult and it may not be possible to maintain such a dense population of a rare species in tandem with long-term management of the heathland itself.

Let us first consider the overall management of a reasonably large piece of lowland heathland. The aim is to prevent invasion of scrub, trees and bracken and to produce, by rotational management, a mosaic of ericaceous vegetation of different ages, representing the entire growth cycle of *Calluna*. There could also be an adequate representation of wet heath and valley bog communities, but this will depend on the topography. First of all, areas to be managed separately for the conservation of a single species should be set aside and not form part of the rotation; the valley bogs, for which different management is needed, are also excluded from the overall plan. The aims may include the maintenance of areas of very old heather, and these would also be excluded from the rotation as they may be important for the conservation of reptiles. When all areas which require management apart from the rotation have been excluded, a plan is drawn up to produce a mosaic of different-aged stands of dry, humid and wet heath communities, bearing in mind that the capacity for heather to regenerate declines with increasing age, and that under ideal management, the maintenance of the correct age structure of the community is important: an adequate representation of the younger age classes is essential to provide replacements should any of the older ones be accidentally lost.

Burning is generally considered to be the most effective way to regulate heathland vegetation and has been a common practice in both the uplands (where it may have originated) and in the lowlands. On grouse and sheep moors, the aim is to provide a crop of either grouse or sheep; for grouse, the structure of the vegetation is important and the moors are burnt in strips to provide young heather for food and older heather nearby for shelter and nesting. Generally, such moors are burnt on a rotation of ten to twelve years (Gimingham, 1971; 1972; 1979). This contrasts with lowland management, which is geared towards conservation and amenity, and in which rotation can be on a fifteen- to twenty-year cycle – or even thirty years (Pickess, 1983). Burning on a fifteen- to twenty-year cycle checks succession to scrub and woodland and matches the accumulation of nutrients (Chapman, 1967).

Not all of the heathland to be burnt should be in one large area, but broken up into plots or up to 2 ha (5 acres) each, preferably surrounded by older heather which acts as a source of colonists. It is important to recognize that under rotational management of any community, very local extinctions of species are to be expected and that there will be recolonization from adjacent areas. It is generally considered that recolonization should take place from within a site rather than from neighbouring ones (see Pickett & Thompson, 1978; Webb & Hopkins, 1984). For this reason, many small heathlands of up to 5 ha (12 acres) in extent are very difficult to manage since there is an insufficient area to maintain a rotation and an inadequate source of colonists.

Controlled burning of heathland is a difficult operation. It is best carried out in the winter; indeed, in lowland Britain heather-burning is prohibited by law between 31 March and 1 November without a licence from the Ministry of Agriculture. For most of the winter, it is impossible to burn heather and gorse, despite their inflammable natures, as they are generally too damp. Occasionally, in a dry autumn, it may be possible to burn during November, but the best period is usually from mid-February until the end of March, when frosts and wind have dried the vegetation and before the new flush of spring growth commences. Heather can only be burned safely when the wind is light, and even under ideal conditions precautions are required to control the fire. A break of 5 m (16 ft) width with an irregular edge is made round the area to be burnt by cutting or swiping, and the cut material must be raked up and burnt (Pickess, 1983). During burning, the most effective control is achieved by directing a fine jet of water from a fire tender to regulate both the spread and intensity of the fire. Adequate results can also be obtained by helpers using fire beaters; such helpers should always be present as a precaution should the fire get out of control.

The aim of heather-burning is to remove all the above-ground vegetation cleanly yet leave the roots unharmed for regeneration. This effect is only obtained where the intensity of the fire is carefully controlled. The most satisfactory result is obtained when the fire is allowed to burn against the wind ('back-burning'). Not only does this produce a clean burn, but it is easier to control both in intensity and the speed at which it moves through the vegetation. If a fire is allowed to burn with the wind, the result is often poor: the flames run through the canopy, which then may be only partly burnt, and most of the woody stems are left unburnt, which is unsightly and hinders the regeneration of the heather. Accidental fires tend to be of this type; they occur in dry conditions in late winter, early spring, or at the height of the summer, and often when it is windy, so that the fire sweeps through the vegetation, out of control. In exceptionally dry conditions, such as the summers of 1975 and 1976, such fires can be very damaging, as not only the vegetation but also the upper layers of the litter and peat may be burnt, leaving only bare mineral soil. When this occurs there may be erosion and gullying, and regeneration is impeded since the seed-bank is depleted (Maltby, 1980a). Under well-controlled prescribed burning, the heather roots remain alive and capable of sprouting rapidly, and a luxuriant growth of young heather, which often flowers profusely, results in the first season. Generally, the capacity of heather to regenerate from roots declines with age (Miller & Miles, 1970; Hobbs & Gimingham, 1984b), and so it is best to have most of the heath under a twenty-year rotation.

In old stands, there is increasing regeneration from seeds, but this is more erratic and also declines with the age of the stand (Hobbs & Gimingham, 1984b). The deep litter layer present in old stands may hinder germination and establishment of seedlings; it should be raked up after a fire.

A mosaic of different-aged stands of heather often acts as an internal fire-break, especially where there is a good representation of the young age classes. On many heathlands, it is impossible to burn heather because of surrounding forestry plantations or houses. Sometimes, the area is too

Heathland management – cutting and baling heather

small to burn safely, although it is sometimes possible to use a flame torch. However, the problem of satisfactory regeneration and recolonisation remains. Cutting may be an alternative, and can be a good one for large heathlands since it does not depend on the weather.

Heather-cutting is a very old practice; it is known that from at least Roman times, bundles of heather were used as road foundations over wet ground and today, in the New Forest, it is still cut and baled commercially for this purpose. Heather can be cut throughout winter using a reciprocating mower, a tractor-mounted swipe or a forage harvester (larger machinery can only be used on flat, uniform areas). The debris can be raked up or collected with a baler. Regeneration from cut stools is generally good but decreases as the plants become older, and if the litter is not raked off, seedling regeneration is poor (Pickess, 1983).

Little, if any, attempt has been made to restore grazing on heathland although there is abundant historical evidence that it used to be widespread. In the Netherlands and Germany, flocks of sheep controlled by a shepherd are used for conservation management – with satisfactory results. It is essential to walk the sheep over the heath and not to allow them to graze freely within an enclosure, since the pattern of grazing is different. Such a flock can be run at a profit and has been shown to be more cost-effective than cutting in Germany (Kottmann et al., 1985).

The management of wet heath and bog communities is less well developed and neglected in many reserves. Frequently during accidental heathland fires these areas are burnt, with beneficial results, but there is seldom prescribed burning. The removal of accumulated litter of Purple Moor Grass, Black Bog Rush, *Calluna*, young birches, and Bog Myrtle, which colonize this habitat, improves it for species such as the Marsh Gentian, which flowers more profusely, setting seed, once the competition for space and nutrients is reduced (see chapter 9). Lack of management of this habitat is one of the reasons why the species has declined. The general floristic diversity of wet heath and bog communities is decreasing because bare areas, resulting from turf- and peat-cutting, are no longer created, and species such as Beak Sedge (*Rhynchospora* spp.) and Marsh Clubmoss (*Lycopodiella inundata*) no longer colonize. The latter species particularly favours bare, algae-covered ground, such as ruts and cart-tracks. On the bogs there are no longer pools of open water, so the succession of species of *Sphagnum* is not maintained; these pools are also important habitats for several dragonfly species. The restoration of conservation-management practices which create the right conditions is much-needed on almost all heaths.

Control of Scrub

Birch, pine and, in some places, gorse have invaded many of the southern heathlands; fire has not always controlled them effectively, and grazing by both domestic animals and rabbits has ceased. Besides birch and pine, Rhododendron can be a pernicious species, smothering ground vegetation and creating sterile conditions which persist even when the bushes have been cut down. Many heathlands in Surrey, north Hampshire and Dorset have been invaded by this ericaceous shrub.

Scrub may be controlled by cutting, spraying with herbicides or a combination of both: all three have limitations. Cutting requires a good deal of labour and is really only effective for coniferous species, which are killed outright, but deciduous species such as birch will sprout vigorously. They can be controlled by spraying with foliar herbicide but the dead scrub and trees remain, and must be cut down later. The cut stumps of small trees and scrub, especially birch and Rhododendron, can be treated with herbicide, either by brushing it on the freshly-cut end or, more effectively, by drilling holes into which a saturated solution of herbicide is poured. Ammonium sulphamate or glyphosate are non-selective herbicides which can be used in these ways, and ensure that the herbicide reaches its target. Other non-selective herbicides may be used as foliar sprays, but care has to be taken with their application as some may damage Heather. Although herbicides are a potent and cost-effective tool for the conservationist, there is resistance to their use since there may be adverse long-term effects. There must be a clear strategy for their application to ensure that only those species to be controlled are treated, that any spray-drift to other organisms is avoided and that there are adequate health and safety procedures for the operators. Foliar sprays can be applied with conventional spraying equipment or, more frequently now, with ultra-low-volume applicators, which produce a very fine haze of droplets. If the spray is too fine, there may be drift onto other species, and if the droplet size is too large, the herbicide will run off the foliage onto other plants. Ultra-low-volume sprays are portable and easy to use on uneven terrain; they do not require large volumes of liquid to dilute the herbicide. If the plants to be treated stand above the other species, a rope-wick applicator which smears the plants is very effective; there are both hand-held and tractor-mounted boom models available (Marrs, 1983).

Bracken is another invasive species on heathland; on many heaths in the south, its control now poses a major problem, especially since grazing and cutting no longer check its growth and over-burning encourages it to spread. Bracken can be controlled with herbicides or by cutting. It should be cut when the reserves of food in rhe rhizome are lowest – from mid-June to late July (Williams & Foley, 1976); if cutting is not confined to thi' time, the plant will have sufficient resources to grow another frond: indeed, a second cut in late July is recommended to check regrowth. A summertime cut reduces the average height of the bracken canopy but increases the frond density in the first year; thereafter, the plants are slowly weakened and eventually killed (Lowday, 1983).

In recent years, the herbicide Asulam has been used for bracken control, but its effect is not total. When sprayed on the fully-open yet young frond, it is translocated to the rhizome, where it impedes meristematic activity, killing developing buds. Asulam does not kill the bracken immediately and its effects are only apparent in the following season, when fewer fronds appear. The effect of the herbicide varies, depending on initial frond density and the type of stand. Reductions of from 63–98%, with an average of 82.5%, have been reported from field trials on Cannock Chase (Bostock, 1980), and in the Breckland, frond density was reduced by 95% and standing crop by 99% in the first season (Lowday, 1983). Without further treatment, the stand will recover and the fronds emerging in subsequent years (even up to 5 or 6 years) need to be sprayed or spot-treated to hold the bracken in check. However, this regrowth may be less easy to control, and increased strengths of herbicide are necessary (Pickess, 1983). There is considerable variability in the results of the trials and Daniels (1983) believes that different treatments are required on every site, involving not only spraying, but cutting and grazing with cattle or sheep. Trampling by animals also helps to eliminate Bracken, but nowhere has this alone been sufficient, and cutting or herbicide treatment is required. In some instances, supplementary food has to be given to the animals (Bostock, 1983).

Clearly, although Asulam cannot eradicate Bracken, it is very useful in controlling it. For instance, where Bracken is invading, the progression of the Bracken front can be held in check, or the invasion of recently-burnt heath controlled, but, generally, as work on Cannock Chase has shown, the eradication of large areas is difficult, not least because it is uncertain what type of plant and animal community will replace it. Beneath dense stands of Bracken there is frequently deep litter, which is unsuitable for the establishment of *Calluna* seedlings; but in less dense stands, where some heather plants persist, there may be recovery of heathland vegetation. Where there has been secondary treatment to check pioneer species, the establishment of heathland may be slow, but this can be accelerated by spreading heather litter or top soil.

Observations on the implications of Bracken control (Cadbury, 1976) suggest that Sheep's Sorrel (*Rumex acetosella*), young *Calluna* plants, some compositae, and some grasses, mainly species of *Poa*, *Holcus* and *Agrostis* (although not Bristle Bent (*A. curtisii*)) may be adversely affected by the spray. Where Bracken has been eliminated, the ground is colonized by pioneer species such as Wavy Hair Grass (*Deschampsia flexuosa*), Creeping Soft Grass (*Holcus mollis*), Rosebay (*Chamaenerion angustifolium*), Foxglove (*Digitalis purpurea*) and Nettle (*Urtica dioica*). These species require further control if heathland is to be established. Drawing mainly on upland examples, Nicholson and Paterson (1976) considered that control, affecting up to 25% of the Bracken area in Scotland, was unlikely to affect bird and mammal populations, but in mixed communities there may be effects on the animal communities. This view would certainly hold in the lowlands where the eradication or control of Bracken is considered desirable for the conservation of many heathland species, particularly the rare vertebrates. Where Bracken control is contemplated, clearly-defined conservation aims must be established, for it is not always the wisest or the simplest procedure to eliminate Bracken and establish another community in its place. It is best to determine whether Bracken is spreading into areas which need protection by marking the boundaries for a few seasons, or whether it is undergoing cyclical regeneration (Watt, 1955). Although it may be increasing in one spot, it may be declining in another, as happens in dense stands where the accumulation of litter checks growth and creates patches into which other heathland plants can spread (Watt, 1976).

As a rule, weedy species are seldom a problem on heathland, even as pioneers, since the soils are too poor. Nevertheless, on many small heathlands which are surrounded by agricultural land or urban areas, there may be invasions of these plants, such as Groundsel (*Senecio vulgaris*) and Annual Meadow Grass (*Poa annua*). These species do not usually establish permanently, but if they do they can be controlled by spot herbicide. Much more of a problem is Rosebay, for which the conditions after fires are ideal. This species, known as Fire Weed in the United States of America, where it is endemic, is characteristic of early successional stages. It can be controlled by handweeding, herbicides and, in some instances, is defoliated by the leaf beetle *Halictus lythri*.

Protection of Individual Species

One can take two views of heathland management. The whole community can be managed in an attempt to maintain a balance between the various species populations, or the community can be managed as the habitat of selected species. Care must be exercised to ensure that the latter view does not predominate, especially in the case of vertebrates, for the rare, space-demanding species may exist at densities too low to form viable populations. Even where these are maintained, they may still be too small to meet the personal preferences of ornithologists and herpetologists, who like to see densities inflated to artificially high levels. This is ecologically unacceptable and will affect the balance that can be struck with other species. At low population densities, genetic effects may be important, but it is considered likely that populations will become extinct through chance effects long before reduction in genetic variability leads to extinction (Berry, 1971; 1977).

Small populations living on isolated patches of heathland are likely to face extinction from chance effects, in the manner of classical island biogeographic theory (MacArthur & Wilson, 1967). An interventionist policy would seek to increase the effective size of the island for such species; the larger resulting population would be less prone to extinction. This may be important, since many of the rare heathland vertebrates, which have a high priority for conservation, are species living at the edges of their ranges in circumstances where random effects, particularly weather, are greatest. The best example is the Dartford Warbler, but isolated populations of Sand Lizard, Natterjack Toad and Smooth Snake are at risk too.

Corbett (1983) considers that general heath management is insufficient to met the needs of the Sand Lizard, and that the use of fire is harmful for this reptile. Its habitat preferences are for mature, dry heathland, where a home range of up to 250 sq m (300 sq yds) can be established round its burrow and in which there is a suitable location for hibernation. In recent years, conservation management for this animal has been directed towards maintaining a structural mosaic in mature heather without resorting to cutting, burning or grazing. If regeneration of scrub and trees is controlled, the heather reaches a mixed-age structure, with patches where there is regeneration from seedlings and adventitious rooting (Corbett, 1983). To further improve the habitat, pioneer trees are felled and bracken controlled, since both tend to create shady conditions unsuitable for the lizards. However, not all trees are removed, as a concession to the needs of some birds and aesthetics; their lower branches are cut – although this makes them useless for Dartford Warblers. Colonies of Sand Lizards with a density of up to 125 adults per ha (50 adults per acre) need about 20% of their habitat area to be bare sand amongst heather. Sand patches of 2 × 1 m (6.6 × 3.3 ft), lying east–west with a southerly aspect for maximum insolation, are recommended for egg-laying (Corbett & Tamarind, 1979); firebreaks may supplement the area of open sand available.

Many suggestions for maintaining Sand Lizard habitat rely on the perpetuation of mature *Calluna* with a mixed-age structure. Yet the Lizard occurs in a much wider range of habitats, and whether it is possible to maintain mixed-age *Calluna* without re-setting the growth cycle is a subject on which opinion is divided. In the short term, monitoring has shown these management prescriptions to be successful at a number of locations in southern England and have led to the restoration and enhancement of breeding populations and an increased number of juvenile and immature Lizards (Corbett & Tamarind, 1979). In some instances, translocations of Lizards from areas where they breed well to those where they have become extinct have been successful. One of the most important needs for all Sand Lizard sites is protection from accidental and uncontrolled fires.

Conservation management for the Sand Lizard has been directed towards habitat management, since the species survives well where the optimum habitat is maintained (decline has been due to habitat loss). Many of the habitat requirements are similar to those of the Smooth Snake, but in the latter species, features of the life history are also important. Smooth Snake population growth is slow and populations live in equilibrium at densities which approach the carrying capacity of their habitat (in evolutionary terms they are said to be 'k-selected'). Such species cannot respond rapidly to sudden changes in their surroundings, and conservation management for the Smooth Snake needs to be directed towards enhancing reproduction. Fecundity is determined by weather and food supply: habitat management should ensure that females have adequate basking conditions for incubation by making use of natural topographic variation or, where this is insufficient, by the creation of embankments. The food supply can be increased by allowing scrub to grow up, providing additional habitat for small mammals which form their prey. It is more difficult to provide invertebrate populations to support larger numbers of rodents. Adequate overwintering conditions have also to be provided (Goddard, 1983).

Because it reproduces slowly and disperses with difficulty, the Smooth Snake is much more at risk from the effects of heathland fragmentation than many species. Since the quality of many isolated fragments is variable, the future of any Smooth Snake population on them looks uncertain. Management of heather by burning is also harmful, since the snakes cannot survive the fire or recolonize quickly afterwards. The Smooth Snake is not entirely confined to heathland, although the structure of this community usually provides it with optimum habitat; various other communities which provide similarly open conditions will meet its requirements and it is plausible that non-heathland or only partly heathy areas could be managed to provide supplementary habitat (Goddard, 1983).

Of all the heathland rarities, the Dartford Warbler was considered by Moore (1962) to have the highest priority for conservation. This bird is a classic example of a species living at the edge of its range, where random effects, particularly bad winter weather, can deplete numbers. Like so many other heathland rarities, site protection is paramount (Bibby, 1978a; Bibby & Tubbs, 1975), and adequately-protected nature reserves are required, since reserves where there is no security of tenure prevent satisfactory management work from being implemented. The Dartford Warbler population of 560 pairs in the New Forest in 1974 represented saturation of all the available habitat; thus, any losses of sites would have reduced the carrying capacity. Bibby considered that the serious damage to heathland caused by the fires of 1975 and 1976, when 11% of all heathland and 20% of Dartford Warbler habitats in Dorset were destroyed, was detrimental to the bird's long-term prospects since the recovery of so large an area of heathland would be slow and its carrying capacity for Dartford Warbler seriously reduced for a long time.

The control and management of gorse, birch, pine, Bracken and grazing are essential features of habitat management. Gorse is vitally important for shelter and as a source of insect food throughout the year, especially during the winter and early spring. Bibby (1978a) recommends that up to 5% of an area of heathland should be gorse; this will support about 25 pairs of Dartford Warbler per sq km (64 per sq mile) by providing about 1000–2000 sq m (1200–2400 sq yds) of gorse in each territory of 2.5 ha (6.2 acres). If a heathland is divided into territories of this size, and about one-fifteenth of the gorse cut or burnt each winter, a rotation is established which meets the needs of the birds. Gorse management aims at maintaining a maximum of dense bushes, lacking the leggy growth and hollow interiors which tend to develop in gorse over twelve years old. When there is insufficient gorse, it should be planted, and this may be encouraged by the creation of embankments, which may also be beneficial to reptiles (Bibby, 1978). Pine encroaching on to open heathland, while remaining young, and while the branches are still in contact with the heather canopy, is also beneficial. These trees should be removed once their branches lose contact with the heather canopy.

The present absence of the Dartford Warbler from the north-east and south-west of its range because there are too few colonists, suggests that the translocation of individuals may be possible: immature birds could be captured in autumn, when they normally disperse, kept in captivity through the winter, and released at new locations in the spring. These birds can be kept easily in captivity and, even in the field, supplementary feeding with meal worms in hard weather may enable larger numbers to survive (Bibby, 1978a). However, it is difficult to envisage how this would be done.

Prescriptions of this detail for the conservation of the Dartford Warbler are based on a thorough study of population dynamics, habitat selection, feeding and carrying capacity, and illustrate how well-executed research enables conservation measures to be planned. For other species of heathland birds there is less information. The Red-backed Shrike is likely to become extinct in Britain as a breeding bird; habitat loss is part of the cause but it has declined throughout its north-west European range and climatic change is a more likely cause. For the Hobby there is insufficient detailed information but, as with all raptors, conservation is difficult because of the relatively large undisturbed areas required. The Woodlark is also poorly known. Habitat management has been successful in the case of the Nightjar (Bibby, 1979b; Berry & Bibby, 1981). This bird is dependent on the ecotone between woodland and heathland, relying on the open heath for nest sites and the woodland edges for feeding. In East Anglia, these authors report that by checking the invasion of birch scrub and providing a broken edge with glades and islands of trees, the habitat was improved. Clearings of up to 0.5 ha (1.2 acres) were used as feeding areas. Nest sites were made by clearing patches 1–2 m (3.3–6.6 ft) wide in mature heather close to a single tree; these sites have increased the number of breeding pairs and have been unusually successful (Bibby, 1983).

Traditionally, it has been the view in conservation management that invertebrate communities will be maintained if the plant communities are managed satisfactorily. It is now realized that this may not be so and that the requirements of many species are precise. This has been ably demonstrated for butterflies, where even a few millimetres difference in turf height renders an area unsuitable for some species, even though its foodplant may still be growing in abundance (Thomas, 1984). Changes in the structure of heathland vegetation affect the composition of the invertebrate populations, but we do not know how to manage heathland optimally for invertebrates, especially since it is important to have an adequate representation for all successional stages. Furthermore, eutrophication of heathland may alter the density of invertebrate populations, and where there is run-off or spray-drift, attempts should be made to control them. In some instances, careful application of some fertilizer, especially nitrogen, might provide a means of regulating invertebrate populations, and hence the food supply of some vertebrates.

The Grayling and the Silver-studded Blue have both declined, largely through habitat loss. General management benefits the Grayling, whose foodplants are grasses. It is a species of heathland margins and not heather communities, and has benefited from the construction of firebreaks. For the Silver-studded Blue, we are hardly in a position to suggest management prescriptions since we know so little of its life history. Most importantly, we do not know to what extent it depends on ants.

Dragonflies are a group for which successful conservation measures have been taken. Requirements vary from ponds and boggy seepages to running water; shelter is also important, particularly at pool margins, where there is maximum insolation. The greatest number occurs in shallow, warm, acid pools and ponds with plenty of aquatic vegetation and well-established emergent vegetation, and suitable areas of mud. Other species need more specialized conditions, such as small pools amongst the *Sphagnum* in the valley bogs or in small seepages (Chelmick *et al.*, 1980). Dragonfly ponds can be dug by hand or created with explosives, and on the Surrey and Dorset heaths, ponds have been established with some success. Pickess (1983) recommends that they should be no less than 20 m (66 ft) in circumference with a depth at the centre of 1.5 m (4.9 ft). Besides digging ponds, the restoration of peat-cutting in the lowland valley bogs would be of inestimable value in providing the early successional stages of the bog communities on which a few species depend.

We know little of the habitat requirements of other invertebrates, such as the Heath Grasshopper (*Chorthippus vagans*), the Speckled Footman (*Coscinia cribraria*), the Ground Beetle (*Carabus nitens*), or the Raft Spider (*Dolomedes fimbriatus*). Many of these species are no rarer than their habitat, but we cannot be certain, and there have been few conservation measures specifically for invertebrates. Diversity is probably the best course of action and the entomologist will probably prefer heathlands with all the successional stages of the heather community represented – some ants and spiders depend on the early open successional stages – and appreciable amounts of gorse, willow and birch scrub. These are all plants with rich herbivore faunas, and much of the alleged richness of the southern heathlands is derived from these species rather than the heather communities.

Other vital habitats that are frequently missing are bare, open, sandy areas in eroded patches, now maintained as heather. Such bare areas are the habitat of Tiger Beetles and Sand Wasps, as well as being valuable to reptiles. An overlooked feature of invertebrate conservation is the fact that many insects require quite different habitats for their larval and adult stages, if not a further one for the pupa, and these need to be provided adjacent to one another for the completion of the life cycle. Sand Wasps require bare sand patches to construct their larval burrows but also need mature heathland vegetation to hunt for the caterpillars with which they provision their burrows.

When reviewing the problems of insect conservation on heathlands, neither Stubbs (1983) nor Webb (1983) were able to make more than general points. To summarize, the continuity of the plant cover should be maintained, with an adequate representation of the different compositional and structural types of vegetation; bare sandy areas are important; the richest fauna is generally associated with the mature and degenerate stands of heather and there should be adequate representation of various type of scrub and aquatic habitats; lastly, the surroundings may modify the composition of the fauna on a heathland, and this is particularly important on small, isolated heathlands (Webb *et al.*, 1984).

This summary of conservation methods on heathlands highlights the problems of meeting the requirements of all species on a single heathland reserve unless it is very large. In some instances, the management for one species may be complementary to the needs of other species; thus, the bare, sandy areas required for reptile conservation may meet the needs of several insects, the creation of additional scrub for birds also increases the insect population, embankments covered with scrub for birds are beneficial to reptiles. But the maintenance of extensive areas of mature heathland does not satisfy the requirements of those insects which need the early successional stages of heather. On small reserves, it is impossible to meet all these needs and management can only be for selected species. However, on large reserves, which are intrinsically more satisfactory, most needs can be met by rotational management. An alternative is to manage each heath of a group for different species which, taken as a whole, would fill the needs of a range of species. The large-scale management of vegetation by burning and cutting is one of the most cost-effective approaches, but this is harmful to many species, especially reptiles, and a balance must be struck. Because heathland vegetation is very inflammable, protection is essential: both swiped and mown firebreaks should be provided, which themselves may add to the range of habitats; fire-beaters should be located at strategic points.

Recreation and Amenity

Within an 80-km (50-m) radius of London there are many heathlands. Most are scattered fragments but some larger areas persist in Surrey and northern Hampshire. Likewise the New Forest, Dorset and Devon where heathlands coincide with areas subjected to severe tourist pressures. Around London, these heathlands are some of the last remaining open spaces and there is a strong case for their maintenance as an amenity, for visitors, riders and motorcyclists and general recreation (Harrison, 1983). Heathland vegetation is about ten times more susceptible to wear than adjacent acid and neutral grasslands (Harrison, 1981). *Calluna* is a most sensitive plant and often dies as a result of trampling or vehicle pressures, leading to erosion and extensive bare areas. On these heathlands, the fire risk is great and directly correlated with the local density of population (Maltby, 1980b); fires are frequent and harmful to the vegetation. If these heathlands are to persist and be of value for both conservation and recreation, it is essential to plan and control their use, by providing car parks, paths, information and education centres, and by managing the vegetation as a grass-heath-scrub mosaic. This would be acceptable to most visitors and would partly meet conservation needs, but the prime conservation areas must be concentrated on the remoter heathlands to the south-west, away from the suburban areas. The heaths nearest London should have management objectives primarily orientated towards amenity, and conservation or dual-purpose management must depend on location (Harrison, 1983).

Restoration

To many, the notion that land can be rehabilitated, restored or manipulated to produce given habitats is an anathema and contrary to the spirit of conservation. It is a paradox that there should be attempts to protect sites and species if other areas can be restored; this, it is argued, tends to encourage wanton destruction of sites. But this need not be the case, and it should be remembered that there are many sites which, although protected, have had their conservation interest destroyed through insufficient, or inappropriate, management. To restore land requires the application of the same ecological knowledge as conservation management, and such a practice can support conservation measures by enabling adjacent land to be improved (in conservation terms) to support a site which is a reserve. Earlier, we have seen how the carrying capacity of heathland for Dartford Warblers can easily be reduced, and it would be beneficial for this bird if adjacent areas could be managed to meet its needs.

Rehabilitation is appropriate on abandoned fields, which were created from heathland, cleared forests, or areas where the heathland plant community has been modified and where there may still be scattered heather plants. The vegetation of such areas may be dominated by grasses, such as Wavy Hair Grass (*Deschampsia flexuosa*), Bristle Bent (*Agrostis curtisii*) or Purple Moor Grass (*Molinia caerulea*) through over-grazing or over-burning. They may also arise as a result of the run-off or spray-drift from fertilizers, or the invasion of agricultural weeds. In the Netherlands, the dominance of Wavy Hair Grass in many communities which were formerly heathland has been attributed to eutrophication caused by agriculture and air pollution. Nitrogen status of heathland vegetation affects the composition and density of its insect fauna. On these Dutch heathlands increased outbreaks of Heather Beetle (*Lochmaea suturalis*) have been attributed to increased nitrogen in the vegetation (Diement & Heil, 1984; Brunsting, 1982), and the damage caused by the beetles has allowed grass communities to replace *Calluna* heathland.

The seed-bank remaining in the soils can be used to restore heathland vegetation with techniques such as mowing, rotovating, turf-stripping or grazing. In these practices, the seeds are exposed and encouraged to germinate; the balance of competition is altered in favour of heathland plants (Bakker, 1978; Bakker *et al.*, 1983; Webb, 1985). Light sheep-grazing has been found to check seedlings of woody species, but at higher densities their dung encourages grasses; however, sheep-grazing on abandoned fields reclaimed from heathland enables vegetation to be restored (Bakker *et al.*, 1983). A single application of nitrogen after turf-stripping enhanced *Calluna* growth, but repeated applications alter the composition of the vegetation (Helsper *et al.*, 1983). Where there is a very small seed-bank in the soil, the application of heather seeds or scattering of litter or topsoil containing seeds may be needed. Rotovating and turf-stripping are both ways in which the buried seed-bank can be exposed to enable heather seeds to germinate. Turf-stripping has the advantage that nutrients are also removed from the upper layers of the soil, helping to maintain a low nutrient status which may offset the input from agriculture and pollution.

Techniques for restoring heathland on derelict areas, disused mineral workings, damaged land, erosion caused by excessive recreation, road schemes and pipelines are now well established (Gillham & Putwain, 1977; Putwain *et al.*, 1982). All these methods rely on the application of propagules of heathland species onto prepared areas. Seed may be obtained from commercial merchants but is often expensive and not of native varieties; it may be collected from existing heathlands, by hand or with a forage harvester. Heather plants can be raised from seeds or from cuttings and transplanted. Heather turves can be laid, but these have to be obtained from existing heathland, which may thus be damaged. How-

Mineral workings suitable for restoration/ N. R. Webb

ever, all methods rely on an existing area of heathland as a source of propagules. An effective method is to use the seed bank in the litter and topsoil of heathland; this also causes damage but does so in a way in which the vegetation can regenerate. It may offer an alternative form of heathland management to cutting or burning and is one which mimics the ancient practice of turf-cutting (turbary), which was in part responsible for maintaining open heathland in the past. To use this method, the vegetation is flailed and the top few centimetres of litter and topsoil rotivated. The resulting loose material is then taken up for spreading on to the site to be restored. The remaining roots and newly-exposed seed-bank on the donor site enable it to regenerate. The litter and topsoil are spread on the new site, which has been prepared to provide the nutrient-poor subsoil required by heathland vegetation. Where there is liable to be erosion, companion grasses with a low productivity, such as *Deschampsia flexuosa* or *Agrostis castellana*, can be sown at low rates of 10–15 kg per ha; and, if the soil is very poor and acid, up to 25 kg per ha of NPK fertilizer with up to 2000 kg (4400 lb) of ground limestone can be applied, but great care must be taken not to encourage non-heathland species (Putwain, 1983).

This type of treatment enables heather communities to be restored on filled mineral workings, road embankments, and places where the vegetation has been destroyed. Disused mineral workings offer considerable scope for restoration schemes as a varied topography can be constructed with earth-moving equipment to create typical heathland basins, with dry heath on the higher surroundings grading into a bog system. By introducing a range of propagules, a whole variety of typical heathland plant communities can be established, from dry heath to a valley bog with *Sphagnum* communities. Once the general vegetation has been established, rarities such as the Marsh Gentian or the Sand Lizard can be introduced.

In recent years, there have been several successful instances of reinstatement following the laying of gas or oil pipelines across heathland, and methods are now well established from the north of England and Scotland (Gillham & Putwain, 1977) and from lowland heath (Burden, 1979). If there is no reinstatement, natural regeneration can be very slow and be mostly of weeds, rushes and grasses, but where care is taken, heathland regenerates. For restoration of pipeline areas, terram sheets are laid either side of the pipeline (Fig. 51); on one side, sand is laid to provide a trackway for vehicles, and on the other the soil from the trench is laid (in order of its horizons), heather turves having been first cut from the line of the pipe. The pipe, which is usually 20–25 cm (8–10 in) in diameter, is laid in the trench and the trench filled in with the material in the reverse order to which it was removed; finally, the heather turves are replaced and the

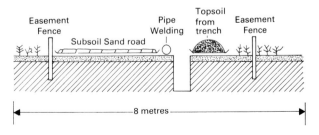

Fig. 51
Pipeline Restoration

sheeting taken up. Very little damage is caused to the heathland vegetation. Some techniques do not provide for a roadway, and in these cases there may be serious damage. The method was adopted on Hartland Moor NNR, where recovery was excellent after two years and the visual impact of the pipeline was minimal (Burden, 1979). One may disagree in principle with the laying of pipelines across nature reserves, but these excellent results suggest that it may be less harmful than imagined. One of the most difficult features of such operations is the control of the contractors doing the work, and this is essential if a high standard of restoration is to result.

Conservation is not ecology; it is one of a number of subjects which draw upon ecological science for its promotion; it is an application of ecological science, and in these later sections we have touched upon aspects of heathland ecology which can be used in the planning and execution of conservation management, amenity and recreation and restoration. The range of heathland ecology has been set out in the earlier chapters: the physical environment of climate and soils, the composition and structure of the vegetation, the dynamics of the plant community, the populations of animals and their interactions with each other and with the whole community, the factors affecting the distribution and abundance of rare species, and the influence of Man which, over many centuries, has regulated the natural succession and the nature of the interactions between the constituent populations. This background of ecological science, which is still incomplete, enables us to understand the existence, structure and functions of heathland communities, and therefore we are able to appraise and derive methods of maintaining them as a characteristic feature of our landscape.

References for Further Reading

Allen, S. E. (1964). Chemical aspects of heather burning. *J. appl. Ecol.* 1:347-67.
Allen, S. E., Evans, C. C. & Grimshaw, H. M. (1969). The distribution of mineral nutrients in soil after heather burning. *Oikos* 20:16-25.
Armstrong, P. H. (1973). Changes in the land use of the Suffolk Sandlings: a study in the disintegration of an ecosystem. *Geography* 58:1-8.
Avery, R. A. (1966). Food and feeding habits of the Common Lizard (*Lacerta vivipara*) in the west of England. *J. Zool. Lond.* 149:115-21.
Avery, R. A. (1971). Estimates of the food consumption by the lizard *Lacerta vivipara* Jacquin. *J. Anim. Ecol.* 40:351-65.

Bakker, J. P. (1978). Some experiments on heathland conservation and regeneration. *Phytocoenosis* 7:347-70.
Bakker, J. P., de Bie, S., Dallinga, J. H., Tjaden, P. & de Vries, Y. (1983). Sheep grazing as a management tool for heathland conservation and regeneration in the Netherlands. *J. appl. Ecol.* 20:541-60.
Bannister, P. (1964a). Stomatal responses of heath plants to water deficits. *J. Ecol.* 52:151-8.
Bannister, P. (1964b). The water relations of certain heath plants with reference to their ecological amplitude. I. Introduction, germination and establishment. *J. Ecol.* 52:423, 432.
Bannister, P. (1964c). The water relations of certain heath plants with reference to their ecological amplitude. II. Field studies. *J. Ecol.* 52:481-497.
Bannister, P. (1964d). The water relations of certain heath plants with reference to their ecological amplitude. *J. Ecol.* 53:499-509.
Bannister, P. (1965). Biological flora of the British Isles. *Erica cinerea* L. *J. Ecol.* 53:527-542.
Bannister, P. (1966). Biological flora of the British Isles: *Erica tetralix* L. *J. Ecol.* 54:795-813.
Barclay-Estrup, P. (1970). The description and interpretation of cyclical processes in a heath community. II. Changes in biomass and shoot production during the *Calluna* cycle. *J. Ecol.* 58:243-9.
Barclay-Estrup, P. (1971). The description and interpretation of cyclical processes in a heath community. III. Microclimate in relation to the *Calluna* cycle. *J. Ecol.* 59:143-66.

Barclay-Estrup, P. (1974). Arthropod populations in a heathland as related to cyclical changes in the vegetation. *Entomologists' mon. Mag.* 109:79-84.
Barclay-Estrup, P. & Gimingham, C. H. (1969). The description and interpretation of cyclical processes in a heath community. I. Vegetational change in relation to the *Calluna* cycle. *J. Ecol.* 57:737-58.
Bayfield, N. G. (1984). The dynamics of heather (*Calluna vulgaris*) stripes in the Cairngorm mountains, Scotland. *J. Ecol.* 72:515-27.
Beebee, T. J. C. (1973). Observation concerning the decline of British amphibia. *Biol. Conserv.* 5:20-4.
Beebee, T. J. C. (1977). Environmental changes as a cause of Natterjack (*Bufo calamita*) declines in Britain. *Biol. Conserv.* 11:87-100.
Beebee, T. J. C. (1983a). Habitat selection by amphibians across an agricultural land–heathland transect in Britain. *Biol. Conserv.* 27:111-24.
Beebee, T. J. C. (1983b). *The Natterjack Toad.* Oxford: Oxford University Press.
Beijerinck, W. (1940). *Calluna*: a monograph on Scotch heather. *Verh. Akad. Wet. Amst* (3rd Sect.). 38:1-180.
Beirne, B. P. (1952). *The Origin and History of the British Fauna.* London: Methuen.
Berry, R. (1979). Nightjar habitats and breeding in East Anglia. *British Birds.* 72:207-18.
Berry, R. & Bibby, C. J. (1981). A breeding study of Nightjars. *Brit. Birds.* 74:161-69.
Berry, R. J. (1971). Conservation aspects of the genetical constitution of populations. In Duffey, E. and Watt, A. S. (eds.) *The Scientific Management of Animal and Plant Communities for Conservation.* Blackwell, Oxford.
Berry, R. J. (1977). *Inheritance and Natural History.* London: Collins New Naturalist.
Betty, J. H. & Wilde, D. S. (1977). The probate inventories of Dorset farmers 1573-1670. *Local Hist.* 12:228-34.
Bhadresa, R. (1981). Identification of leaf epidermal fragments in rabbit faeces (with special reference to heathland vegetation). Rogate Papers No. 4, King's College, London.
Bhadresa, R. (1984). In press. Faecal analysis and exclosure studies. In Moore, P. D. & Chapman,

REFERENCES FOR FURTHER READING

S. B. (eds.) *Methods in Plant Ecology*, 2nd edition. Blackwell Scientific Publications, Oxford.

Bibby, C. J. (1973). The Red-backed Shrike: a vanishing British species. *Bird Study*. 20:103–10.

Bibby, C. J. (1978a). Conservation of the Dartford Warbler on English lowland heaths: a review. *Biological Conservation*. 13:299–307.

Bibby, C. J. (1978b). A heathland bird census. *Bird Study*. 25:87–96.

Bibby, C. J. (1979a). Food of the Dartford Warbler *Sylvia undata* on southern English heathland. *J. Zool. Lond*. 188:557–76.

Bibby, C. J. (1979b). Mortality and movement of Dartford Warblers in England. *Brit. Birds*. 72: 10–22.

Bibby, C. J. (1983). Heathland management for birds. In Farrell, L. (ed.) Focus on Nature Conservation No. 2. Heathland Management. Nature Conservancy Council, Shrewsbury.

Bibby, C. J. & Tubbs, C. R. (1975). Status, habitats and conservation of the Dartford Warbler in England. *British Birds*. 68:477–95.

Boer, P. J. den (1977). Dispersal power and survival: Carabids in a cultivated countryside. Miscellaneous Papers 14 (1977). Landbouwhogeschool Wageningen, The Netherlands.

Bøcher, T. W. (1943). Studies on the plant geography of the north Atlantic heath formation. II. Danish dwarf shrub communities in relation to those of northern Europe. *K. Danske vidensk. Selsk., Biol. Skr*. 2:1–129.

Bostock, J. L. (1980). The effects of spraying and respraying bracken (*Pteridium aquilinum* L. Kuhn) in heathland with asulox. *Bull. Soc. Ecol. Fr*. 11: 717–23.

Bostock, J. L. (1983). Countryside Commission management experiments on Cannock Chase. In Farrell, L. (ed.) Focus on Nature Conservation No. 2. Heathland Management. Nature Conservancy Council, Shrewsbury.

Brian, A. D. (1957). Differences in flowers visited by four species of bumble bees and their causes. *J. Anim. Ecol*. 26:71–98.

Brian, M. V. (1964). Ant distribution in a southern English heath. *J. Anim. Ecol*. 33:451–61.

Brian, M. V. (1977). *Ants*. Collins New Naturalist, London.

Brian, M. V., Mountford, M. D., Abbott, A. & Vincent, S. (1976). The changes in ant species distribution during ten years post-fire regeneration of a heath. *J. Anim. Ecol*. 45:115–33.

Bridges, E. M. (1970). *World Soils*. Cambridge: Cambridge University Press.

Brightmore, D. (1968). Biological Flora of the British Isles. *Lobelia urens* L. *J. Ecol*. 56:613–20.

Brøndsted, J. (1965). *The Vikings*. Harmondsworth: Penguin.

Brown, A. & MacFadyen, A. (1969). Soil carbon dioxide output and small scale vegetation pattern in a *Calluna* heath. *Oikos*. 20:8–15.

Brown, S. C. S. (1960). A note on the early history of *Coscinia cribrum* L. *Entomologists' Record*. 72:92–4.

Brunsting, A. M. H. (1982). The influence of the dynamics of a population of herbivorous beetles on the development of vegetation patterns in a heathland system. In Visser, J. H. & Minks, A. K. (eds.) *Proc. 5th Int. Symp. Insect–Plant Relationships*, Wageningen, 1982, pp. 215–23. Pudock, Wageningen.

Burden, R. F. (1979). Landscape scientist in a county planning office. *Landscape Design* 126, 9.

Burgess, C. (1980). *The Age of Stonehenge*. London: Dent.

Burnham, C. P. (1983). The vegetation of Ashdown Forest and its management. *Seesoil* 1:100–107.

Cadbury, C. J. (1976). Botanical implications of bracken control. *Bot. J. Linn. Soc*. 73:285–95.

Cameron, A. E., McHardy, J. W. & Bennett, T. T. (1944). The heather beetle (*Lochmaea suturalis*); its biology and control. British Field Sports Society, Petworth.

Chadwick, L. (1982). *In Search of Heathland*. Durham: Dobson.

Chapin, F. S. (1980). The mineral nutrition of wild plants. *Annual Review of Ecology and Systematics* 11:223–60.

Chapman, S. B. (1967). Nutrient budgets for a dry heath ecosystem in the south of England. *J. Ecol*. 58:445–52.

Chapman, S. B. (1970). The nutrient content of the soil and root system of a dry heath ecosystem. *J. Ecol*. 58:445–52.

Chapman, S. B. (1975). The distribution and composition of hybrid populations of *Erica ciliaris* L. and *Erica tetralix* L. in Dorset. *J. Ecol*. 63:809–23.

Chapman, S. B. (1979). Some inter-relationships between soil and root respiration in lowland *Calluna* heathlands in southern England. *J. Ecol*. 67:1–20.

Chapman, S. B. (1984). The phosphorus economy of lowland heathland. *Annu. Rep. Inst. terr. Ecol*. 1983. pp. 81–3.

Chapman, S. B., Hibble, J. & Rafarel, C. R. (1975a). Net aerial production by *Calluna vulgaris* on lowland heath in Britain. *J. Ecol*. 63:233–58.

Chapman, S. B., Hibble, J. & Rafarel, C. R. (1957b). Litter accumulation under *Calluna vulgaris* on a lowland heathland in Britain. *J. Ecol*. 63:259–71.

Chapman, S. B. & Clarke, R. T. (1980). Some relationships between soil, climate, standing crop and organic matter accumulation within a range of *Calluna*-heathlands in Britain. *Bull. Soc. Ecol. Fr*. 11:221–32.

Chapman, S. B. & Rose, R. J. (1980). The establish-

ment of seedling on lowland heaths. *Annu. Rep. Inst. terr. Ecol.* 1979. pp. 86–8.
Chapman, S. B. & Rose, R. J. (1983). Ecological studies on the Marsh Gentian (*Gentiana pneumonanthe*). *Annu. Rep. Inst. terr. Ecol.* 1982, 74–7.
Chapman, S. B. & Webb, N. R. (1978). The productivity of *Calluna* heathland in southern England. In Heal, O. W. & Perkins, D. F. (eds.) Production Ecology of some British Moors and Montane Grasslands. pp. 247–62. Springer-Verlag, Berlin.
Chapple, F. J. (1952). *The Heather Garden*. London: Collingridge.
Chapuis, J. L. (1980). Analyse de la distribution spatiale du lapin de garenne *Oryctolagus cuniculus* (L.) sur une lande bretonne. *Bull. Soc. Ecol. Fr.* 11:571–85.
Chapuis, J. L. & Lefeuvre, J. C. (1980). Evolution saisonniere du régime alimentaire du lapin de garenne *Oryctolagus cuniculus* (L.) sur une lande bretonne. *Bull. Soc. Ecol. Fr.* 11:587–97.
Chelmick, D., Hammond, C., Moore, N. & Stubbs, A. (1980). The conservation of dragonflies. Nature Conservancy Council.
Conway, E. (1957). Spore production in bracken (*Pteridium aquilinum* (L.) Kuhn). *J. Ecol.* 45: 273–84.
Coppins, B. J. & Shimwell, D. W. (1971). Cryptogram complement and biomass in dry *Calluna* heath of different ages. *Oikos* 22:204–9.
Cooke, A. S. & Ferguson, P. F. (1975). Is the Palmate Newt a montane species? *Brit. J. Hrrpetol.* 5:460–3.
Cooke, A. S. & Frazer, J. F. D. (1976). Characteristics of newt breeding sites. *J. Zool. Lond.* 178:223–36.
Coombe, D. E. & Frost, L. C. (1956a). The heaths of the Cornish serpentine. *J. Ecol.* 44:226–56.
Coombe, D. E. & Frost, L. C. (1956b). The nature and origin of the soils over the Cornish serpentine. *J. Ecol.* 44:605–15.
Corbett, K. (1983). Heathland management for the Sand Lizard. In Farrell, L. (ed.). Focus on Nature Conservation No. 2. Heathland Management. Nature Conservancy Council, Shrewsbury.
Corbett, K. F. & Tamarind, D. L. (1979). Conservation of the Sand Lizard, *Lacerta agilis*, by habitat management. *Brit. J. Herpetol.* 5:799–823.
Cormack, E. & Gimingham, C. H. (1964). Litter production by *Calluna vulgaris* (L.) Hull. *J. Ecol.* 52: 285–97.

Damman, A. W. H. (1957). The south Swedish *Calluna*-heath and its relation to the Calluno-Genistetum. *Bot. Notiser.* 110:363–98.
Daniels, J. L. (1983). Bracken control in mixed heather and bracken stands. In Daniels, J. L. (ed.). Heathland Management in Amenity Areas. Countryside Commission, Cheltenham.
Daniels, R. E. & Pearson, M. C. (1974). Ecological studies at Roydon Common, Norfolk. *J. Ecol.* 62: 127–50.
Derby, H. C. & Welldon Finn, R. (1967). *The Domesday Geography of South-west England*. Cambridge: Cambridge University Press.
Delany, M. J. (1953). Studies on the microclimate of *Calluna* heathland. *J. Anim. Ecol.* 22:227–39.
Delany, M. J. (1954). Studies on the life history and ecology of *Dilta littoralis* (Wormersley, 1930) (Thysanura: Machilidae). *Trans. R. ent. Soc. London* 105:31–63.
Delany, M. J. (1956). The animal communities of three areas of pioneer heath in south-west England. *J. Anim. Ecol.* 25:112–26.
Diemont, W. H., Blanckenborg, F. G. & Kampf, H. (eds.). (1982). Blij op de hei. Innoveties in het heidebeheer. *Rapport. werkgr. verwerking/afzet heide plaggen.* Statsbosbeheer, Utrecht, Netherlands.
Diemont, W. H. & Heil, G. W. (1984). Some longterm observations on cyclical and seral processes in Dutch heathlands. *Biol. Conserv.* 30:283–91.
Dimbleby, G. W. (1962). The development of British heathlands and their soils. Oxford Forestry Memoirs. 23:1–121.
Dimbleby, G. W. (1967). The history and archaeology of heaths. In Sankey, J. H. P. & Mackworth-Praed, H. W. The Southern Heathlands. Surrey Naturalists' Trust.
Diver, C. (1933). The physiography of South Haven Peninsula, Studland Heath, Dorset. *Geogrl. J.* 81: 404–27.
Duffey, E. (1962). A population study of spiders in limestone grassland. Description of study area, sampling methods and population characteristics. *J. Anim. Ecol.* 31:571–99.
Duffey, E. (1976). Breckland. In Nature in Norfolk: a heritage in Trust. Norfolk Naturalists' Trust/Jarrold, Norwich.

Etherington, J. R. (1981). Limestone heaths in south-west Britain: their soils and the maintenance of their calcicole–calcifuge mixtures. *J. Ecol.* 69: 277–94.
Eyebert, M. C. (1980). Dynamique de la reproduction de la Linotte melodieuse (*Ancanthis cannabina*) sur une lande bretonne. *Bull. Soc. Ecol. Fr.* 11:543–58.
Elmes, G. W. (1971). An experimental study on the distribution of heathland ants. *J. Anim. Ecol.* 40: 495–9.
Elton, C. S. (1927). *Annimal Ecology*. London: Sidgwick & Jackson.
Evans, C. C. & Allen, S. E. (1971). Nutrient losses in smoke produced during heather burning. *Oikos* 22:149–54.

Farrell, L. (1983). The current state and objectives of management of British heaths. In Daniels, J. L. (ed.). Heathland Management in Amenity Areas. Countryside Commission, Cheltenham.

Farrow, E. P. (1925). *Plant life of East Anglian Heaths.* Cambridge: Cambridge University Press.

Findley, R., Young, M. R. & Findlay, J. A. (1983). Orientation behaviour in the Grayling butterfly: thermoregulation or crypsis. *Ecol. Entomol.* 8: 145–53.

Forrest, G. I. (1971). Structure and production of north Pennine blanket bog vegetation. *J. Ecol.* 59: 453–79.

Forrest, G. I. & Smith, R. A. H. (1975). The productivity of a range of blanket bog vegetation types in the northern Pennines. *J. Ecol.* 63:173–202.

Frazer, D. (1983). *Reptiles and Amphibians in Britain.* London: Collins New Naturalist.

Fritsch, F. E. & Salisbury, E. J. (1915). Further observations on the heath association of Hindhead Common. *New Phytol.* 14:116–38.

Froment, F. (1981). Conservation of Calluno–Vaccinietum heathland in the Belgian Ardennes, an experimental approach. *Vegetatio.* 47:193–200.

Fussell, G. E. (1952). Four centuries of farming in Dorset, 1500–1900. *Proc. Dorset. nat Hist. archaeol. Soc.* 73:116–40.

Gillham, D. A. & Putwain, P. D. (1977). Restoring moorland disturbed by pipeline installation. *Landscape Design.* 119:34–6.

Gimingham, C. H. (1960). Biological flora of the British Isles: *Calluna vulgaris* (L.) Hull. *J. Ecol.* 48:455–83.

Gimingham, C. H. (1961). North European heath communities: a network of variation. *J. Ecol.* 49: 655–94.

Gimingham, C. H. (1964). Dwarf shrub heathlands. In Burnett, J. H. (ed.). *The Vegetation of Scotland.* Edinburgh: Oliver & Boyd.

Gimingham, C. H. (1971). British heathland ecosystems: the outcome of many years of management by fire. *Proc. Annu. Tall Timbers Fire Ecol. Conf.* 10:293–321.

Gimingham, C. H. (1972). *Ecology of Heathlands.* London: Chapman & Hall.

Gimingham, C. H. (1981). Conservation: European heathlands. In Specht, R. L. (ed.). Ecosystems of the World Vol. 9B. Elsevier, Amsterdam.

Gimingham, C. H., Chapman, S. B. & Webb, N. R. (1979). European heathlands. In Specht, R. L. (ed.). Ecosystems of the World Vol. 9A. Heathlands and Related Dwarf Shrublands. Elsevier, Amsterdam.

Gimingham, C. H. & de Smidt, J. T. (1983). Heaths as natural and semi-natural vegetation. In Holzner, W., Werger, M. J. A. & Ikusina, I. (eds.). Man's Impact upon Vegetation. Junk, The Hague.

Goddard, P. (1983). Heathland management and the Smooth Snake. In Farrell, L. (ed.). Focus on Nature Conservation No. 2 Heathland Management. Nature Conservancy Council, Shrewsbury.

Goddard, P. (1984). Morphology, growth, food, habits and population characteristics of the Smooth Snake *Coronella austriaca* in southern Britain. *J. Zool. Lond.* 204:241–57.

Goddard, P. & Spellerberg, I. F. (1980). Reproduction as a factor in the conservation of *Coronella austriaca* Laur. in southern England. *Bull. Soc. Ecol. Fr.* 11:535–41.

Godwin, H. (1944). Age and origin of the Breckland heaths of East Anglia. *Nature, Lond.* 154:6.

Godwin, H. (1975). *The History of the British Flora.* Cambridge: Cambridge University Press.

Golightly, W. H. (1962). Biological control of *Lochmaea suturalis* (Thompson) (Col: Chrysomelidae). *Entomologists' mon. Mag.* 98:196.

Good, R. (1948). A Geographical Handbook of the Dorset Flora. Dorset Natural History & Archaeological Society, Dorchester.

Gaebner, P. (1925). Die Heide Norddeutschlands. Leipzig.

Grace, J. & Marks, T. C. (1978). Physiological aspects of bog production at Moor House. In Heal, O. W. & Perkins, D. F. (eds.). Production Ecology of some British Moors and Montane Grasslands. Springer-Verlag, Berlin.

Grace, J. & Woolhouse, H. W. (1974). A physiological and mathematical study of growth and productivity of a *Calluna–Sphagnum* community IV a model of growing *Calluna. J. appl. Ecol.* 11:281–95.

Grant, S. A. (1971). Interactions of grazing and burning on heather moors. II. Effects on primary production and level of utilisation. *J. Brit. Grassld. Soc.* 26:173–81.

Grant, S. A. & Hunter, R. F. (1966). The effects of frequency and season of clipping on the morphology, productivity and chemical composition of *Calluna vulgaris* (L.) Hull. *New Phytol.* 65: 125–33.

Gray, A. J., Stephens, D. & Ambrosen, H. E. (1985). Demographic genetics of the perennial heathland grass *Agrostis curtisii. Annu. Rep. Inst. terr. Ecol.* 1984. pp. 96–100.

Grubb, P. J., Green, H. E. & Merrifield, R. C. J. (1969). The ecology of chalk heath: its relevance to the calcicole-calcifuge and soil acidification problems. *J. Ecol.* 57:175–212.

Haes, E. C. M. (1984). An expansion of the known ranges of *Conocephalus discolor* into the New Forest and the heathlands of east Dorset. *Entomologists' Gazette* 35:64–5.

Hagerup, O. (1950). Thrips pollination in *Calluna*. *Biol. Meddr.* 18:1–16.
Harrison, C. M. (1970). The phytosociology of certain English heathland communities. *J. Ecol.* 58:573–89.
Harrison, C. M. (1981). Recovery of lowland grassland and heathland in southern England from disturbance by seasonal trampling. *Biol. Conserv.* 19:119–30.
Harrison, C. M. (1983). Lowland heathland: the case for amenity management. In Warren, A. & Goldsmith, F. B. (eds.). Conservation in Perspective. Wiley, London.
Haskins, L. E. (1978). The vegetational history of south-east Dorset. Ph.D. Thesis, University of Southampton.
Haywood, V. H. (1978). *Flowering Plants of the World*. Oxford: Oxford University Press.
Hazel, V. (1983). Hampshire's Countryside Heritage 4. Heathland. Hampshire County Council, Winchester.
Heal, O. W. & Perkins, D. F. (eds.). (1978). Production ecology of some British moors and montane grasslands. Ecological Studies 27. Springer-Verlag, Berlin.
Heath, J. (1946). The life history of *Pachythelia villosella* Ochs. (× *nigricans* Curt.) (Lep., Psychidae). *Entomologist's mon. Mag.* 82:59–63.
Heath, J., Pollard, E. & Thomas, J. A. (1984). *Atlas of British Butterflies*. London: Viking Press.
Heil, G. W. & Diemont, W. H. (1983). Raised nutrient levels change heathland into grassland. *Vegetatio*. 53:113–20.
Helsper, H. P. G., Glenn-Lewin, D. & Werger, M. J. A. (1983). Early regeneration of *Calluna* heathland under various fertiliser treatments. *Oecologia*. 58:208–14.
Hill, M. O. & Stephens, P. A. (1981). The density of viable seed in soil of forest plantations in upland Britain. *J. Ecol.* 69:693–709.
Hobbs, R. J., Currall, J. E. P. & Gimingham, C. H. (1984). The use of 'thermocolor' pyrometers in the study of heath fire behaviour. *J. Ecol.* 72:241–80.
Hobbs, R. J. & Gimingham, C. H. (1984a). Studies on fire in Scottish heathland communities. I. Fire characteristics. *J. Ecol.* 72:223–40.
Hobbs, R. J. & Gimingham, C. H. (1984b). Studies on fire in Scottish heathland communities. II. Post-fire development. *J. Ecol.* 72:585–610.
Hobbs, R. J., Mallik, A. U. & Gimingham, C. H. (1984). Studies on fire in Scottish heathland communities. III. Vital attributes of the species. *J. Ecol.* 72:963–76.
Hodkinson, I. D. (1973). The population dynamics and host plant interactions of *Strophingia ericae* (Curt.) (Homoptera: Psylloidea). *J. Anim. Ecol.* 42:565–83.

Hopkins, J. J. (1980). Turf huts in the Lizard district: an alternative suggestion for their interpretation. *J. Royal Institution of Cornwall, N.S.* 8:241–9.
Hopkins, J. J. (1983). Studies of the historical ecology, vegetation and flora of the Lizard district, Cornwall, with particular reference to heathland. Ph.D. Thesis, University of Bristol.
Hopkins, P. J. & Webb, N. R. (1984). The composition of the beetle and spider faunas on fragmented *Calluna*-heathland. *J. appl. Ecol.* 935–46.
House, S. M. & Spellerberg, I. F. (1983a). Comparison of *Lacerta agilis* habitats in Britain and Europe. *Brit. J. Herpetol.* 6:305–8.
House, S. M. & Spellerberg, I. F. (1983b). Ecology and conservation of the Sand Lizard (*Lacerta agilis* L.) habitat in southern England. *J. appl. Ecol.* 20:417–37.

Iversen, J. (1964). Retrogressive vegetational succession in the post-glacial. *J. Ecol.* 52 (suppl.), 59–70.
Iversen, J. (1969). Retrogressive development of forest ecosystem demonstrated by pollen diagrams from fossil mor. *Oikos Suppl.* 12:35–49.
Ivimey-Cook, R. B., Proctor, M. C. F. & Rowland, D. M. (1975). Analysis of plant communities of a heathland site: Aylesbere Common, Devon. *Vegetatio*, 31:33–45.

Jackson, H. C. (1978). Low May sunshine as a possible factor in the decline of the Sand Lizard (*Lacerta agilis* L.) in north west England. *Biol. Conserv.*, 13:1–12.
Jackson, H. C. (1979). The decline of the Sand Lizard *Lacerta agilis* L. populations on the sand dunes of the Merseyside coast, England. *Biol. Conserv.* 16:177–93.
Jones, H. E. (1971a). Comparative studies of plant growth and distribution in relation to waterlogging. II. An experimental study of the relationship between the uptake of iron in *Erica cinerea* L. and *E. tetralix* L. *J. Ecol.* 59:167–78.
Jones, H. E. (1971b). Comparative studies of plant growth and distribution in relation to waterlogging. III. The response of *Erica cinerea* L. to waterlogging in peat soils of differing iron content. *J. Ecol.* 59:583–91.
Jones, H. E. & Etherington, J. R. (1970). Comparative studies of plant growth and distribution in relation to waterlogging. I. The survival of *Erica cinerea* L. and *Erica tetralix* L. and its apparent relationship to iron and manganese uptake in waterlogged soil. *J. Ecol.* 58:487–96.
Jong, J. T. de & Klinkhamer, P. G. L. (1983). A simulation model for the effects of burning on the phosphorus and nitrogen cycle of a heathland ecosystem. *Ecological Modelling* 19:263–84.

Kenworthy, J. B. (1963). Temperatures in heather burning. *Nature, Lond.* 200:1226.

Kerr, B. (1968). *Bound to the Soil. A Social History of Dorset.* Wakefield: EP Publishing.

Kottmann, H. J., Schwoppe, W., Willers, T. & Wittig, R. (1985). Heath conservation by sheep grazing: a cost benefit analysis. *Biol. Conserv.* 31:67–74.

Kyall, A. J. (1966). Some characteristics of heath fires in NE Scotland. *J. appl. Ecol.* 3:29–40.

Lack, D. (1935). The breeding bird population of British heaths and moorland. *J. Anim. Ecol.* 4:43–51.

Lamb, H. H. (1965). The early medieval warm epoch and its sequel. *Palaeogeogr. Palaeoclimatol. Palaeocol.* 1:13–37.

Lawton, J. H. & Schroder, D. (1977). Effects of plant type, size of geographical range and taxonomic isolation on the insect species associated with British plants. *Nature, Lond.* 265:137–40.

Leslie, A. S. & Shipley, A. E. (1912). *The Grouse in Health and Disease.* London: Smith, Elder & Co.

Lewis, T. (1973). *Thrips: their Biology, Ecology and Economic Importance.* London: Academic Press.

Linssen, E. F. (1959). *Beetles of the British Isles.* London: Warne.

Lowday, J. (1983). Bracken control on lowland heaths. In Farrell, L. (ed.) *Nature Conservation in Focus No. 2. Heathland Management.* Shrewsbury: Nature Conservancy Council.

Lucas, A. T. (1960). *Furze: A survey and history of its uses in Ireland.* Dublin: National Museum of Ireland.

MacArthur, R. H. & Wilson, E. O. (1967). *The Theory of Island Biogeography.* Princeton: Princeton University Press.

MacFadyen, A. (1963). *Animal Ecology: Aims and Methods.* London: Pitman.

MacFadyen, A. (1971). The soil and its total metabolism. In Philipson, J. (ed.) *Methods of study in quantative soil ecology.* I.B.P. Handbook No. 18. Oxford: Blackwell Scientific Publications.

McNeil, S. & Prestige, R. A. (1982). Plant nutritional strategies and herbivore community dynamics. In Visser, J. H. & Minks, A. K. (eds.) Proc. 5th Int. Symp. Insect–Plant Relationships. Wageningen, 1982. Wageningen: Pudoc.

Mackney, D. (1961). A podsol development sequence in oak woods and heaths in southern England. *J. Soil Sci.* 12:23–40.

Mallik, A. U. & Gimingham, C. H. (1981). Regeneration of heathland plants following burning. *Vegetatio*, 53:45–58.

Mallik, A. U., Gimingham, C. H. & Rahman, A. A. (1984a). Ecological effects of heather burning. I. Water infiltration, moisture retention and porosity of surface soil. *J. Ecol.* 72:767–76.

Mallik, A. Y., Hobbs, R. J. & Legg, C. J. (1984b). Seed dynamics in *Calluna-Arctostaphylos* heath in north-eastern Scotland. *J. Ecol.* 72:855–71.

Malloch, A. J. C. (1971). Vegetation of the maritime cliff-tops of the Lizard and Land's End peninsulas, west Cornwall. *New Phytol.* 70:1155–97.

Maltby, E. (1980a). The impact of severe fire on *Calluna* moorland in the North York Moors. *Bull. Soc. Ecol. Fr.* 11:683–708.

Maltby, E. (1980b). The environmental fire hazard. In Doornkamp, J. C., Gregory, K. J. & Burns, A. S. (eds.) *Atlas of Drought in Britain.* London: Institute of British Geographers.

Mangenot, F. (1966). Etude microbiologique des litières. *Bull. Ecol. Nat. Sup. Agron. Nakcy.* 8:113–25.

Margules, C. & Usher, M. B. (1984). Conservation evaluation in practice. I. Sites of different habitats in north-east Yorkshire, Great Britain. *J. Environmental Management* 18:153–68.

Marrs, R. H. (1983). Scrub control on lowland heaths. In Farrell, L. (ed.) *Focus on Nature Conservation No. 2. Heathland Management.* Shrewsbury: Nature Conservancy Council.

Marrs, R. H. & Procter, J. (1978). Chemical and ecological studies of heath plants and soils of the Lizard Peninsula, Cornwall. *J. Ecol.* 66:417–32.

Merrett, P. (1967). The phenology of spiders on heathland in Dorset. *J. Anim. Ecol.* 36:363–74.

Merrett, P. (1968). The phenology of spiders on heathland in Dorset. *J. Zool., Lond.* 156:239–56.

Merrett, P. (1969). The phenology of linyphid spiders on heathland in Dorset. *J. Zool., Lond.* 157:289–307.

Merrett, P. (1976). Changes in the ground-living spider fauna after heathland fires in Dorset. *Bull. Br. Arachnol. Soc.* 3:214–21.

Miles, J. (1972). Experimental establishment of seedlings on a southern English heath. *J. Ecol.* 60:225–34.

Miles, J. (1973a). Early mortality and survival of self-grown seedlings in Glenfeshie, Inverness-shire. *J. Ecol.* 61:93–8.

Miles, J. (1973b). Natural recolonisation of experimentally bared soil in Callunetum in north-east Scotland. *J. Ecol.* 61:399–412.

Miles, J. (1974). Experimental establishment of new species from seed in Callunetum in north-east Scotland. *J. Ecol.* 62:527–51.

Miles, J. (1975). Performance after six growing seasons of new species established from seed in Callunetum in north-east Scotland. *J. Ecol.* 63:891–901.

Miles, J. (1979). *Vegetation Dynamics.* London: Chapman & Hall.

Miles, J. (1981). *Effect of Birch on Moorland.* Cambridge: Institute of Terrestrial Ecology.
Miles, J. & Young, W. F. (1980). The effects on heathland and moorland soils in Scotland and northern England following colonisation by birch (*Betula* spp.). *Bull. Soc. Ecol. Fr.* 11:233–42.
Miller, B. J. F. (1974). Studies of changes in the populations of invertebrates associated with cyclical processes in heathland. Ph.D. Thesis, University of Aberdeen.
Miller, G. R. (1979). Quantity and quality of the annual production of shoots and flowers by *Calluna vulgaris* in north-east Scotland. *J. Ecol.* 67:109–29.
Miller, G. R. & Miles, J. (1970). Regeneration of heather (*Calluna vulgaris* (L.) Hull) at different ages and different seasons in north-east Scotland. *J. appl. Ecol.* 7:51–60.
Miller, G. R. & Watson, A. (1978). Heather productivity and its relevance to the regulation of Red Grouse populations. In Heal, O. W. & Perkins, D. F. (eds.) *The Ecology of some British Moors and Montane Grasslands.* Berlin: Springer-Verlag.
Minchinton, W. E. (1956). Agriculture in Dorset during the Napoleonic Wars. *Proc. Dorset. Nat. Hist. archaeol. Soc.* 77:162–73.
Mohamed, B. F. & Gimingham, C. H. (1970). The morphology of vegetative regeneration in *Calluna vulgaris*. *New Phytol.* 69:743–50.
Moore, N. W. (1962). The heaths of Dorset and their conservation. *J. Ecol.* 50:369–91.
Moore, N. W. (1964). Intra- and interspecific competition among dragonflies (Odonata). *J. Anim. Ecol.* 33:49–71.
Moore, P. D. & Bellamy, D. J. (1974). *Peatlands.* London: Elk Science.

Nicholson, I. A. & Patterson, I. S. (1976). The ecological implications of bracken control to plant animal systems. *Bot. J. Linn. Soc.* 73:269–83.
Nicholson, A. M. (1980). The ecology of the Sand Lizard (*Lacerta agilis* L.) in southern England and comparisons with the Common Lizard (*L. vivipara* Jacquin). Ph.D. Thesis, University of Southampton.
Norrevang, A. & Meyer, T. J. (1975). Hede, Overdrev – og Eng. In Bøcher, T. W., Nielsen, C. O. & Schon, A. (eds.) *Danmarks Natur* Vol. 7. Politiken Forlag, Kobenhavn.
Noirfalise, A. & Vanesse, R. (1976). *Heathlands of Western Europe.* Strasbourg: Council of Europe.

Page, C. N. (1976). The taxonomy and phytogeography of bracken – a review. *Bot. J. Linnl Soc.* 73:1–34.
Parkinson, J. D. & Whittaker, J. B. (1975). A study of two physiological races of the heather psyllid *Strophingia ericae* (Curtis) (Homoptera: Psylloidea). *Biol. J. Linn. Soc.* 7:73–81.
Passmore, A. H. (1969). *New Forest Commoners.* Printed privately.
Pearsall, W. H. (1950). *Mountains and Moorlands.* London: Collins New Naturalist.
Pennington, W. (1969). *The History of the British Vegetation.* London: English Universities Press.
Perring, F. H. & Walters, S. M. (eds.) (1976). *Atlas of the British Flora.* Wakefield: EP Pubplishing.
Perring, F. H. & Farrell, L. (1977). Vascular Plants. British Red Data Book No. 1. Royal Society for Nature Conservation, Nettleham, Lincs.
Pickard-Cambridge, O. (1886). *Coronella laevis*, Boie. *Proc. Dorset. nat. Hist. archaeol. Soc.* 7:83–92.
Pickess, B. P. (1980). The dragonflies of Arne nature reserve and their conservation. *Proc. Dorset. nat. Hist. archaeol. Soc.* 100:109–11.
Pickess, B. P. (1983). Heathland management at Arne nature reserve. In Ferrell, L. (ed.) Focus on Nature Conservation No. 2. Heathland Management. Nature Conservancy Council, Shrewsbury.
Pickett, S. T. A. & Thompson, J. N. (1978). Patch dynamics and the design of nature reserves. *Biol. Conserv.* 13:27–37.
Pigot, B. (1960). *The New Forest commoners.* In The New Forest. London: Galley Press.
Pollard, E., Hooper, M. D. & Moore, N. W. (1974). *Hedges.* London: Collins New Naturalist.
Prestt, I., Cooke, A. S. & Corbett, K. F. (1974). British amphibians and reptiles. In Hawksworth, D. L. (ed.) *The Changing Flora and Fauna of Britain.* London: Academic Press.
Prestt, I. (1971). An ecological study of the Viper *Vipera berus* in southern Britain. *J. Zool., Lond.* 164:373–418.
Proctor, M. C. F. (1965). The distinguishing characters and geographical distributions of *Ulex minor* and *Ulex gallii*. *Watsonia* 6: 177–87.
Putwain, P. D., Gillham, D. A. & Hollidey, R. J. (1982). Restoration of heather moorland and lowland heathland, with special reference to pipelines. *Environmental Conserv.* 9:225–35.
Putwain, P. D. (1983). Restoring heather cover on bare areas. In Daniels, J. L. (ed.) *Heathland Management in Amenity Areas.* Cheltenham: Countryside Commission.

Rackham, O. (1976). *Trees and Woodland in the British Landscape.* London: Dent.
Ratcliffe, D. A. (1977). *A Nature Conservation Review.* Cambridge: Cambridge University Press.
Ragge, D. R. (1965). *Grasshoppers, Crickets and Cockroaches of the British Isles.* London: Warne.
Richards, O. W. (1926). Studies on the ecology of English heaths. III. Animal communities of the

REFERENCES FOR FURTHER READING

felling and burn successions at Oxshott Heath, Surrey. *J. Ecol.* 14:244–81.

Robinson, R. K. (1972). Importance of soil toxicity in relation to the stability of plant communities. In Duffey, E. & Watt, A. S. (eds.) *The Scientific Management of Animal and Plant Communities for Conservation*. Oxford: Blackwell Scientific Publications.

Rose, F. (1976). The vegetation of heaths. In Sankey, J. H. P. & Mackworth, Praed, H. W. (eds.) *The Southern Heathlands*. Surrey Naturalists' Trust.

Rubel, E. A. (1914). Heath and steppe, macchia and garigue. *J. Ecol.* 2:232–7.

Rymer, L. (1976). The history and ethnobotany of bracken. *Bot. J. Linn. Soc.* 73:151–76.

Sharrock, J. T. R. (1976). *The Atlas of Breeding Birds in Britain and Ireland*. Carlton Staffordshire: Poyser.

Sheail, J. (1971). *Rabbits and their History*. Newton Abbot: David & Charles.

Sheail, J. (1979). Documentary evidence of changes in the use, management and appreciation of the grass-heaths of Breckland. *J. Biogeogr.* 6:277–92.

Simms, C. (1969). Recolonisation of burnt heath by lizards *Lacerta vivipara* Jacquin. *Brit. J. Herpetol.* 4:117–20.

Simms, C. (1972). Shift in a population of northern Vipers. *Brit. J. Herpetol.* 4:268–71.

Simmons, I. G. & Dimbleby, G. W. (1974). The possible role of Ivy (*Hedera helix* L.) in the mesolithic economy of western Europe. *J. Archaeol. Sci.* 1:291–6.

Sinclair, G. (1970). *The Vegetation of Exmoor*. Dulverton: Exmoor Press.

Smidt, J. T. de (1967). Phytogeographical relations of the north west European heaths. *Acta Bot. Neerl.* 15:630–47.

Smidt, J. T. de (1977). Interaction of *Calluna vulgaris* and Heather Beetle (*Lochmaea suturalis*). In Tuxen, R. (ed.) Vegetation and Fauna 1976. Berichte uber die internationalen Symposien der Internationalen Vereinigung fur Vegetationskunde in Stolzenau und Rinteln. Vaduz: Cramer.

Smith, M. A. (1951). *British Amphibians and Reptiles*. London: Collins New Naturalist.

Southwood, T. R. E. & Leston, D. (1959). *The Land and Water Bugs of the British Isles*. London: Warne.

Southwood, T. R. E., Brown, V. K. & Reader, P. M. (1979). The relationship of plant and insect diversities in succession. *Biol. J. linn. Soc.* 12:327–48.

Specht, R. L. (1979). Heathlands and related shrublands of the world. In Specht R. L. (ed.) Ecosystems of the World Vol. 9A. Amsterdam: Elsevier.

Spellerberg, I. F. (1975). Conservation and management of Britain's reptiles and their ecological and behavioural requirements: a progress report. *Biol. Conserv.* 7:289–300.

Spellerberg, I. F. (1977). Behaviour of a young Smooth Snake *Coronella austriaca* Laurenti. *Biol. J. Linn. Soc.* 9:323–400.

Spellerberg, I. F. & Phelps, T. E. (1977). Biology, general ecology and behaviour of the snake *Coronella austriaca* Laurenti. *Biol. J. Linn. Soc.* 9:158–64.

Spellerberg, I. F. & House, S. M. (1982). Relocation of the lizard *Lacerta agilis*: an exercise in conservation. *Brit. J. Herpetol.* 6:245–8.

Stoutjesdijk, P. (1959). Heaths and inland dunes of the Veluwe. *Wentis* 2:1–96.

Stubbs, A. (1983). The management of heathland for Invertebrates. In Farrell, L. (ed.) Focus on Nature Conservation No. 2. Heathland Management. Shrewsbury: Nature Conservancy Council.

Stubbs, A. E. & Falk, S. J. (1983). *British Hoverflies*. London: British Entomological and Natural History Society.

Summerhayes, V. S., Cole, L. W. & Williams, P. H. (1924). Studies on the ecology of English heaths. I. The vegetation of the unfelled portions of Oxshott Heath and Esher Common, Surrey. *J. Ecol.* 12:287–306.

Summerhayes, V. S. & Williams, P. H. (1926). Studies on the ecology of English heaths. II. Early stages in the recolonisation of felled pinewood on Oxshott Heath and Esher Common, Surrey. *J. Ecol.* 14:203–43.

Summers, C. F. (1978). Production in montane dwarf shrub heaths. In Heal, O. W. & Perkins, D. F. (eds.) *Production Ecology of some British Moors and Montane Grasslands*. Berlin: Springer-Verlag.

Tansley, A. G. (1939). *The British Islands and their Vegetation*. Cambridge: Cambridge University Press.

Taylor, C. C. (1970). *The Making of the English Landscape: Dorset*. London: Hodder & Stoughton.

Thiele, H.-U. (1977). *Carabid Beetles in their Environments*. Berlin: Springer-Verlag.

Thomas, C. D. (1985a). Specializations and polyphagy of *Plebejus argus* (Lepidoptera) in North Wales. *Ecol. Entomol.* 10:325–40.

Thomas, C. D. (1985b). The status and conservation of the butterfly *Plebejus argus* L. (Lepidoptera: Lycaenidae) in north west Britain. *Biol. Conserv.* 33:29–51.

Thomas, J. A. (1980). Why did the Large Blue become extinct in Britain? *Oryx* 15:243–7.

Thomas, J. A. (1984). The conservation of butterflies in temperate countries: past efforts and lessons for the future. In Vane-Wright, R. I. & Ackery, P. R. (eds.) *The Biology of Butterflies*. London: Academic Press.

Tubbs, C. R. (1965). The development of the smallholding and cottage stock-keeping economy of the New Forest. Agricultural History Review, 13: 23–39.

Tubbs, C. R. (1967). Numbers of Dartford Warblers in England during 1962–6. British Birds 60:87–9.

Tubbs, C. R. (1968). The New Forest, an Ecological History. Newton Abbot: David & Charles.

Tubbs, C. R. (1985). The decline and present status of the English lowland heaths and their vertebrates. Focus on Nature Conservation No. 11. Peterborough: Nature Conservancy Council.

Tubbs, C. R. & Jones, E. L. (1964). The distribution of gorse (*Ulex europaeus* L.) in the New Forest in relation to former land use. Proc. Hampshire Field Club 23:1–10.

Tye, A. (1980). The breeding biology and population size of the Wheatear (*Oenanthe oenanthe*) on the Breckland of East Anglia, with implications for its conservation. Bull. Soc. Ecol. Fr. 11:559–69.

Wallen, B. (1980). Structure and dynamics of *Calluna vulgaris* on sand dunes in southern Sweden. Oikos 35:20–30.

Wallen, C. C. (1970). Climates of Northern and Western Europe. World Survey of Climatology Vol. 5. Amsterdam: Elsevier.

Waloff, N. (1968). Studies on the insect fauna on Scotch Broom *Sarothamnus scoparius* (L.) Wimmer. Advances in Ecological Research Vol. 5. London: Academic Press.

Ward, L. K. (1973). The conservation of Juniper. I. Present status of Juniper in southern England. J. appl. Ecol. 10:165–88.

Ward, S. D. (1970). The phytosociology of *Calluna-Arctostaphylos* heaths in Scotland and Scandinavia. I. Dinnet Moor, Aberdeenshire. J. Ecol. 58:847–63.

Watt, A. S. (1937). Studies in the ecology of Breckland. II. On the origin and development of blow-outs. J. Ecol. 25:91–112.

Watt, A. S. (1947). Pattern and process in the plant community. J. Ecol. 35:1–22.

Watt, A. S. (1955). Bracken versus heather, a study in plant sociology. J. Ecol. 43:490–506.

Watt, A. S. (1971a). Factors controlling the floristic composition of some plant communities in Breckland. In Duffey, E. & Watt, A. S. (eds.) The Scientific Management of Animal and Plant Communities for Conservation. Oxford: Blackwell Scientific Publications.

Watt, A. S. (1971b). Rare species in Breckland: their management for survival. J. appl. Ecol. 8:593–609.

Watt, A. S. (1976). The ecological status of Bracken. Bot. J. Linn. Soc. 73:217–39.

Webb, N. R. (1972). Cryptostigmatid mites recorded from heathland in Dorset. Entomologists' mon. Mag. 107:228–9.

Webb, N. R. (1983). Habitat isolation and its effects on the distribution and abundance of invertebrates on the Dorset heathlands. In Farrell, L. Focus on Nature Conservation No. 2. Heathland Management. Nature Conservancy Council, Shrewsbury.

Webb, N. R. (1985). Restoring heathlands. Annu. Rep. Inst. terr. Ecol. 1984. pp. 46–7.

Webb, N. R. & Haskins, L. E. (1980). An ecological survey of heathland in the Poole Basin, Dorset, England in 1978. Biol. Conserv. 17:281–96.

Webb, N. R. & Hopkins, P. J. (1984). Invertebrate diversity on fragmented *Calluna*-heathland. J. appl. Ecol. 21:921–33.

Webb, N. R., Clarke, R. T. & Nicholas, R. T. (1984). Invetebrate diversity on fragmented *Calluna* heathland: effects of surrounding vegetation. J. Biogeogr. 11:41–6.

Webster, J. R. (1962a). The composition of wet heath vegetation in relation to aeration of the ground water and soil. I. Field studies of ground water and soil aeration in several communities. J. Ecol. 50: 619–38.

Webster, J. R. (1962b). The composition of wet heath vegetation in relation to aeration of the ground water and soil. II. Response of *Molinia caerulea* to controlled conditions of soil aeration and ground-water movement. J. Ecol. 50:639–50.

Whitehead, G. K. (1964). The Deer of Great Britain and Ireland: an Account of their History, Status and distribution. London: Routledge & Kegan Paul.

Witherby, H. F., Jourdain, F. C. R., Ticehurst, N. F. & Tucker, B. W. (1940). The Handbook of British Birds. London: Witherby.

Whittaker, E. (1961). Temperatures in heath fires. J. Ecol. 49:709–15.

Whittaker, E. & Gimingham, C. H. (1962). The effects of fire on regeneration of *Calluna vulgaris* (L.) Hull from seed. J. Ecol. 50:815–22.

Whittaker, R. H. (1975). Communities and Ecosystems. London: Macmillan.

Williams, G. H. & Foley, A. (1976). Seasonal variation in the carbohydrate content of bracken. Bot. J. Linn. Soc. 73:95–104.

Yates, E. M. (1972). The management of heathlands for amenity purposes in south-east England. Geographica Polonica 24:227–40.

Heathland Nature Reserves

The range of the southern heathlands was described in chapter 5. There is an extensive series of reserves which protect this community. Reserves are managed by the Nature Conservancy Council (NCC) as National Nature Reserves (NNRs) or by private organizations such as the Royal Society for the Protection of Birds (RSPB) or one of the 42 county nature conservation trusts. Elsewhere, heathland is protected by the National Trust or by landscape designations such as National Parks, Areas of Outstanding Beauty or Heritage Coasts. The following is not exhaustive, but lists the main reserves or similar areas and the organization responsible for their maintenance. Further details are contained in *A Nature Reserves Handbook* (A. E. Smith ed.), published by the Royal Society for Nature Conservation or 'A Guide to Britain's Nature Reserves' (J. Hywel-Davies & V. Thom eds.), published by Macmillan. Many of the managing bodies publish guides to their own reserves. Reserves marked * have restrictions on access but in some instances there are rights of way from which the heathland can be seen.

Purbeck c. *1899, Dorset County Museum*

Bedfordshire
The Firs, Ampthill — Bedfordshire County Council

Berkshire
Edgebarrow Woods — Bracknell District Council
Inkpen Common — Berkshire, Buckinghamshire & Oxfordshire Naturalist's Trust (BBONT)
Snellsmore Common Country Park — Newbury District Council

Cheshire
Little Budworth Country Park — Cheshire County Council
Thurstaston Common — National Trust

Cornwall
North Cornish Coast
Land's End Peninsula
Chapel Porth
Isles of Scilly — Duchy of Cornwall/NCC
Lizard NNR — NCC
  Kynance — Cornish Trust for Nature Conservation
  Goonhilly
  Predannack

Devon
Aylesbeare Common* — RSPB
Chudleigh Knighton Heath — Devon Trust for Nature Conservation

Dartmoor National Park
Lundy Island — National Trust/Landmark Trust

Dorset
Arne Neath* — RSPB
Avon Forest Park — Dorset County Council
Cranborne Common* — Dorset Trust for Nature Conservation
Hartland Moor NNR* — NCC
Holt Heath NNR — NCC
Holton Heath NNR* — NCC
Morden Bog NNR* — NCC
Stoborough Heath NNR* — NCC
Studland & Godlingston Heaths NNR — NCC
Tadnol* — Dorset Trust for Nature Conservation
Higher Hyde Heath* — Dorset Trust for Nature Conservation
Woolsbarrow — Dorset Trust for Nature Conservation

Essex
Tiptree Heath — Tiptree Parish Council

HEATHLAND NATURE RESERVES

Dyfed
Dowrog Common — West Wales Naturalists' Trust

Greater London
Wimbledon Common

Hampshire
Broxhead Common — Hampshire County Council
Fleet Pond — Hart District Council
Ludshott Common — National Trust
New Forest — Forestry Commission
Yateley Common — Hampshire County Council

Hereford & Worcester
Broadmoor Common — Hereford & Worcester County Council
Devil's Spittleful — Worcestershire Nature Conservation Trust
Hartlebury Common — Hereford & Worcester County Council

Hertfordshire
Hertford Heath — Hertfordshire & Middlesex Trust for Nature Conservation
Marshall's Heath — Hertfordshire & Middlesex TNC

Kent
Hothfield Common — Kent Trust for Nature Conservation/Ashford Borough Council

Leicestershire
Bradgate Park — Bradgate Park Trust

Lincolnshire & South Humberside
Kirkby Moor* — Lincolnshire & South Humberside Trust for Nature Conservation
Linwood Warren* — Lincolnshire & South Humberside TNC
Scotton Common — Lincolnshire & South Humberside TNC

Norfolk
East Winch Common* — Norfolk Naturalists' Trust
East Wretham Heath* — Norfolk Naturalists' Trust
Norfolk Coast — Area of Outstanding Natural Beauty
Roydon Common* — Norfolk Naturalists' Trust
Sandringham Country Park — Sandringham Estate
Weeting Heath NNR* — NCC
Winterton Dunes NNR — NCC

Staffordshire
Cannock Chase — Staffordshire County Council
Highgate Common Country Park — Staffordshire County Council

Somerset
Exmoor National Park
Langford Heathfield* — Somerset Trust for Nature Conservation

Suffolk
Cavenham Heath NNR — NCC
Dunwich Common — National Trust
Knettishall Heath Country Park — Suffolk County Council
Minsmere* — RSPB
Thetford Heath NNR* — NCC
Walberswick NNR* — NCC
Wangford Glebe* — Suffolk Trust for Nature Conservation
Westleton Heath NNR* — NCC

Surrey
Chobham Common — Surrey County Council
Frensham Country Park — Waverly District Council
Devil's Punch Bowl, Hindhead — National Trust
Headley Heath — National Trust
Horsell Common — Horsell Common Preservation Society
Lightwater Country Park — Surrey Heath Borough Council
Thursley Common NNR — NCC
Whitley Common — National Trust

Sussex
Ashdown Forest — Conservators of Ashdown Forest
Chailey Common & Warren* — East Sussex County Council/ Sussex Trust for Nature Conservation
Iping Common — West Sussex County Council
Lullington Heath NNR* — NCC

Warwickshire
Sutton Park — City of Birmingham District Council

Yorkshire
Allerthorp Common* — Yorkshire Wildlife Trust
North Yorks Moors — National Park
Skipwith Common* — Yorkshire Wildlife Trust
Strensall Common* — Yorkshire Wildlife Trust

Index

Acalles ptinoides 153
Adder *see* Viper
Aeolothrips ericae 141
Aescodes mento 156
Aeshna
  Common 143
  Scarce 143
  Southern 143
Aeshna
  cyanea 143
  juncea 143
  mixta 143
Agrostis
  capillaris 73
  curtisii 45, 56–60, 65, 66, 122
Ajuga chamaepitys 71
Alder 33, 34
Aldershot 66
Allerthorp Bog 76
Alnus 34
Altica spp. 157
Amara infirma 152
Ambersham Common 65, 66
Amenity 197
Ammophila spp. 157
Ammophila arenaria 75, 77
Amphibia 161–3
Anglesey 76
Apanteles spp. 148
Apera interrupta 71
Apion spp. 153
Apodemus sylvaticus 167, 177
Anagallis tenella 123
Anarta myrtilli 149
Anax imperator 143
Andersen, Hans Christian 12
Andrena spp. 157
Anergetes atratulus 159
Anglo Saxons 36, 37
Anguis fragilis 163
Ants 137, 158
Araneae 138, 140
Archaeology 29, 31, 36
Aristotelia ericinella 151
Armeria maritima 55, 59
Arne 38
Artemisia spp. 31, 71
Ashdown Forest 43, 45, 46, 67, 68

Asilus crabroniformis 160
Askham Bog 76
Asphodel, Bog 57, 58, 63, 122
Astata boops 157
Asulam 191
Atapus affinis 140
Atlantic Period 27, 30, 31, 33, 35
Autographa gamma 150
Autumnal Moth 149
Aylesbeare Common 58

Back-burning 99, 188
Bagshot Heath 12
Bagworm, Large 150, 151
Bartsia, Yellow 130
Beak-sedge
  Brown 60, 66, 123
  White 63, 66, 123
Beaulieu Road 67
Beautiful Yellow Underwing 149
Beauveria bassiana 156
Bedstraw, Heath 70, 121
  Slender Marsh 63
  Wall 71
Beech 25
Bees 157
Beetles
  Carabid 151–3
  Chrysomelid 153
  Dor 153
  Dung 133, 153
  Ground 151–3
  Heather 98, 144, 153–6
  Minotaur 153
  Oil 153
  Tiger 133, 151
Beijerinck, W. 18, 27
Belgium 17
Bent, Bristle *see Agrostis curtisii*
Berkshire 12, 66
Berners Heath 73
Betula spp. 34, 106, 190
Bexley Heath 173
Bicton Common 58
Bilberry 34, 59, 76
Bimastos eiseni 140
Birch 34, 106, 190
Birds 169

INDEX

Birds-foot Trefoil, Slender 55
Black Bog Rush 55, 58, 63, 123
Blackdown 64
Bladderworts 65, 130
Blue
 Common 145
 Mazarine 150
 Silver-studded 145–7, 196
Bocher, T. W. 78
Bodmin Moor 57
Bog Myrtle 63
Bombus spp. 157
Bordered Grey 149
Boreal 30, 31, 33
Bracken 12, 35, 51, 55, 57, 67, 76
 control 76, 191
Bramshott Heath 64
Breckland 13, 32, 33, 35, 38, 39, 43, 46, 68–73, 87, 175
 Invertebrates 73
 rarities 71
 vegetation 70
Brilliant Emerald 68, 143
Bristle Tails 91, 114
Brittany 17
Bronze Age 27, 31, 34, 35, 37, 48
Broom 59, 129
Bryophytes 105
Bufo bufo 161
 calamita 65, 161–3, 193
Bugs 143, 144
Burning 48, 97, 98, 188
Bush-Cricket, Bog 142
Bustard, Great 73
Butterflies 145–6
Butterworts 123, 130
Buxton Heath 74
Buzzard, Common 63, 175
 Honey 63

Caenopsis fissirostris 153
Callophrys rubi 145, 146
Calluna vulgaris 108–114
 distribution 18, 109
 effects of fire 101–2
 flowering 108
 frost damage 111
 germination 110
 growth form 111–12
 growth phases 89, 113
 insects of 132
 light 110
 name, use of 16
 requirements 18
 seeds 109
 uses 120
 variation 109

water relations 111
Campanula rotundifolia 121
Cannock Chase 67, 76, 191
Carabus problematicus 151
 nitens 152, 196
 violaceus 151
Cardiganshire 76
Carex arenaria 69, 71, 74, 77, 122
 binervis 123
 ericetorum 71
 hostiana 58
 panacea 123
 pilulifera 123
Cartographic evidence 43
Case moths 151
Catchfly 71, 73
Cavenham Heath 73
Centaury, Yellow 63, 122
Ceratophytes typhaeus 153
Ceratothrips ericae 141
Ceriagrion tenellum 63, 66, 68, 143
Chamaenerion angustifolium 133
Chenopodium spp. 31
Chobham Common 66, 157
Chorthippus brunneus 142
 parallelus 142
 vagans 61, 142, 196
Chrysops reticulatus 160
Chrysotoxum octomaculatum 159
Cicadelidae 145
Cicendela spp. 151
Cicendia filiformis 63, 122
Cirsium dissectum 58
Cladonia spp. 70, 105, 122
Cleora cinctaria 149, 151
Clethrionomys glareolus 177
Climate 18, 26, 27
Clouded buff 150
Clovers 55
Clubmoss, Fir 59
 Marsh 65, 67, 68, 123
 Stagshorn 123
Cobbett, William 41, 46
Coccidae 145
Coccinella hieroglyphica 156
Cockroaches 142
Coenagrion mercuriale 143
Coenonympha pamphilus 145
Coleophora spp. 151
Coleoptera 151–7
Collaton Raleigh Common 58
Collembola 23, 140
Colletes spp. 157
Common Heath 149
Coneheads 142
Coniocleonus nebulosus 153
Conocephalus spp. 142

INDEX 217

Conservation 181-7
Coral Necklace 63
Coranus subapterus 145
Cordulea aenea 143
Cordulegaster boltoni 143
Cornwall 36, 47, 53, 57
Coronella austriaca 61, 64, 163, 167-9, 193, 194
Corylus avellana 30, 34, 62
Corynephros canescens 71
Coscinia cribraria 61, 151, 196
Coastal Heaths 53, 57
Cotton Grass 57, 58, 59, 63, 123
Cowberry 59, 76
Cow Wheat 130
Crag 73
Cranberry 65, 123
Cranborne Chase 37
Crassula tillea 60, 71, 122
Creeping Ladies Tresses 71
Crowberry 59, 76, 77
Cuculionidae 153
Cudweed, Heath 122
Curlew 172
Curlew, Stone 72, 175
Cuscuta epithymum 122, 130
Cyaniris semiargus 150
Cybosia mesomella 150
Cycles 87-9
Cytisus scoparius 59, 129

Dactylorhiza spp. 123
Dale, J. C. 151
Damselfly, Small Red 63, 66, 60, 143
    Southern 143
Danish Heath Society 182
Danthonia decumbens 67
Dark Tussock 150
Dartmoor 57
Darwin, Charles 129
Dasychira fascelina 150
Decomposition 22, 92
Deer 179-180
Deer Grass 58, 59, 123
Defoe, Daniel 12
Denmark 12, 17, 32, 37, 182
Dense Silky Bent 71
Deschampsia flexuosa 59, 76, 122
Devils-bit Scabious 58
Devon 57, 59
Diacrisia sannio 150
Diapensiaceae 15
Dicranium scoparium 122
Dilta littoralis 91, 140
Diver, Capt. C. 61, 186
Diversity 184
Dodder 122, 130

Dolomedes fimbriatus 141, 146
Domesday Survey 37-9
Dorset 13, 24, 33, 38, 42, 44, 45, 47, 60, 157
Downy Emerald 143
Dragonflies 61, 143, 196
Dragonfly, Emperor 143
    Gold-ringed 143
    White-faced 66, 143
Drosera spp. 63, 66, 129
Dry Heath 79, 80, 82
Dunes 24, 69, 86
Dwarf shrub structure 14
Dynamics of vegetation 86

Earthworms 22, 96, 140
East Devon Commons 58
Ectobius spp. 142
Eeyore 67
Egdon Heath 13
Eggars 149
Elasmostethus interstinctus 144
Elm 30, 31, 34
Ematurga atomaria 149
Emperor Moth 147
Empetriaceae 15, 107
Empetrum nigrum 34, 59, 76, 77
Enchytraeidae 140
Entephria caesiata 59
Epacridaceae 15, 107
Episyrphus balteatus 159
Eresus niger 140
Erica ciliaris see Dorset Heath
Erica cinerea see Bell Heather
Erica lusitanica see Lusitanean Heath
Erica mackaiana see MacKay's Heath
Erica mediterranea see Irish Heath
Erica scoparia see Besom Heath
Erica tetralix see Cross-leaved Heath
Erica vagans see Cornish Heath
Ericaceae 15, 32, 107
Ericaphis ericae 145
Eriophorum angustifolium 57, 59, 63, 123
    vaginatum 57, 59, 123
Esher Common 133
Euchlora dubia 153
Eupithecia spp. 149
Euphrasia spp. 130
Eurhynchium pulchellum 71
Eutrophication 26, 185
Evapo-transpiration 23
Exmoor 12, 47, 59
Exposure 26
Eyebrights 130

Fagus sylvaticus 25
Farnborough 66

INDEX

Fat Hen 31
Fertilizers 200
Festuca ovina see Fescue, Sheep's
Fescue, Sheep's 55, 56, 57, 65, 70, 73, 122
Field Southernwood 71
Fiennes, Celia 50
Finland 18
Fire, effects of 99, 101
  post-fire succession 102–6
  temperatures during 100–1
Flandrian 27
Fleet 66
Flies 160
Footman, Four-dotted 150
  Scarce 150
  Speckled 61, 151, 196
Formica spp. 159
Forest clearance 27, 37
Forvie, Sands of 77, 86
Foxhole Heath 73
Fox Moth 148
France 17
Frankiniella intonsa 141
Frensham Common 64
Frog, Common 161
Froghoppers 145
Frost, effects of 20, 111
Fuel gathering 39, 48, 50
Furze *see* Gorse
Furze cutters 51
Furze, Needle 68
Furze Wren *see* Dartford Warbler
Fynbos 15

Galium debile 63
  parisiense 71
  saxatile 70, 121
Gatekeeper 145
Gaultheria spp. 108
Genista anglica 68, 122, 128
  pilosa 128
  tinctoria 128, 146
Gentian, Marsh 60, 63, 67, 68, 123, 151
Gentiana pneumonanthe see Marsh Gentian
Geology 24, 27
Geotrupes spp. 153
Germany 12, 17, 18, 190
Glaciation 29
Gladiolus, Wild 63
Gnaphalium sylvaticum 122
Goldcrest 170
Goodyera repens 71
Gorse, Common 34, 43, 55, 56, 62, 125–8

Dwarf 34, 60, 61, 62, 65–7, 125–8
Western 34, 55, 56, 58, 59, 60, 61, 73, 125–8
Gorse cutting 48, 50
  differences 127
  distributions 125–6
  pollen 34
  uses 128
Grape Hyacinth 71
Grasses 31–3
Grasshopper 142
  Heath 61, 142, 196
  Large Marsh 61, 142
Grass Emerald 149
Grass Snake 163
Grayling 136, 145, 146, 196
Grazing 25–7, 39, 46, 47, 69, 188, 190
Greensands 64
Greenweeds 128
Grey Hair Grass 71
Grey Mountain Carpet 59
Grimes Graves 33
Groundhopper, Common 142
Grouse, Black 59, 64, 172
  Red 171
Growth Phases 89
Grubbiaceae 15, 107

Hadena irregularis 73
Hairstreak, Green 145, 146
Halictus spp. 157
Hampshire 12, 43, 44, 64–5, 157
Hampshire Purslane 63
Hankley Common 64, 66
Hardy, Thomas 13, 25, 51
Harebell 121
Harpalus spp. 152
Harrier, Hen 59, 175
  Montagu's 59, 63, 175
Hawkweed, Mouse-eared 121
Hawthorn 62
Hazel 30, 34, 62
Heath, Cornish 16, 55–6, 79, 120
Heath, Cross-leaved 116–18
Heath, Dorset 60, 118–19
Heath, Irish 120
Heath, Lusitanean 120
Heath, MacKay's 120
Heath Grass 67
Heath Sedge 71
Heathland
  burning 48, 99, 188
  climate 18, 26, 27
  climax theory 25
  definition 11
  derivation 14
  difference from moorland 14

distribution, European 17
distribution, world 15
fire, effect 99–102, 188
fragmentation 45
growth phases 89
grazing 25–7, 188, 190
human influences 25, 27, 31
litter production 95
losses 44, 45, 70, 73, 182
nutrients 97
origins 25
plant communities 78–85
productivity 92
regeneration 101, 189
seedbank 102
soils 21
succession 86, 102–6
uses 46, 52
variation, range of 78–85
Heather, Bell 114–16
Heather, Common *see Calluna vulgaris*
Heather, Besom 79
Hedgehog 176
Hemiptera, Heteroptera 143
Hemiptera, Homoptera 145
Herbicides 191
Herniaria ciliata 55
 glabra 71
Hieraceum pilosella 121
Hipparchia semele 136, 146, 147, 196
Historical ecology 25
Hobby 63, 73, 175, 176, 195
Hockham Mere 32, 35, 69
Hollesley Common 73
Holley 62
Holt Lowes 74
Horn Heath 73
Horse Chestnut Moth 150
Horsford Heath 74
Hothfield Common 66
Humid heath 81
Hoverflies 159
Hymenoptera 157
Hypericum humifusum 122
 pulchrum 121
Hypnum cupressiforme 122

Ice retreat 29
Iceland 18
Illecebrum verticillatum 63
Ilex aquilifolium 62
Insect conservation 196–7
Insectivorous plants 129
Invertebrates 132
 succession 133–9
Iping Common 65, 66
Ireland 18, 48

Iron Age 36, 37
Ischnura, Scarce 63, 143
Isoetes histrix 55

Jasione montana 122
Juncus acutifolius 123
 bulbosus 123
 capitatus 55
 pygmaeus 55
 squarrosus 123
July Belle 149
Juniper 122
Jutland 12, 17, 18, 32, 50, 71, 182
Jydefolk 12

Kelling Heath 74
Kent 66
Kestrel 175
Kite 63
Knawlweed, Perennial 71
Knotgrass, Sea 55

Lacerta agilis 61, 64, 66, 163–6, 193, 194
 vivipara 163
Lakenheath Warren 69, 73, 114
Landbridge with continent 30
Landnam 32
Lapwing 172
Lasiocampa spp. 149
Lasius spp. 137
Leaves, form of 19, 108
Leiston Common 73
Leith Hill 64
Lestes, Green 143
Lestes sponsa 143
Leucorrhinia dubia 66, 143
Libellula, Scarce 143
Libellula fulva 143
Lichens 105
Light 18, 32
Lime Tree 30, 34
Lincolnshire 74, 75
Ling *see Calluna vulgaris*
Liphook 64
Linnet 170–2
Lithosia complana 150
Litter 95–6
Livilla ulicis 145
Lizard, Common 163
 Sand 61, 64, 66, 163–6, 193, 194
Lizard Peninsula 36, 43, 45, 47, 49, 51
Lizard Rarities 55
Lleyn Peninsula 76
Lobelia, Heath 122
Lobelia urens 122
Lochmaea suturalis 98, 144, 153–6
London Basin 66, 157

INDEX

Long Mynd 76
Losses of heathland 44, 45, 70, 73, 183
Lotus angustissimus 55
Lousewort 123, 130
Ludshot Heath 64
Ludwigia palustris 63
Lundy Island 59
Luneberger Heide 17
Lusitanean flora 30
Luzula spp. 70, 122
Lycophotia porphyrea 149
Lycopodiella indundata 65, 68, 123
Lycopodium clavatum 123
  selago 59

Macrothylacia rubi 148
Malaxis paludosa 63, 66, 123
Mammals 176
Man, effects of 25, 27, 31, 35, 38
Management, aims 187
  burning 188
  cutting 188
  grazing 190
  herbicides 191
  rare species 193
  scrub 190
  turf cutting 190
Maniola jurtina 145
Maps 40, 43
Market Rasen 75
Marram Grass 75, 77
Massingham Heath 74
Mat Grass 57, 59, 76
Meadow Brown 145
Meassingham heath 75
Medicago spp. 71
Medicks 71
Meloe proscrabaeus 153
Melanpyrum spp. 130
Merlin 59, 175
Mesolithic Man 31, 37, 66
Mesophilous heath 85
Metasyrphus corollae 159
Metrioptera brachyptera 142
Micrellus ericae 153
Micro-arthropods 22, 96
Micro-climate 89–91
Micro-lepidoptera 151
Micro-organisms 22, 96
Microdon eggeri 159
Microtus agrestis 167, 177
Middle Ages 36
Midlands 76
Milkwort, Heath 121
Millipeds 22, 96, 140
Mineral workings 200
Minsmere 73

Mites 23, 96, 140
Mole 176
Molinia caerulea see Purple Moor Grass
Morden Bog 33
Mor 22
Morphology of heath plants 15, 18
Moths 146
Mountain heaths 80
Mousehold Heath 39
Models, computer 98
Moder 23
Mugwort 31, 32
Mull 22
Muscari atlanticum 71
Mutilla europaea 158
Mycorrhiza 108
Mynydd Prescelly 76
Myrmeleotettix maculatus 142
Myrica gale 63
Myrmica spp. 137, 146, 159

Nabis ericetorum 145
Nardus stricta 57, 59, 76
Narthecium ossifragum 57, 63, 122
National Vegetation Classification 82
Natrix natrix 163
Neolithic Man 31–4
Netherlands 17, 18, 50, 71
Nettles 31
New Forest 12, 37, 39, 43, 47, 48, 50, 62–4
Newts 161
Newton Heath 74
Nightjar 64, 73, 170, 172, 173, 195
Nitrogen 132
Norfolk 32, 66
Normandy 17
Norway 17
Nutrients 97

Oak 25, 30, 62
Ochlodes venatus 145
Omocestus viridis 142
Oporinia spp. 149
Organic matter 94
Orchid
  Bog 63, 66, 123
  Heath Spotted 123
  Marsh 123
Orthetrum coerulescens 143
Orthetrum, Keeled 143
Ortholitha plumbaria 149
Orthotylus ericetorum 144
Oxshott Heath 133

Pachycnemia hippocastanaria 150
Pachythelis villosella 150, 151

Palomena prasina 143
Palynology 25, 36
Pansy, Wild 71
Paragus spp. 159
Parasitic plants 130
Parentucellia viscosa 130
Parley Common 67, 150, 168
Pearsall, W. H. 16
Peat 21
Peat cutting 48
Pebble Beds 58, 76
Pedicularis sylvatica 123, 130
Pelecocera tricinctaria 159
Pembrokeshire 76
Pentatoma rufipes 144
Pickard-Cambridge, Revd. O. 168
Picromerus bidens 144
Piezodorus lituratus 143
Pimpernel, Bog 123
Pine, Ground 71
Pine, Scots 25, 27
Pinguicula spp. 123, 130
Pipelines 200
Pipit, Meadow 170
  Tree 73, 172
Pironotaceae 15
Pisaura mirabilis 141
Phleum arenarium 71
  phleoides 71
Plaggen 50
Plant lice 145
Plantain 31, 32, 33
Plebejus argus 145-7, 196
Pleorochaete squarrosa 71
Pleurozium schreberi 70, 122
Podalonia spp. 157
Podsols 21, 23, 24, 25, 31
Pollen analysis 25, 28
  types 29, 32, 34
  profiles 32
Polygala serpyllifolia 121
Polygonium maritimum 55
Polyommatus icarus 145
Polytrichum spp. 122
Polyxenus largurus 140
Pompilidae 157
Pohh, Winnie-the- 67
Poole Basin 12
Poole Harbour 33, 50
Post-Allerod 29
Pot worms 140
Potentilla erecta 103, 121
Pre-boreal 30
Production, vegetation 92
Pseudoterpna pruniata 149
Psyllids 145
Pteridium aquilinum see Bracken

Pugs 149
Purple Moor Grass 45, 55, 56-60, 63, 67, 68, 76, 122
Purple-stemmed Catstail 71
Pyronia tithonus 145

Quercus spp. 25, 30, 34, 62
Quillwort 55

Rabbit 26, 69, 177-9
Rabio-carbon dating 29, 31
Rana temporaria 161
Rare species protection 193
Rarity 185
Reclamation 41, 42
Recreation on heathland 197
Redpoll 172
Redshank 172
Reptiles 163-9
Reserves, choice of 183-7
  size of 183
Restoration 198
Return of the Native 13, 39, 51
Rhacognathus punctatus 144, 155
Rhinanthus minor 130
Rhingia campestris 159
Rhododendron 34, 107, 191
Rhytidium rugosum 71
Rhyncospora alba 63, 123
  fusca 63, 66, 123
Ringed Carpet 149, 151
Risby Warren 75
Roman times 35, 36
Roots
  production 93-4, 96
  regeneration from 104, 188
  system 93
  viability 102
Rosebay 133
Roydon Common 66, 74
Rumex acetosella 31, 32, 70, 121
Rupturewort, Fringed 55
  Glabrous 71
Russia 18
Rustic Moths 150

Salix repens 121
Salthouse Heath 74
Sand Catstail 71
Sandringham Warren 74
Saturna pavonia 147
Saw-wort 68
Scale insects 145
Scaeva pyrastri 159
Schoenus nigricans 56, 58, 63, 123
Scilla verna 80
Scilly, Isles of 53

INDEX

Scirpus cespitosus 58, 59, 123
Scleranthus perennis 71
Scolopostethus decoratus 144
Scotland 12, 77
Scotton Common 75
Scrub control 190-2
Scunthorpe 75
Scutellaria hastifolia 71
Sedge, Carnation 123
    Green-ribbed 123
    Pill 123
    Sand 69, 71, 74, 77, 122
    Tawny 58
Seeds 102-3
Selidosema brunnearia 149
Serratula tinctoria 68
Sheep's Bit 122
Sheep's Fescue *see Festuca ovina*
Sheep's Sorrel 31-3, 70, 121
Shepherd's Cress 70, 122
Sherwood Forest 76
Shieldbugs 143
Shouldenham Heath 74
Shrews 167, 177
Shrike, Red-backed 64, 73, 172, 195
Shropshire 76
Silene spp. 71, 73
Silver-Y 150
Sitona spp. 153
Skippers 145
Skipwith Common 75
Skullcap, Spear-leaved 71
Slow Worm 163
Small Autumnal Moth 149
Small Heath 145
Smooth Snake 61, 64, 163, 167-9, 193, 194
Snape Warren 73
Snipe 172
Snow protection 18
Soil, brown forest 23, 27, 31, 34
    buried profiles 27, 31
    carbon dioxide 94
    deterioration 25, 27, 30, 34
    eutrophication 26
    formation 23
    fauna 96
    horizons 21
    nutrients 18, 23, 28, 97
    pH 18
    temperatures 90, 100
Somatochlora metallica 68, 143
Somerset 59
Soerx spp. 167, 177
South Africa 15
Spain 18
Speedwells 71

Sphaerophoria 159
Sphagnum spp. 57, 58, 63
Sphecidae 157
Spiders 138, 140, 141, 196
Spider mites 141
Spring Squill 80
Springtails 23, 140
Standing Crop 92
Stanford 71
Stenoptilia pneumonanthes 151
Stethophyma grossum 61
St John's Worts 121, 122
Stoat 177
Stonechat 170, 172
Stonecrop, Mossy 60, 71, 122
Strensall Common 76
Strongylognathus testaceus 158
Strophingia spp. 145
Strophosomus spp. 153
Studland Heath 86
Sub-boreal 31, 33, 35
Sub-fossil remains 32
Succession 86, 182
Succisa pratensis 58
Suffolk Sandlings 37, 44, 45, 46, 69, 73
Sundews 63, 66, 129
Surrey 12, 64-6, 157
Sussex 46, 47, 64-6
Sweden 17, 182
Sympetrum, Black 143
Syritta pipiens 159
Syrphidae 159

Tabanus spp. 160
Tachysphex pompiliformis 157
Taeniothrips ericae 141
Tansley, Sir Arthur 26
Teesdalia nudicaulis 71, 122
Tetralicia ericae 145
Tetramorium caespitosum 137, 158
Tetranychus lintearicus 141
Tetrix undulata 142
Thetford 32, 38, 69, 73
Thrift 55, 59
Thrips 141
Thomisus onustus 141
Thursley Common 64, 66
Thymelicus flavus 145
Thyme, Wild 71
Thysanura 91, 140
Tilia spp. 30, 34
Toad, Common 161, 162
    Natterjack 65, 161-3, 193
Tormentil 103, 121
Tortula ruraliformis 71
Trichiura crataegi 149
Triturus spp. 161

INDEX

Trifolium spp. 55
Trolius luridus 144
True-lovers Knot 149
Tuddenham Heath 73
Tundra 29
Turbary 49, 50, 190
Turf cutting 39, 49–50, 182, 190

Ulex spp. *see* Gorse
Ulmus spp. 30, 31, 34
Ulopa reticulata 145
Urtica sp. 31
Utricularia spp. 65, 130

Vaccinium myrtillis 34, 59, 76
 oxycoccos 65, 123
 vitis-idaea 59, 76
Vegetation, classification 78–85
 dynamics 86–106
 nutrients 97
 production 92
Velvet Ant 158
Venn Ottery Common 58
Veronica spp. 71
Vertebrates 161–180
Vikings 37
Viola tricolor 72
Viper 163, 166–7
Viper's Bugloss Moth 73
Voles 167, 177

Walberswick Heath 73
Wales 76
Wangford Warren 69, 73, 87
Warbler, Dartford 61, 64, 66, 170, 172, 173–5, 193–5
 Willow 170, 172

Wasps 157
Watt, Dr. A. S. 70, 113, 186
Wavy Hair Grass *see Deschampsia flexuosa*
Weald 64
Weasel 177
Weather Heath 73
Weevils 153
Weichselsian times 29
Westleton Heath 73
Wet heath 79, 81, 85
Wheatear 73, 172
Whin, Petty 122, 128
Whinchat 172
White, Gilbert 12, 48
Whitethroat 170, 172
Willow, Creeping 121
Windsor 66
Wood Hall Spa 75
Wood, Mouse 167, 177
Wood Rushes 70, 122
Woodbury Common 58
Woodlark 73, 172, 195
Woodpecker, Green 170, 171
Woolmer Forest 12, 43, 48, 64, 65
Wren 170, 171

Xestia spp. 150

Yellow Hammer 170, 172
Yellow Rattle 130
York, Vale of 75
Yorkshire 24, 74–5
Young, Arthur 41